650 mc
01

The Broken Center

WITHDRAWN
UTSA LIBRARIES

The William Lyon Phelps Lectures   1965

Also by Nathan A. Scott, Jr.

Rehearsals of Discomposure:
    Alienation and Reconciliation in Modern Literature (1952)
Modern Literature and the Religious Frontier (1958)
Albert Camus (1962)
Reinhold Niebuhr (1963)
Samuel Beckett (1965)

Edited by Nathan A. Scott, Jr.

The Tragic Vision and the Christian Faith (1957)
The New Orpheus: Essays Toward a Christian Poetic (1964)
The Climate of Faith in Modern Literature (1964)
Man in the Modern Theatre (1965)
Four Ways of Modern Poetry (1965)
Forms of Extremity in the Modern Novel (1965)

New Haven and London, Yale University Press

Nathan A. Scott, Jr. THE
BROKEN
CENTER *Studies in the*
Theological Horizon of Modern Literature

To Leslie,
whose radiant joyousness lights her father's days
and to Charlotte,
dearest companion of twenty years—without whom,
nothing

Preface

This book resumes the effort that I was undertaking in my book of 1958, Modern Literature and the Religious Frontier, *to search out and explore those areas of interrelationship in the modern period that unite the literary and the religious imagination, whether in a state of accord or of tension. Ours has, of course, been a literature that has involved itself relentlessly in those questions with which it has traditionally been the office of religious faith to deal—those questions that, in the ugly language of our time, we call existential. Both the sense of life and of death in modern literature (the one, incidentally, never being sharply distinguishable from the other) have often carried a dark, feral intensity that is suggestive of a kind of "transcendence," a secular transcendence—toward such a vision of the human enterprise as entails secularity, as it were, surpassing itself, into a modality at least incipiently religious.*

Indeed, what seems to underlie most of the representative poetry, drama, and fiction of our period, as something of a basic premise, is a sense that the anchoring center of life is broken and that the world is therefore abandoned and adrift. "We need a theme? then let that be our theme," said Conrad Aiken in one of his finest poems, thereby expressing with poignant candor a lament that has often been heard as a deep, resounding undertone in the literature of this century. And it is this negatively *theological character of modern literature that compels the critic to enter an essentially theological order of*

*discourse and evaluation. In fact just such a critical responsive-
ness in the last few years—in the work of men like R. W. B.
Lewis, Fr. William Lynch, Cleanth Brooks, Fr. Walter Ong,
Frederick Hoffman, and Murray Krieger—has made for one of
the more notable new developments in American criticism.
Therefore, having found a sort of corroboration (at least in the
general direction of my own interests) in the work of critics so
acutely perceptive as these and others, I am no longer troubled
by the uncertainty about this general direction that I still felt
intermittently after I had finished* Modern Literature *and the*
Religious Frontier, *for then there was too small a body of
critical work to give me any sense of confirmation in my own
belief that the theological horizon is centrally important in the
literary landscape of our period. The accuracy, truthfulness,
and relevance of what I say must, of course, be certified by
others; but at least I no longer have any doubt about the
validity of the general enterprise to which this book is committed. For not only does the literature of our time most emphatically initiate theological inquiry, but my conviction also
grows that the major poetry and fiction and drama of the
modern period do indeed form a great literature and that
Christian theology as a result of its dialogue with the literary
imagination will find itself more richly repaid (in terms of
deepened awareness both of itself and of the age) than by any
similar transaction into which it may enter. But, so far as these
pages themselves are concerned, I have no sense of anything
remotely resembling finality: they form, like my book of 1958,
only "an interim report"—which I offer with tentativeness and
with no small sense of what is both rough and derivative in its
formulations.*

*The material in Chapter 5 was delivered as the first William
Lyon Phelps Lectures at Yale University in the Winter of 1965;
and it is an occasion of pleasure for me to be able here to record my gratitude for having been invited to hold this lecture-
ship honoring one of Yale's great men of a generation ago. The
Lectures are jointly sponsored by the Divinity and the English
faculties of the University; and I am glad also to record here*

Preface

my very great appreciation of courtesies generously extended to me by friends in both departments while I was in New Haven: I am most especially grateful for the warm hospitality of Dr. and Mrs. B. Davie Napier, Dr. and Mrs. W. K. Wimsatt, Dr. and Mrs. Jaroslav Pelikan, and Dr. and Mrs. J. Edward Dirks.

I continue to be indebted to my colleague, Preston Roberts, for fidelity in friendship and for encouragement in all the affairs of our common professional involvement. And, with the passing of each year, I have a larger sense of the marvelous grace of my students at the University of Chicago—whose lively intelligence, whose impatience with inexactitude, and whose patience with me have been one of the great blessings of my life. My "chief," Dean Jerald C. Brauer, is one of those rare and remarkable administrators in the academic community who conceives it his main duty to make it possible for his colleagues to get on with the job of teaching and reflection; and not only in his official capacity has he smoothed my course, but also outside our official relation, in countless ways, of which I know he is unaware, his friendship has been a stay and a support. And my wife and children do each day offer the environment in which all self-doubt is finally swallowed up in the Mystery of companionship and love—and this is the best gift of all.

N. A. S., JR.

The Divinity School
The University of Chicago
9 August 1965

Acknowledgments

The material in Chapter One was first written, in slightly different form, as an article entitled "The Broken Center: A Definition of the Crisis of Values in Modern Literature," for the volume Symbolism in Religion and Literature, edited by Rollo May (New York, 1960), and also appeared in The Chicago Review, 13 (1959). It is used here by permission of George Braziller, Inc., and the American Academy of Arts and Sciences.

The material in Chapter Two first appeared, in slightly different form, in The Scope of Grace: Essays in Honor of Joseph Stitler, edited by Philip J. Hefner (Philadelphia, 1964), and is used here by permission of The Fortress Press.

Chapter Three was first published, in slightly different form, in The Christian Scholar, 44 (1961) and also appears in Comedy: Meaning and Form, edited by Robert W. Corrigan (San Francisco, 1965). It is used here by permission of the editor of The Christian Scholar.

Chapter Four first appeared, in slightly different form, in the Anglican Theological Review, 45 (1963), and is used here with the permission of the editor of that journal.

The discussions in Chapter Six were first published, in slightly different form, as two separate articles in motive: "Art and the Renewal of Human Sensibility in Mass Society," 21 (1960), and "Faith and Art in a World Awry," 22 (1961). The first article was reprinted in Christian Faith and the Contemporary Arts, edited by Finley Eversole (New York-Nashville,

1962), and the second in The Climate of Faith in Modern Literature, *edited by Nathan A. Scott, Jr. (New York, 1964). The material is used here with the permission of the Abingdon Press and The Seabury Press.*

The material in Chapter Seven was originally written, in slightly different form, for the volume The Search for Identity, *edited by Roger L. Shinn. Copyright © 1964 by The Institute for Religious and Social Studies. Reprinted by permission of Harper & Row, Publishers.*

Quotations from Four Quartets *by T. S. Eliot, copyright © 1943 by T. S. Eliot, are reprinted by permission of Harcourt, Brace & World, Inc., and Faber and Faber.*

Contents

The Broken Center

Things fall apart; the center cannot hold;
Mere anarchy is loosed upon the world;

. . .

The best lack all conviction, while the worst
Are full of passionate intensity.
    —William Butler Yeats, "The Second Coming"

We need a theme? then let that be our theme:
that we, poor grovellers between faith and doubt,
the sun and north star lost, and compass out,
the heart's weak engine all but stopped, the time
timeless in this chaos of our wills—
that we must ask a theme, something to think,
something to say, between dawn and dark,
something to hold to, something to love.
                    —Conrad Aiken, *Time in the Rock*

Chapter One THE NAME
AND NATURE
OF OUR PERIOD-STYLE

One of the characters in the late Richard Chase's brilliant dialogue, *The Democratic Vista*, gives me a kind of text for this first chapter when he remarks, "It seems that the greatest writers of the first half of the twentieth century lived in a high, tense world of strenuous and difficult metaphysics, moral doctrine, political ideology, and religious feeling."[1] The young man who says this is a graduate student of literature who, together with his wife and two children, is spending a late summer week end on the Massachusetts coast in the home of a professor at his university, and it is to his senior friend that he offers his observation. He is perhaps being characteristic of his generation when he argues that "it is no longer possible to share" the intellectual and spiritual preoccupation of the great heroes of the modern tradition, of people like Eliot and Joyce and Pound. But though his foreclosure may be too narrow and too premature, he does identify accurately the most important distinguishing feature of the great classic tradition of modern letters, for that is most certainly a tradition that posits "a high, tense world of strenuous and difficult metaphysics . . . and religious feeling."

When we think, for example, of Mann and Lawrence and Kafka and Faulkner, it becomes immediately apparent, of

1. Richard Chase, *The Democratic Vista: A Dialogue on Life and Letters in Contemporary America* (Garden City, Doubleday, 1958), p. 16.

course, that all of these writers cannot easily be sheltered under the same umbrella: their methods of practicing the arts of fiction and the various gestures they make toward reality represent enormous diversity and the amazing differentiation of attitude and language that is a chief hallmark of literary art in our period. But, despite this multifariousness of creative technique and fundamental point of view, they are writers whom we feel impelled to regard as constituting in some sense a genuine community and a unitary tradition. We take this view, I believe, because these are writers whose most emphatic insistence has been upon the fact of their being unsustained by any vital and helpful traditions: the community which they have formed has been rooted in their common awareness of their isolation. And this is an isolation which has not been primarily an affair of the artist's tenuous position in the polity of modern society: to be sure, that has been something uncertain and problematic, and the artist's social marginality has undoubtedly at times greatly added to his unease; but what has most fundamentally given his life the aspect of crisis has been that recession of faith and that erosion of the religious terrain announced by Nietzsche in the nineteenth century, and, in our own time, by Sartre.

In an age when all is in doubt and when, as Yeats says, "Things fall apart" and "the center cannot hold," the philosopher may not be utterly crippled if he is willing to have his vocation confined to the analysis of nothing more than the structure of sentences; and the social critic can always be kept busy in notating the tics and the spasms that are the signs of our distress. In similar reduced ways the other custodians of cultural life may in some manner continue to function when overtaken by a late bad time. But when the traditional premises regarding the radical significance of things have collapsed and when, therefore, there is no longer any robust common faith to orient the imaginative faculties of men with respect to the ultimate mysteries of existence—when, in other words, the basic presuppositions of a culture have become just yawning question marks—then the literary artist is thrust upon a most desolate frontier indeed. For, though his role is sometimes spoken of as though it involved presiding over an act of *communication*, this is a vulgar version of it which could pass muster only in an age of television and of what is called the mass-audience. The writer may, to be sure, take his stand before a microphone and speak to a crowd in whose fate he is not at all implicated; and, when he does this, he may perhaps play a part in something that might be called a process of communication. But, when this is his position, surely it is impossible for anything to be "shared, in a new and illuminating intensity of awareness," as Allen Tate has reminded us. Indeed, the very concept of literature as communication may well, in its currency, betoken a tragic victory of modern secularism over the human spirit. "Our unexamined theory of literature as communication could not," he says,

> have appeared in an age in which communication was still possible for any appreciable majority of persons. The word communication presupposes the victory of the secularized society of means without ends. The poet, on the one hand, shouts to the public, on the other (some distance away), not the rediscovery of the common experience, but a certain pitch of sound to which the well-conditioned adrenals of humanity obligingly respond.[2]

No, says Mr. Tate, the language of communication may be the language of radio and television; but the language which the artist seeks sensitively to supervise is the language not of communication but of *communion*: it is that language into which an effort has been made to put a deep and authentic knowledge of what is involved in the life together of free men, and it is, therefore, a language which invites us to reenter what Martin Buber calls "the world of *I* and *Thou*."

This is, of course, to say that the language of imaginative

2. Allen Tate, *The Forlorn Demon* (Chicago, Regnery, 1953), pp. 13, 12.

literature is not the ethically and spiritually neutral jargon of any science: it is, rather, a language which, if it is to do its proper work, needs to be heavily weighted with the beliefs, sentiments, and valuations that are the deep source in a culture of its "hum and buzz of implication"[3] and that bind its people together with ties that separate them from the people of other cultures. Only when the artist's language bears this kind of freight can it be something more than a vehicle of communication. Only then can it become an instrument of communion and—what all art is ultimately intended to be—a servant of love.

We are now brought back to that desolate frontier on which I have said the modern writer has found himself, for what has made his position as an artist so insecure has been precisely the very great difficulty he has had in making contact with any significant body of belief that, having vital authority in our period, might furnish his imagination with the premises of its functioning and facilitate the transaction between himself and his reader. "In the profoundest human sense," said Kenneth Burke in one of his early books, "one communicates in a *weighted* vocabulary in which the weightings are shared by [one's] group as a whole."[4] But it is just at this point that modern culture has presented great privation. There is, in fact, little of profound significance that is widely shared by modern men. The dominant dispensation has, of course, been of a scientific character, but, as Max Planck once reminded us, "there is scarcely [even] a scientific axiom that is not now-a-days denied by somebody."[5] And, outside the realm of our scientific culture, the resistant pressure that has been offered to the relativizing tendencies of our time has been negligible indeed.

3. Lionel Trilling, *The Liberal Imagination* (New York, Viking, 1950), p. 206.
4. Quoted in Herbert Muller, *Modern Fiction* (New York, Funk and Wagnalls, 1937), p. 10.
5. Quoted in Harry Slochower, *No Voice Is Wholly Lost* (New York, Creative Age, 1945), p. vii.

of Our Period-Style

In his important book *Diagnosis of Our Time*, the late Karl Mannheim proposes the interesting and cogent hypothesis that the despiritualization of modern life is best understood in terms of the gradual evaporation in our period of authentic "paradigmatic experience" and of those great "primordial images or archetypes" which, being formed out of this kind of experience, have directed the human enterprise in the most genuinely creative moments of cultural history. By the term paradigmatic experience, Mannheim refers to those "basic experiences which carry more weight than others, and which are unforgettable in comparison with others that are merely passing sensations." Without experiences of this kind, he says,

> no consistent conduct, no character formation and no real human coexistence and co-operation are possible. Without them our universe of discourse loses its articulation, conduct falls to pieces, and only disconnected bits of successful behaviour patterns and fragments of adjustment to an ever-changing environment remain.[6]

And his contention is that paradigmatic experience, insofar as it yields some conviction as to what is radically significant also, in effect, yields a kind of "ontological hierarchy" in accordance with which we say, "This is bad, this is good, this is better." But, of course, the whole drive of the positivistically oriented secularism of modern culture has been towards such "a neutralization of that ontological hierarchy in the world of experience" as encourages the belief that one experience is as important as any other and that the question of right or wrong is merely one concerning the most efficient environmental adjustments. So the result has been the evaporation of those primordial images which objectify a people's faith and provide the moral imagination with its basic premises. And when there are no paradigmatic experiences, then nothing is any longer revealed as having decisive importance, and men are

6. Karl Mannheim, *Diagnosis of Our Time* (New York, Oxford, 1944), pp. 146–48.

5

ruled, said Mannheim, by a kind of kaleidoscopic concept of life which, in giving equal significance to everything, does, in effect, attribute no radical significance to anything. In such an age, the individual is condemned to the awful prison of his own individuality, since nothing means the same thing to any broad segment of people—the primary fact about the human community is disclosed as being the complete collapse of anything resembling genuine community.

This is a fact which has been dramatized by much recent social criticism in its notation of the astonishing lack of drama in modern society. The life of the average megalopolitan today is ungraced by any rituals which strengthen the ties of sympathy and fellow-feeling that bind him to his neighbors. Nor is the civic scene complicated and enlivened by any round of celebrations and festivities comparable to the religious liturgies or the secular rites which figured so largely in the common life of earlier times. In the great cities of our day we are cave-dwellers, scurrying about the urban wilderness from one vast compound to another, like "bits of paper, whirled by the cold wind," says T. S. Eliot in "Burnt Norton." Like the members of Captain Ahab's crew, we are, in Melville's words, "nearly all Islanders," none "acknowledging the common continent of men, but each *Isolato* living on a separate continent of his own."

This, then, is the intractable and unpromising reality which the modern writer has been up against. Mr. Burke says that the artist's task is to supervise a weighted language whose weightings are shared by the commonalty. But it has been the fate of the modern artist to live in a time when the commonalty, as anything more than a statistical assemblage of unrelated atoms, is something remembered only by the historical imagination. And this is why the problem of understanding modern literature so largely involves the problem of understanding the stratagems that become inevitable for the artist when history commits him to the practice of his vocation in a vacuum of belief.

What the modern artist has most deeply needed are systems

of value, appropriate to the experience of the age, in which his art could find a principle of order and unity. This is, indeed, what the artist has always needed; and, when the circumstances of his culture have afforded a good soil for art, the ethos of his community has provided him with coordinating analogies, key-metaphors, myths, and symbols which, in flowing out of the funded memories and experience of his people, could well serve him as instruments for the full evocation of the human communion. Surely it is no merely willful or sentimental nostalgia that leads us, when we roam back through the tradition, to account in these terms for the greatness of the achievement of Sophocles and Dante, of Shakespeare and Racine, or, on a far less exalted level, of, say, Madame de Lafayette or Jane Austen. In these older writers we feel a freedom and a security of reference that strike us as being a consequence of their having had the good fortune to live in cultures which, having a vital unity, could liberally provide them with those primordial images and archetypes which centralize and order the poetic imagination. These older writers were the lucky ones, for they did not have to invent for themselves ways of construing or making sense of experience: they were fortunate, because the writer who has to expend energy on philosophical and theological enterprises before he can get his literary project underway will have squandered reserves of imaginative power that, in more favorable circumstances, would be used up in the practice of his art. And when one thinks, say, of Jane Austen in relation to the woman of our own time who wrote such a book as *Nightwood*, we cannot help but feel that the older writer was more fortunate because, in receiving her ultimate terms of reference from her culture, she was relieved of any uncertainty about how to establish contact with her readers and was, therefore, enabled in her fundamental terms of speech to make the kinds of assumptions that facilitate the poetic transaction.

This is precisely the kind of good fortune that the writer in the modern period has not enjoyed. He has inherited no traditional and widely accepted frame of values from his culture.

Before his art could be steadied by some executive principle of valuation, it has been necessary for the artist to try to construct some viable system of belief for himself by an effort of personal vision: he has had to become, in a sense, his own priest, his own guide, his own Vergil. He has been condemned by the cultural circumstances of his time to draw from himself everything that forms and orders his art. The waters in which he has swum have been the deep waters of his own mind into which he has descended to search for a clue to the principles by which the anarchy of experience might be controlled and given a shape and a significance. This is why it might be said that the reigning law of the modern movement in the arts has been that of the *principium individuationis*.

Indeed, much of the great literature of the modern period might be said to be a literature of metaphysical isolation, for the modern artist—and this is perhaps the fundamental truth about him—has experienced a great loneliness, the kind of loneliness known by the soul when, unaided by ministries either of Church or of culture, it undertakes the adventure of discovering the fundamental principles of meaning. And this is unquestionably the reason for the obscurity of so many great modern texts—of Rimbaud's *A Season In Hell*, of Rilke's *Duino Elegies*, of Joyce's *Finnegans Wake*, of Malcolm Lowry's *Under the Volcano*. For, amid the confusion of values of this age, the artist is attempting to invent a system of attitudes and beliefs that will give meaning to his world. And it is this idiosyncrasy, this extreme individuality, of modern poetic vision that has often made our finest literature so difficult to penetrate. What has been most distinctive of the great heroes of the modern tradition is, as Stephen Spender says, that they assumed the task "of re-experiencing everything as though it had never been experienced before, and then expressing it not in terms with which traditions and education have made us familiar but in new ones minted out"[7] of their separate sensibilities. In a time when

7. Stephen Spender, *The Creative Element* (London, Hamish Hamilton, 1953), p. 176.

of Our Period-Style

> So various
> And multifoliate are our breeds of faith
> That we could furnish a herbarium
> With the American specimens alone[8]

the writer has felt himself to be without a common background of reference by which his own imaginative faculties and those of his readers might be oriented and brought into profound rapport with one another. So he has turned inward, pursuing a system of values or beliefs in the world of his own subjectivity. The result is that "it becomes increasingly difficult for the reader to understand the significance of the writer's symbols and language, without his having experienced the process of the writer's experiencing. . . . Hence a vast literature explaining texts and the circumstances of each writer's life has grown up around the modern movement."[9] This development has tended to institutionalize the originally unique experimentations of the great modern pioneers and to make them, indeed, a staple of the new academic tradition—as is indicated, for example, by the statement on the jacket of William York Tindall's book, *James Joyce*, that Mr. Tindall "is a member of the James Joyce Society, and has made the pilgrimage to Dublin." Yet this is precisely what the appropriation of Joyce's work demands—membership in scholarly societies devoted to its study and foundation-sponsored tours to Dublin in search of scraps of information that may assist in unraveling the bafflements of Joyce's incredibly complex art. For this writer does in himself constitute a cosmos and a culture and a total mythology. And the necessity we confront, when we tackle a book like *Finnegans Wake*, is that of trying to make some coherent sense out of a vast chaotic array of notes toward what its author heroically strove to make the great modern novel.

Indeed, the Joycean experiment, however stillborn it may in

8. Karl Shapiro, *Essay on Rime* (New York, Reynal and Hitchcock, 1945), p. 63.
9. Spender, pp. 176–77.

part have been, does at least succeed in stating significant questions and in drawing attention to what has been a fundamental dilemma of the artist in our period. We may say the lesson of Joyce's career teaches us that, though the artist cannot by fiat produce adequate surrogates for traditions of faith and culture that are no longer available to him, he may, in attempting to do so, vividly dramatize what it is that makes his task difficult in the modern period. And that is what Joyce succeeded in doing. As T. S. Eliot put the issue in his famous review of *Ulysses* in 1923:

> In using the myth, in manipulating a continuous parallel between contemporaneity and antiquity, Mr. Joyce is pursuing a method which others must pursue after him. . . . It is simply a way of controlling, or ordering, of giving a shape and a significance to the immense panorama of futility and anarchy which is contemporary history.[10]

The radicalism of his effort to find this shape and this significance makes Joyce the great exemplar of the literary artist in the modern age: he gives the age away—he puts us in mind of how much "the greatest writers of the first half of the twentieth century lived in a high, tense world of strenuous and difficult metaphysics . . . and religious feeling." When we think not only of Joyce but also of Proust, Kafka, Lawrence, and Gide, we immediately remember how much these artists, amid the disintegration and incoherence of our intellectual systems, in the quest for a viable body of beliefs or first principles expended energies that in a more fortunate age could have been directed into the labor of composition. These are all writers who, in various ways, were handicapped in not having been given by their culture an adequately objective framework of religious commitments and metaphysical beliefs. But these writers, like many other great artists of our period, are also notable by reason of the ardor with which they sought to com-

10. T. S. Eliot, "*Ulysses*, Order and Myth," in *Critiques and Essays on Modern Fiction*, ed. John V. Aldridge (New York, Ronald Press, 1952), p. 426.

pensate for this disability by religious and philosophic improvisations whose virtuosity is perhaps without previous parallel in literary history. Indeed, the real religious power and greatness we feel in the great classic tradition of modern literature is, I believe, a direct consequence of the immense courage with which the chief protagonists of this tradition have steered their lonely, separate courses through the spiritual void of our time.

Now it is precisely the extreme self-reliance in the quest for first principles that I have been positing as the inescapable necessity facing the modern writer—it is precisely this that makes evident his descendance from the great Romantics of the nineteenth century and also makes evident the fact that the literature of the age of Joyce and Kafka is essentially a late development of the Romantic movement. Here we must not be misled by the vigorous anti-Romanticism that informs so much of twentieth-century literature. It is true, of course, that men like Valéry and Eliot and Pound in poetry, and Joyce and Proust in the novel, have sponsored programs of one sort or another whose aim has been to encourage a rejection of the legacy of Romanticism—its inspirationist aesthetic, its cult of sincerity, its artlessness, and its confusions of art and religion. But, steady as this quarrel with the Romantic movement has been in our time, it is a family quarrel, and the fact remains that the great tradition of twentieth-century literature is, fundamentally, a product of the Romantic dispensation. Robert Langbaum has observed:

> Whatever the difference between the literary movements of the nineteenth and twentieth centuries, they are connected . . . by their response to the same wilderness. That wilderness is the legacy of the Enlightenment, of the scientific and critical effort of the Enlightenment which, in its desire to separate fact from the values of a crumbling tradition, separated fact from all values—bequeathing a world in which fact is measurable quantity while value is man-made and illusory. Such a world offers no objective verification for

just the perceptions by which men live, perceptions of beauty, goodness, and spirit. It was as literature began in the latter eighteenth century to realize the dangerous implications of the scientific world-view that Romanticism was born. It was born anew in at least three generations thereafter as men of genius arrived intellectually at the dead-end of the eighteenth century and then, often through a total crisis of personality, broke intellectually into the nineteenth. As literature's reaction to the eighteenth century's scientific world-view, Romanticism connects the literary movement of the nineteenth and twentieth centuries.[11]

This recognition of the havoc wrought by Enlightenment iconoclasm did not, in the great English Romantics, lead to an exacerbation of spirit so extreme as that which is often noticeable in their French and German contemporaries, but we can, nevertheless, detect the signs of this unrest in Coleridge and Wordsworth and in Keats and Shelley. They all make us feel that for them the traditional archetypes and systems of faith had ceased to be effective and that they, as a result, in their dealings with the world were thrown back upon their own private resources. They had all felt what Keats in "Lamia" called "the touch of cold philosophy," and they knew themselves, as a consequence, to be deprived of that mythical machinery for ordering experience which writers in earlier periods of the tradition had been blessed in having: they knew themselves to be fated by the logic of their culture to bear, alone and unassisted, what Wordsworth called "the weight of all this unintelligible world." So, in works like "Tintern Abbey," the "Immortality" ode, "The Rime of the Ancient Mariner," "Adonais," the "Ode to the West Wind," and the "Ode to a Nightingale," these men attempted to perform what Coleridge believed to be the poet's task "of spreading the tone, the *atmosphere,* and with it the depth and height of the ideal world around forms, incidents, and situations, of which, for the com-

11. Robert Langbaum, *The Poetry of Experience* (New York, Random House, 1957), pp. 11–12.

mon view, customs had bedimmed all the lustre, had dried up
the sparkle and the dew drops."[12]

When we turn, however, to continental Romanticism, particularly in France, and here not to such relatively early figures
as Rousseau, Chateaubriand, and Lamartine but to such later
writers of this Romantic tradition as Baudelaire, Rimbaud,
and Lautréamont, then we leave the elegiac temper of the English school and come to a new kind of intensity and violence
that point directly towards the *Angst*-ridden literature of the
twentieth century. It was with this tradition in mind that the
distinguished French critic Jacques Rivière remarked in his
essay, "La Crise du concept de littérature," that "with Romanticism . . . the literary act began to be conceived as a kind of
assault on the absolute, and its result as a revelation," the
writer becoming a kind of priest. Indeed, said Rivière, this
whole literature is "a vast incantation toward the miracle."[13]

But not only does the artist working under the dispensation
of Baudelaire and Lautréamont become a priest, he also becomes a kind of scientist: for, wanting to rescue himself from
the metaphysical void of his culture, he is so much in the grip
of a great passion for knowledge that the poetic process itself
becomes not primarily a process of the artist's *making* but
rather a process of the artist's *discovering* the ultimate fron-
tiers of human existence and of there staking out his claim to
dominion. Rimbaud, for example, in a letter to his friend, Paul
Demeny, says:

> The first study for a man who wants to be a poet is the
> knowledge of himself, entire. He looks for his soul, inspects
> it, learns it. As soon as he knows it, he cultivates it: it seems
> simple. . . . But the soul has to be made monstrous, that's
> the point. . . .
> One must, I say, be a *seer*, make oneself a *seer*.
> The poet makes himself a *seer* through a long, a prodi-

12. S. T. Coleridge, *Biographia Literaria*, ed. J. Shawcross (London,
Oxford, 1907; Impression of 1954), *1*, 59.

13. Jacques Rivière, "La Crise du concept de littérature," *Nouvelle
Revue Française* (Feb. 1, 1924).

gious and rational disordering of *all* the senses. Every form of love, of suffering, of madness; he searches himself, he consumes all the poisons in him, keeping only their quintessences. Ineffable torture in which he will need all his faith and superhuman strength, the great criminal, the great sickman, the utterly damned, and the supreme Savant! For he arrives at the unknown! Since he has cultivated his soul— richer to begin with than any other! He arrives at the unknown: and even if, half crazed, in the end, he loses the understanding of his visions, he has seen them! Let him croak in his leap into these unutterable and innumerable things: there will come other horrible workers: they will begin at the horizons where he has succumbed.[14]

Here we have an inner dislocation which this particular poet called a sacred disorder, but it is clear that what it really signified was his having yielded to "an invasion of vertigo" and lost his footing. Therefore, it is not surprising that he abandoned poetry in 1873 at the age of nineteen to spend the rest of his brief life in exotic adventure and in angry defiance of bourgeois Philistinism. But, despite Rimbaud's abdication from literature, his prophecy was borne out, and other laborers did come after him, "who began," as Jacques Maritain says, "at the horizons where he had collapsed."[15] A horizon, of course, is the place where the extremes of earth and sky meet, and the particular horizon where Rimbaud collapsed was the point at which his own desperate need, as an artist and as a man, for metaphysical and religious order collided with the spiritual void of the nineteenth century. And this is the precise horizon on which we may locate that great modern procession that includes, in addition to Baudelaire, Rimbaud, and Lautréamont, such earlier writers as Hölderlin, Leopardi, and Vigny as well as such later writers as Mallarmé, Valéry, Joyce, Hart Crane, André Gide, André Malraux, St.-John Perse, and many others.

14. Arthur Rimbaud, *Prose Poems from the Illuminations*, trans. Louise Varèse (New York, New Directions, 1946), pp. xxvi–xxvii.
15. Jacques Maritain, *Creative Intuition in Art and Poetry* (New York, Pantheon Books, 1953), p. 186.

For all these, in the sense that I am claiming for the term, are Romantics: that is, they are writers bent upon *improvising* perspectives and principles in terms of which a shape and a significance may be given to the immense panorama of modern experience, thus making it accessible to art. This is their passion and their chosen task; and such a dedication makes them candidates for the special kind of sainthood that the avant-garde has tended to produce in the modern period. That is, in a way they have been martyrized by the dislocations of the time, in having to bear upon their own souls the stigmata of the bent and broken world to which they were committed by modern history.

This, it seems to me, is the first major observation to be made about the great classic tradition of contemporary letters: we must say that in its tone and style and outlook it incorrigibly follows in the Romantic tradition. This is seen, for example, even in apparently so non-Romantic a figure as T. S. Eliot, who, to be sure, made his way back to a classical tradition of religious faith and found in Christian history the deepest inspiration for the work of his last thirty-five years. But the particular tradition of Christian faith in which Eliot chose to live—the tradition, say, of Origen and Dame Julian of Norwich and Jacob Boehme and St. John of the Cross—is hardly one which strikes us as belonging to the great central tradition of Christian culture: it is very special and irregular, and its reclamation by a contemporary Christian poet suggests that even his "orthodoxy" did, in its attainment, represent something of the improvisation that has tended generally to characterize the modern artist's philosophic and religious stratagems.

But, now, a second major specification must be made of the modern tradition in literature, for we shall not fully comprehend it until we recognize it as a tradition which represents that particular late development of the Romantic movement that comprises the whole experiment of Existentialism. Not only must we say that this is a Romantic literature: we must say that it is an Existentialist literature as well. Of course, when I denominate the central tradition in our literature as

15

Existentialist, it must be apparent that I do not refer merely to certain recent writers, particularly in France, who have found a theoretical sanction for their vision in the doctrines of Existentialist philosophy. I use the term in a much broader sense and intend it to define the literature of the past hundred years in which we find reflected an experience of existence as fundamentally and, perhaps even, essentially problematic.

It will doubtless be our first impulse to regard this experience as having been occasioned by those ultimate exigencies in the history of the modern spirit to which Nietzsche called attention in his announcement of the death of God. But the death of God, as a cultural fact of the modern age, is itself something whose fundamental cause is to be sought in the "death of man" in our time, for this is the really primary fact in modern experience. What we confront, throughout the whole polity of modern society, is a tragic devitalization of the very concept of the person. That special sort of life en masse, so distinctive of our period, has been made possible by a system whose inner logic has necessitated a high degree of specialization in all fields of man's labor. And this, in turn, by a dreadful kind of inexorability has accomplished what might even be said to be a mutation in human nature itself, insofar as the habit of requiring a man to justify himself by his ability to perform a special task has weakened in us the capacity to make the crucial distinction between the function and the human being who performs it. Not only has the distinction become difficult to make but the human act by which a man transcends his various social and economic functions has, under the pressures of a commercialized culture, also become an act that it is increasingly more difficult to perform. Many of the most thoughtful observers of modern life have noticed how the logic of a technocratic culture reduces the concrete particularity of the unique individual to a purely abstract and functional identity; and they also have noticed the gray anonymity of life that this reduction accomplishes. What every reporter on the present human condition has, indeed, to take into ac-

count is the sense that men have today of being thrust into the
nudity of their own isolated individual existence. Though
"huddled together" in the great metropolises of the contemporary world "like dust in a heap," that which figures most
prominently in their awareness is a sense of the world's va-
cancy, and the loss of which they are most acutely conscious is
the loss of the real *proximity* of friends and neighbors. Life
seems, Karl Jaspers says, to have grown "indefinitely vast"; it
no longer has that "interlinkage" which holds it together, "so
that it is not frittered away" and disintegrated into "the brief
perspective of the [immediate] present."[16] A man has the function that he performs for eight hours a day, and he has his bit
of breathing-space somewhere in the urban or the suburban
wilderness. But, as we are told in one of the choruses in T. S.
Eliot's *The Rock:*

> The desert is squeezed in the tube-train next to you,
> The desert is in the heart of your brother.

So, though all the time we live closer and closer together in
our great urban compounds, we find it more and more difficult
to recognize one another or even to retain a sense of our own
identities. Amid this gray, dreary anonymity, we know that
we live in a world from which all the gracious marks of "presence" have been banished.

"Just as primitive man believed himself to stand face to
face with demons and believed that could he but know their
names he would become their master," so too, says Karl Jaspers, contemporary man is faced by something that is "incomprehensible, which disorders his calculations. . . . the nameless powers of Nothingness are, in our world whence the gods
have been driven forth, the analogy of the demons that confronted primitive man."[17] I believe this is why men in the modern period have believed God to be silent and absent and even

16. Karl Jaspers, *Man in the Modern Age*, trans. Eden and Cedar Paul
(Garden City, Doubleday Anchor, 1957), pp. 209, 202, 210.
17. Ibid., p. 191.

dead. This has been their conclusion, because they have not lived out their days in real nearness to one another; and, not having known the gracious reality of presence in their relations with their neighbors, their imaginations have been unable to grasp the possibility of the world itself being grounded in a transcendent Presence.

In a world, where the human communion has been destroyed and man's condemnation is to an empty and unfertile solitude, what Gabriel Marcel calls *Présence*[18] appears to be, irretrievably, a thing of the past: not only does it appear that God is dead but also that an obituary notice is to be written that will memorialize the disappearance of man as well. In this "place of disaffection" (to use T. S. Eliot's phrase), the only available dispensation seems to be that of loneliness and exile. And the sober acceptance of this icy alienation as the inescapable ground of human existence constitutes that special modern sensibility which the Existentialist movement has brought most sharply into focus.

The "existentialist experience" is not, of course, the sole property of those contemporary theorists whose program goes under the name of Existentialism. Their nineteenth-century predecessors were, to be sure, among the first to give it emphatic definition. It first became a public fact in the Berlin lectures of Schelling (*Die Philosophie der Mythologie und der Offenbarung*) during the Winter of 1841–42, and in later writings of men like Kierkegaard and Marx and Feuerbach and Nietzsche and Max Weber. But the existentialist experience may also be dated from that morning when Baudelaire looked out upon the Paris landscape—"that vast cemetery that is called a great city"—and felt an immense disgust. We find it in such writers as Baudelaire, Rimbaud, Dostoievski, and Strindberg, and also in artists like Cézanne, Van Gogh, and the American, Albert Pinkham Ryder. These were all men who belonged to that nineteenth-century vanguard of revolution-

18. See Gabriel Marcel, *The Mystery of Being* (Chicago, Regnery, 1951), *1*, Chs. 9, 10 (trans. O. S. Fraser); *2*, Ch. 1 (trans. René Hogue).

aries who were distinguished by the clarity and courage with which they acknowledged the bitter facts of alienation and estrangement as the central facts of modern existence. And when, as Paul Tillich says in *The Courage to Be*, "the nineteenth century came to an end" on the thirty-first of July, 1914, the existentialist experience ceased to be the experience of a sensitive minority and became the dominant experience of the age. In this century it has furnished the perspectives of the philosophic tradition that has been established by such thinkers as Berdyaev, Chestov, Heidegger, Jaspers, Sartre, and Marcel; it is the experience that one feels in Stravinsky's *Petrouchka*, in Schoenberg's *Pierrot Lunaire*, in Alban Berg's *Wozzeck*, in Bartók's second *Quartet*, and in much of the great music of our time. It is also the experience that has been painted into many canvases of such classic moderns as Picasso and Rouault and the early de Chirico or of such recent artists as Willem de Kooning and Jackson Pollock and Hans Hofmann.

This strain of sensibility is central in much of twentieth-century literature: we recognize it in such poets as Rainer Maria Rilke, Hart Crane, Robert Penn Warren, and Gottfried Benn, and in such poets of the novel as Conrad, Kafka, Faulkner, and Malraux. Indeed, as Lionel Trilling has remarked, "There is carcely a great writer of our own day who has not addressed himself to the ontological crisis, who has not conceived of life as a struggle to be—not to live, but to be."[19] What one feels to be formative in much representative literature of our period is the profound need for a deep restoration of confidence in the stoutness, reliability, and essential healthiness of the things of earth. The trauma that has been suffered is the trauma inflicted upon the imagination when it appears that both God and man are dead.

Thus the narrative at the center of our literature is a narrative of estrangement and alienation: the story told is a tale of

19. Lionel Trilling, *The Opposing Self* (New York, Viking, 1955), p. 140.

our abandonment "in some blind lobby," "or corridor of Time." "And in that dark," says Robert Penn Warren, "no thread."[20] No thread! We are given some measure of how emphatic is the insistence upon our lostness by the apocalypticism and hyperesthesia of the modern literary imagination, "its feeling," as Richard Chase says, "that no thought is permissible except an extreme thought: that every idea must be directly emblematic of concentration camps, alienation, madness, hell," "that every word must bristle and explode with the magic potency of our plight."[21]

In our American tradition, the figure of William Dean Howells as a novelist has suffered a very considerable eclipse. We may be helped at least in part to understand the decline of his prestige by remembering the observation made many years ago by Henry James when he said of Howells, "He is animated by a love of the common, the immediate, the familiar, and the vulgar elements of life, and holds that in proportion as we move into the rare and strange we become vague and arbitrary."[22] And, when today we reread books like *The Rise and Fall of Silas Lapham* and *A Hazard of New Fortunes* and *A Modern Instance,* we realize that, with his customary acuteness, James put his finger exactly on one of Howells' primary qualities. Thus it is not surprising that the contemporary reader finds it so difficult to enter into a happy and reciprocal relation with his work, for, as Mr. Trilling has reminded us, "We consent to the commonplace [only] as it verges upon and becomes the rare and the strange": we "want something that has affinity with the common, the immediate, the familiar," but "we like them represented in their extremity to serve as a sort of outer limit of the possibility of our daily lives, as a kind of mundane hell."[23]

20. Robert Penn Warren, *Brother to Dragons* (London, Eyre & Spottiswoode, 1953), p. 7.

21. Richard Chase, "Christian Ideologue," in *The Nation* (April 8, 1950), p. 330.

22. Henry James, *The American Essays* (New York, Vintage Books, 1956), p. 152.

23. Trilling, *The Opposing Self*, p. 88.

of Our Period-Style

All the great charismatic seers of modern literature from Baudelaire to Kafka and from Pirandello to Faulkner, in one way or another, have wanted us to understand that we are lost in a dark wood and that, in this maze, what is least trustworthy is the common, the immediate, the familiar. Therefore, the motion that the modern artist has very often performed before the revolving universe has been one of recoil. Sometimes, like Rimbaud, he has fallen in love with what Jacques Maritain calls "the blind glitter of nothingness" and made of his art a kind of incantatory magic. Or, like the author of *Finnegans Wake*, sometimes he himself has decided to be God and to create *ex nihilo* a universe of his own. On occasion, his retreat, like Mallarmé's, has been into *la poésie pure*—or, like the early Hemingway or the Dos Passos of the *U.S.A.* trilogy, it has been into the neutral factuality of naturalistic documentation. The recoil has also been expressed in the subjectivistic perspectives of a Proust or a Virginia Woolf, or as that distress which provokes the belch of disgust, say, in Jean-Paul Sartre's *La Nausée*. Various as the configurations are, it can, nevertheless, be said that many major literary artists of our time, whether they knew it or not, have had as their patron saint not St. Athanasius but Dionysius the Areopagite, for, in their dealings with the body of this world, their Way has been not the Way of Affirmation but the Way of Rejection. That is, they have not known the kind of confidence in the world and in temporal reality that was managed in happier moments in the literary tradition.

Those Roman Catholic apologists who explain this attrition in terms of the anti-sacramentalism of a Protestant ethos are doubtless right in part—but they are right only in part, for the authentic sacramentalism of Christian faith has also been obscured by what has often been the theological and cultural obscurantism of post-Tridentine Romanism. Nor can we forget the role that has been played in this development by the deep fears generated by the continual expansion of the universe being mapped out by modern science and modern cosmology. In the seventeenth century, Pascal was already conscious of the anxiety caused by contemplating "the infinite immensity of spaces" being revealed by the new science, and, in what is one of the great expressions of modern consciousness, he said, "The eternal silence of these infinite spaces frightens me."[24] Of course, even far more frightening than the universes of modern physics have been the perils of modern historical existence itself which have tended increasingly to involve a global insecurity unexperienced in previous times. But by far the deepest cause of the despondency and sense of alienation in modern literature is to be found in the collapse of any real certainty that what is Radically and Ultimately Significant is not absolutely secluded from that which is only provisionally significant in nature and in history. To the men of our age, God seems, as Heidegger says, to be "withholding" Himself: he seems to be absent and perhaps even dead. As a consequence, our journey through the world seems to be a terribly uncertain and perilous journey: as Stanley Hopper puts it, "the familiar trails to reality are swallowed up in thickets of confusion: the spoors are thickly overlaid,"[25] and the artist's recoil before this dark and threatening wood is but type and example of the deep mistrust with which modern man faces today the indigence and privation of the world of finite, historical existence.

W. H. Auden tells us that Kafka bears to our own age the kind of relation that Dante bore to his, and, I am certain, a part of what he means is that, whereas the hero of Dante's poem is a pilgrim and the movement of the poem is from an initial darkness to a final light, the hero of the Kafkan fable, at the end of his journeying, is no nearer the Castle than he was at the beginning and remains forever quavering in the dungeon of his dereliction. In the one case, we have the Christian drama of rebirth and redemption; in the other, we have a story of the soul's exclusion from the Courts of the Most High and

24. Blaise Pascal, *Pensées*, trans. W. F. Trotter, Fragment 206 (New York, Dutton, 1943), p. 61.
25. Stanley R. Hopper, "On the Naming of the Gods in Hölderlin and Rilke," in *Christianity and the Existentialists*, ed. Carl Michalson (New York, Scribner's, 1956), p. 156.

of the despair which overtakes the soul in its abandonment and isolation—the story, in other words, that embodies the characteristic judgment of the human condition that is rendered by the Existentialist imagination in modern literature.

Ours is, then, an "extreme" literature which plunges us into "extreme" situations. Conrad's Decoud, Kafka's K., Gide's Lafcadio, Malraux's Kyo, Faulkner's Joe Christmas, and Penn Warren's Jeremiah Beaumont are all men who have been cast into a world that offers no place of safety or security. Their lives have to be lived at a great distance from whatever are the sources of ultimate meaning, and, as a consequence, the salient stigmata of the modern hero are to be seen in his scepticism and in his despondency and alienation. However, the miracle that occurs in the existentialist universe of a Conrad or a Kafka or a Malraux or a Faulkner is that, through the grace of some power that is unnamed and perhaps unknown, this scepticism and this despondency are prevented from so completely encircling the hero as to undo his humanity, so that he, in his great moments, has had what Tillich calls "the courage of despair"—the courage, despite everything problematic and uncertain in his world, to affirm his humanity. And since, despite all the nihilism in modern literature, this courage is an expression of a kind of faith—faith, as Dr. Tillich says, is simply "the state of being grasped by the power of being-itself"[26]—it is not surprising that the redefinition in our time of classical traditions of faith has often been deeply informed by this whole body of testimony. The Orthodox thinker Nicolas Berdyaev, the Roman Catholics Romano Guardini and Jacques Maritain, and the Protestant theologian Paul Tillich are representative of many other leading strategists of contemporary religious thought who have been alert to the fact that, if the high forms of faith are once again to appear at least *possible* for us, their reinterpretation must be informed by the kind of awareness that comes from facing the distresses of life without

26. Paul Tillich, *The Courage To Be* (New Haven, Yale University Press), p. 172.

any of the supports and consolations of religious faith. And so, in the attentiveness with which the religious community today often listens to our poets and novelists and dramatists, we may discern some earnest of the reconstructive role that may yet be played by modern negation and denial.

—for Joseph Sittler

Human life is drenched in time, in its restless rhythm and dynamic periodicity. And since man, as Unamuno said, is "of flesh and bone," the time in which he dwells comes to him as flux, as passing and perishing, as a powerfully inexorable fatality that is forever pushing life toward its final limit. Though we sing in our chains like the sea, said Dylan Thomas, Time holds us green and dying. For we are but the merest reeds in nature, feeble at best, and soon withering away: we are not creatures of permanence: nothing stays for us, and there is no escaping what Camus called "the cruel mathematics that command our condition." The time in which man dwells is the time of the hourglass, and this is a time which not only constitutes the encompassing structure of human life but which also forms the basic environment of all living things. For the career of everything that grows and develops is bracketed within the consecutive flow of temporality, and death is the form that finality takes for all living things, whether they be vegetal or animal or human.

To man alone, however, is reserved the vocation of living under the shadow of this ultimate and inescapable threat, and the burden that he bears by virtue of being human is a burden that in part entails the privilege and the obligation of anticipating his eventual annulment, of *knowing* that he shall die. Among all the creatures of the earth, it is alone the distinction of humankind to claim death as the capital possibility of its existence. And it may well be that our very awareness of time itself is arrived at by some process of vitally immediate and non-discursive inference from our knowledge of death's impendence: this is indeed frequently hinted at in the profound meditations on death that form so large a part of Martin Heidegger's great book of 1927, *Being and Time,* where it is suggested that the existential structure of our being-in-the-world is a being-toward-the-end, toward-death, toward that point beyond which we shall be no more. And if a running-toward-death constitutes one of the essential modalities of human existence, it may well be that, insofar as it situates man in the future, it is just this impending threat of the ultimate *annihilatio* that elicits in us the sense of passage, of transit, of chronology.

But time is something more than merely transience toward death, for it is bent not only toward the future but also toward the past. Indeed, in the very anticipation of death itself there is implicit the realization of having *been* committed to the world and of *being* therefore very largely constituted by what one's place in the world has been. For man to live in the presence of death is, in other words, for him to be made deeply aware of his createdness: the very contingency of his existence, as it is disclosed in the awareness that he must die, tells him that the origin and meaning of his life are not wholly immanent within himself: he did not create himself: life itself is received, it is a gift. And not only is man, in the ontological order, a creature, that is, a created being—but, in the historical order, he also *is* very largely what he has *become:* he is a product of what the Greeks called *paideia,* of that deep process of formation through which the social and cultural actualities of one's inheritance give shape and form to personal existence.

So, though we are *un*made by time, there is also a sense in which it appears that we are *made* by time, not so much by natural time as by cultural and historical time, by the rich bequests that we inherit (through family and church and the educational community and the nation) from the funded wisdom and experience of the human community. We are bent *toward* the future, and the human situation may therefore from a certain angle be viewed as being-toward-the-end. But we are also bent *by* the past. The Spanish philosopher Julián Marías quotes a passage from his master, Ortega, which reminds us that "the task of being a man was obviously a very different one [in 1862 A.D.] from what it had been in 1862 B.C.," and Ortega means, presumably, to call our attention to the fact that the human enterprise of a hundred years ago was qualified by an inheritance of norms and values and experience that was profoundly different from that which was known by men of the second millennium before Christ. This is to say that, though "time *passes* and its manner of being consists in passing or flowing by . . . it is also something which *remains*, something which is kept and stored up,"[1] and that man's life, always bearing the pressure of the past, is therefore radically historical.

Hence the temporality of human existence is expressed in the fact that man is at once projected forward toward what he *will be* and is also constituted by what he has *become*. Human time is both the inheritance of the past and the promise of the future (which is, ultimately, a promise of despair and utter woe, if it is untransfigured by the alchemy of religious faith). But, if time is somehow in a future that is not yet and in a past that is no more, the question must inevitably arise as to where it really is, if in fact it has any actual location at all. If "we live from that which is no more toward what is not yet through a slender, fragile boundary called 'now' "[2] that is too fugitive ever really to be laid hold of, where, then, is time? This question has perennially occasioned perplexity, but its perplexity has just as perennially been dispelled by the recovery of the answer which was given by Augustine and which has been immensely influential in Western thought. For it was Augustine who first gave conceptual clarity to the profound truth that if

1. Julián Marías, *Reason and Life* trans. Kenneth H. Reid and Edward Sarmiento (New Haven, Yale University Press, 1956), pp. 360, 120.
2. Roger Hazelton, *God's Way With Man* (New York, Abingdon Press, 1956), p. 101.

we would discover where time is we need look no farther than ourselves, for there, he said, within the self, is where it lies. Book XI of his *Confessions* is very largely given over to an analysis of the problem of time, and the line that he takes is summarily indicated by the concluding paragraph of Chapter 28:

> I am about to repeat a psalm that I know. Before I begin, my attention is extended to the whole; but when I have begun, as much of it as becomes past by my saying it is extended in my memory; and the life of this action of mine is extended both ways between my memory, on account of what I have repeated, and my expectation, on account of what I am about to repeat; yet my consideration is present with me, through which that which was future may be carried over so that it may become past. The more this is done and repeated, by so much (expectation being shortened) the memory is enlarged, until the whole expectation be exhausted, when that whole action being ended shall have passed into memory. And what takes place in the entire psalm, takes place also in each individual part of it, and in each individual syllable: this holds in the longer action, of which that psalm is perchance a portion; the same holds in the whole life of man, of which all the actions of man are parts; the same holds in the whole age of the sons of men, of which all the lives of men are parts.

What Augustine suggests through this illustration is that the unity of time has its real ground in the soul, in the imagination, and that this in fact is *where* time is: the past *exists* in the mind's capacity for recollection, and the future *exists* in our intentions and expectations, and the present *emerges* out of the imagination's fusion of its memory of the past and its anticipation of the future. As Augustine says, in his twenty-eighth chapter of Book XI of the *Confessions*, time is "in the human mind, which expects, considers, and remembers." And, significantly, his testimony is at this point deeply in accord with a fundamental perspective of Biblical thought. For, as

Paul Minear reminds us, "in the Bible, time is primarily a category of history rather than of nature."[3] That is, the Biblical community, characteristically, took little interest in clock-time, in those linear orders of temporal sequence which are measured by chronometers: its tendency was to grasp an event in terms of its content rather than in terms of its position in a uniform series of quantitatively defined units of objective time. And, for the men of the Bible, all the occasions of life have as their most significant content a human response to divine purpose: all times are of God's appointment, and they move with a momentum arising out of the dynamic stuff of human volition. Time is what it is not by reason of being dateable by a calendar or measurable by a clock but by reason of being the theatre within which human life reaches its fulfillment: it is "a fabric woven of the warp of opportunity and the woof of human response."[4] And time is used to "press toward the mark for the prize of the high calling of God in Christ Jesus" (Philippians 3:14); that is, the knight of faith is no slave to any merely objective order of temporal sequence: he can bend it in the pursuit of his "high calling": time dwells *in him:* and it is not surprising that, in his meditations on the nature of time in Book XI of the *Confessions,* Augustine should have been led to recall this passage from the Epistle to the Philippians.

The existentialist realism about time that we encounter in Biblical thought and in Augustine is also frequently to be encountered in modern intellectual tradition, and often in thinkers otherwise as radically divergent from one another as Kant and Kierkegaard, Marx and Bergson, Whitehead and Heidegger: for these and many others, the time that it is felt to be most important to study is *le temps humain*—that is, *our* time, the time that bears the imprint of human purpose and decision, the time which is not merely the infinite extension that is ticked off by a chronometer but which is filled with human

3. Paul S. Minear, *Eyes of Faith* (Philadelphia, Westminster Press, 1946), p. 98.
4. John Marsh, *The Fulness of Time* (London, Nisbet, 1952), p. 22.

intentionality and therefore dwells within the deep recesses of man's own creativity.

In the most primary sense, then, in which any predication can be made, the reality of human existence is a temporal reality, for in every dimension of man's life his most vital and immediate horizon is the horizon of time. It is the basic environment not only of man but of all forms of organic life, and everything that it touches is afflicted with transitoriness. But though time moves in the direction ultimately of death, in all the anterior phases of its motion it may be viewed not only (in Whitehead's phrase) as a "perpetual perishing" but also as a force of creativeness. For, as Sr. Marías says, "though it is true that time uses up and puts an end to our lives, is it not even truer . . . that living is always living more time, that life makes itself not merely in time but *with* time, that time is the substance out of which life weaves its web?"[5] Man lives, in other words, not only in time but on time. And, lastly, as we have noticed, time lives also in him.

Time is, in short, both the milieu and the medium of human life; and this is why it, inevitably, is also the medium of the arts of story, of all those forms of literature which present a narrative account of the human adventure in the concrete terms of action and plot and character. The arts of the word, however, are involved in time not merely by reason of the radically temporal character of human existence itself but also by reason of what is intrinsically the nature of literary art. This is an aspect of the matter that Aristotle was to some extent mindful of—as, for example, in his notion that the action of a play needs to be confined "within the limits of a single revolution of the sun"—though he was not nearly so preoccupied with the problem of time as the Renaissance theorists of Italy (Robortelli, Scaliger, Castelvetro) and England (Sidney, Jonson, Dryden) tended to suggest, when they implied a clear Aristotelian sanction for the rigorism with which they converted unity of time into an absolute requirement for drama. Indeed, it was not until the second-half of

5. Marías, *Reason and Life*, p. 120.

the eighteenth century that what is essentially temporal in the nature of the literary medium began to win some clear acknowledgment and recognition. And the crucial event is of course Lessing's notable work of 1766, the *Laocoön*, with its famous distinction between the arts of space and the arts of time.

The immediate provocation of Lessing's essay was provided by the archaeologist Johann Joachim Winckelmann, who, in attempting to contrast the Greek genius with the Latin, had turned, on the one hand, to Vergil's *Aeneid* and, on the other, to the famous group of Hellenistic sculptures (excavated on the grounds of Hadrian's villa in 1506) that in the eighteenth century was lodged in the Vatican Museum. Winckelmann contended that the reason why the priest Laocoön, in the statue that bears his name, is exhibited with calm and undistorted features, despite being locked in mortal combat with two serpents, is that the Greek genius was characteristically given to sobriety and a noble restraint. On the other hand, Vergil's Laocoön, said Winckelmann, bellows and shrieks in his agony because the Latins were lacking in a certain maturity and reserve, and therefore had no capacity for curbing violent outbursts of strong emotion. Lessing accepted this contrast which Winckelmann drew between the two Laocoöns (as he would surely not have done, had he had access to the statute and been able to observe that in point of fact the Laocoön in the marble group is by no means represented as silent and impassive), but he regarded Winckelmann's manner of interpreting the contrast as a gratuitous slur on Vergil and the Latin world: for, said he, what is at issue is not such a factitious distinction between the Greeks and the Latins as Winckelmann was attempting to establish but simply the inner logic of plastic art. As he explained, the plastic arts represent bodies coexistent in space; whereas poetry (that is, the literary arts in general) deals with situations and actions in which there is movement through time. "If it is true," he wrote, "that painting employs in its imitations quite other means or signs than poetry employs—the first, form and color in space; the second, articulated sounds in time—if these symbols indisputably require a suitable relation to the thing signified, then it is clear that symbols arranged together side by side can express only subjects which, or the various parts of which, exist thus side by side, whilst symbols which succeed each other can express only subjects which, or the various parts of which, are themselves consecutive" (Section XVI). And because the plastic arts are spatial, the artist working in these media, in painting or sculpture, has always to settle upon the "single moment" which best represents the total history of his subject, since he is prevented from exhibiting the flow and evolution of that history by the very nature of his medium. So, the Laocoön of the Greek sculpture, though caught in a death grip by serpents, presents a countenance undistorted by agony not for the reason adduced by Winckelmann but simply because the artist who created the figure, having no way in which to represent the complete history of the priest, was confined to a "single moment" and had therefore to carve the facial expression of a soul at rest, because a gape and a grimace are (as Lessing reasoned) formal faults in sculptural art. But Vergil, though he represents Laocoön as shrieking aloud in the Second Book of the *Aeneid,* is not confined to the "single moment": "this shrieking Laocoön we already know and love as the wisest of patriots and the most affectionate of fathers" (Section IV). And since the poet can give us a more temporally spacious view of his subject, when he portrays him as racked by death-agonies, he does not run the risk of encouraging us to attribute the cries to the subject's character: that has *already* been established, and we refer the cries, therefore, not to the subject's character but only to his unendurable suffering. In short, the mere fact of Vergil's portrayal of Laocoön's torment need not be attributed to any special conception of his character but merely to what is possible within the medium in which he was working.

In this way, then, Lessing moved toward a fundamental conception of form in the literary arts. And however out-of-date certain phases of his argument may be today by reason of his dependence upon the now-antiquated archaeological researches of Winckelmann or by reason of his polemic against the pictorial poetry of his period which has long since ceased to have any interest for the modern reader, he presents us with one of the great seminal insights into the nature of literature and stands, along with Plato and Aristotle and Longinus and Coleridge and Croce, among the few truly original thinkers in the history of poetics. For it was Lessing who first brought into public view the fact that the arts of the word have time, in a very special sense, as their essential medium. Literature is an art of time because, as Lessing realized, it is built out of language which is itself composed of sequences of words following one another in time. And thus a work of literary art requires time, simply in order to be itself: a poem or a novel does, of course, exist as so many characters on a printed page or as a thick chunk of pages bound between hard covers; but the poem or novel does not exist as a work of art until it is read, and the reading happens not in an instant but in a period of time, thus marking a certain difference between a novel, say, and a painting or a statue—for whereas "you [can] move round the statue," and have it, "always there in its entirety before you,"[6] if, when you are halfway through Tolstoy's *War and Peace*, you find that you have *forgotten* what went before, then the novel has ceased to exist as a work of art. It may be of course—indeed, it most surely is the case —that the *deepening* of apprehension of a work of plastic art also requires time: but at least one's *first* apprehension of a painting can be immediate in a way that can never be the case with a work of literary art, for a novel or a drama cannot even begin to exist without the passage of time. And it was Lessing who first laid hold of and clearly enunciated this fundamental truth about the nature of literature.

But literary art is not only involved in time because its human subject is temporal and because its own nature is temporal: it has also within itself, characteristically, a profound

6. Wyndham Lewis, *Time and Western Man* (New York, Harcourt, Brace, 1928), p. 174.

awareness of time. It is, of course, aware of time insofar as it is deeply aware of the "dark backward and abysm" of the human mystery itself: but I am now referring not to historical time but to what may be called literary time. For our present understanding of this aspect of the matter, we are perhaps most largely indebted to T. S. Eliot and to his celebrated essay of 1917 on "Tradition and the Individual Talent." For it was Eliot, more than any other modern critic, who taught us to understand how "nearly indispensable to anyone who would continue to be a poet beyond his twenty-fifth year" is "the historical sense." By this he meant such a grasp of tradition as "compels a man to write not merely with his own generation in his bones, but with a feeling that the whole of the literature of Europe from Homer and within it the whole of the literature of his own country has a simultaneous existence and composes a simultaneous order."[7] Literature exists, in other words, in something like that "imaginary museum" where, as André Malraux supposes, modern photography has made the entire history of visual art immediately available to the contemporary artist. But the analogy is not quite exact, since, in that ideal order which each new poet enters, it is not the quiet decorum of a museum that prevails but rather the assertive debate of a forum, for the tradition is undergoing a constant process of alteration as a result of pressures exerted upon it by each fresh addition. Not only does every authentic work of art exert its own pressure upon the tradition, but it also bears upon itself the pressure of the tradition: and its particular way of bearing this burden, its special "sense of the past," constitutes an important element of the unique datum which it presents to the reader.

Thus, in several large ways literature is deeply involved in time. And the central tradition in the poetics of our period has, it now seems, too greatly obscured this whole dimension of things. Ironically stemming in part from Eliot himself and

7. T. S. Eliot, *Selected Essays: 1917–1932* (New York, Harcourt, Brace, 1932), p. 4.

chiefly represented in America by the movement which John Crowe Ransom in 1941 named "the New Criticism," this tradition has had a great reluctance to acknowledge how deeply immersed literature is in the stuff of time and history. In reaction against the historicist biases of an earlier literary scholarship, the New Criticism has wanted to confront the poem not as a marginal gloss on social and intellectual history nor as a symptomatic puff of the Zeitgeist but as a poem; and its admirable program, as it was once formulated by Cleanth Brooks, has been to "put the reader in possession of the work of art." To account for the strenuous attention which aesthetic experience involves, these theorists developed a view of the literary work as an autonomous system of verbal constructs among which there is an interaction so dynamic as to lure the reader out of the circumambient world into the "new" and autotelic world of the poem's unicity. In line with this definition of the work, distinctively literary "meaning" arises solely out of the complex mutual qualifications that the constituent terms of a poetic discourse practice upon one another: it is a purely "reflexive" meaning, an affair of "irony" and "tension": and the language of literary art, in this canon, is unstained by either the historicity of human existence or of literature or of the inherited language itself.

Increasingly in recent years, however—despite the special kind of brilliance that this poetic fostered in the work of its best exponents—a certain dissatisfaction with the whole concept of literature on which the New Criticism was based has been making considerable headway. The most thoughtful spokesmen for the new attitude are not at all ungrateful for the lessons in the reading of texts that they were taught by the New Criticism—by men like Brooks and Ransom and Allen Tate and R. P. Blackmur—and they are by no means generally inclined rudely to launch a frontal assault. But they are concerned so to widen and deepen the hermeneutics of the New Criticism as to win a new enfranchisement for the recognition that the true function of literature is today, and always has been, to awaken in us a greater lucidity about our common *humanitas*[8] and its commitment to the manifold burdens of time and history, as this is made manifest not only through the account that literature gives us of man's existential plight but also through the inner history of literature itself. This new interest was first expressed with compelling cogency by Lionel Trilling in his essay of the early forties, "The Sense of the Past,"[9] and in the last few years it is what one feels to be the controlling motive behind many diverse developments in criticism—the theory of "open" form in the work of Robert Adams,[10] the new "historicism" of Roy Harvey Pearce,[11] the existentialist personalism of Fr. Walter Ong,[12] and the elusively absorbing mythography of Northrop Frye[13] being significant examples.

It begins to be possible, then, once again to repossess the dimension of time as a central index of drift or tendency in the realm of the literary imagination. Indeed this is an angle from which the literature of the modern period most insistently asks to be considered, as Wyndham Lewis reminded us in his crankily brilliant book of 1928, *Time and Western Man*. For with most of the characteristic writers of our period—Proust, Joyce, Mann, Virginia Woolf, Eliot, Ezra Pound, and Faulkner, to mention only a few—time is an abiding problem: ours is a literature obsessed with time, with time lost and time recaptured, with time as duration and time as disintegration: and most of the texts in our poetry and especially in our fiction

8. My choice of this term stems from the suggestive use made by Roy Harvey Pearce in the essay cited in n. 11.

9. Trilling, *The Liberal Imagination*.

10. See Robert M. Adams, *Strains of Discord: Studies in Literary Openness* (Ithaca, Cornell University Press, 1958).

11. See Roy Harvey Pearce, "Historicism Once More," *Kenyon Review*, 20 (1958), 554–91; also Pearce, *The Continuity of American Poetry* (Princeton, Princeton University Press, 1961).

12. See Walter J. Ong, S. J., *The Barbarian Within* (New York, Macmillan, 1962), Part 1.

13. See Northrop Frye, *Anatomy of Criticism* (Princeton, Princeton University Press, 1957).

prove, on examination, to be various types of metaphors on the nature of time.

The special sensibility that lies behind this fascination has perhaps its most immediate root in the sheer crowdedness of the time that has been experienced by people living in the Western world during the last hundred years. Since Wendell Willkie first taught us at the outbreak of World War II to think of the human community today as forming "one world," we have grown accustomed to the use of the phrase in purely political discussions that emphasize the impossibility of conducting politics any longer on the assumption that the nation-state retains its traditional autonomy. But, fearsomely as this lesson has been proved by the events of the past quarter-century, there is a deeper, spiritual sense in which ours is one world, though here too the meaning is by no means unconnected with the technological advance that has created many of our political dilemmas. For the same marvellous techniques of modern communication that bring Washington and London and Paris and Moscow into such close proximity not only set the terms within which our statesmen have to work but also contribute very largely to the formation of the whole evanescent atmosphere in which the men and women of our time experience what the psychologists call "human identity." What is at issue here is simply the fact that an event today can, as it were, be instantly recorded by our newspapers and radio and television networks: we live in an age in which there is no longer any real interim between a significant ocurrence and its being learned about all across the globe: thus, through the immediate ripples of reaction that are set up, and through the waves of counterreaction that follow, indeed through large complex chains of reaction, our various reportorial agencies can, and actually do, initiate what Erich Kahler speaks of as a "mass production of events." "The result of all this," he says, "is a crowding of events in the domain of our vision and consciousness, an oppressive closeness and overwhelming shiftiness of events, an excess of details and complexities in every single event—in short, what I would call an *overpopulation of the surfaces.*"[14] To leaf through the pages of so characteristic a phenomenon of our culture as *Life* magazine —as one looks at bathing beauties in Atlantic City and Negro civil rights-demonstrators on the streets of Birmingham and the bier of Pope John in the Vatican and a fancy house-party in Connecticut and a Buddhist priest burning himself to death on a thoroughfare in Saigon—is to feel that one is being flicked at by something like an antique movie. And the whole of contemporary life is very much like an early cinema show: the sensation everywhere felt is that of being flicked at: the surfaces are overpopulated because of the sheer mass-production of events, and time has a crowdedness unexperienced by men in earlier periods of history.

This enormous density of what may be called "modern time" gives rise to our characteristic vertigo, to the sense that "all time is eternally present," that all the fragments of all possible experience are somehow simultaneously coexistent in the present. For the present has taken on a kind of kaleidoscopic boundlessness; and, as a consequence, it seems no longer possible for the mind to distinguish between and define its own fundamental categories: everything appears to be whirling into everything else, to be flowing into the heterogeneous and unstable present. Indeed, the very principle of temporality seems no longer possible of assumption, for not only is time spatialized in the simultaneity of the kaleidoscopic present but the violence of international politics has also given the spaces of modern life a new kind of temporal character, so that space itself is no longer a fact of nature but rather a fact of culture—an issue of contention between statesmen that has entered into the continuum of historical time.

Whereas life once appeared to be a pilgrimage and like a journey, it now seems to be very much like Grand Central Station (on a busy, holiday week end). And thus Arnold Hauser speaks of ours as "the film age," for it is the cinema which is

14. Erich Kahler, *The Tower and the Abyss* (New York, Braziller, 1957), p. 95–96.

not only the invention of the modern age but which has come to be the artistic medium that, through its commingling of space and time, most perfectly symbolizes our sense of the fluidity of experience. In the temporal medium of a film, says Dr. Hauser, time "loses, on the one hand, its uninterrupted continuity, on the other, its irreversible direction. It can be brought to a standstill: in close-ups; reversed: in flash-backs; repeated: in recollections; and skipped across: in visions of the future. Concurrent, simultaneous events can be shown successively, and temporally distinct events simultaneously—by double-exposure and alternation; the earlier can appear later, the later before its time."[15] And it is just this irregularity of cinematic time that forms so large a part of the distinctively modern experience.

Since the tempo of human existence in this late stage of modern history leads men to experience time as scattered, as amorphous and fluid, inevitably there arises the anxious surmise that there may be nothing any longer that can be counted on to hold time together, to order it and stabilize it and give it firm anchorage. Eternity is felt to be in eclipse and all is in doubt: for time has lost all coherence: one instant is indistinguishable from another or is merely engulfed by another, and all moments have fallen into a strange impoverishment and mediocrity in which they know neither design nor repose. All is turmoil, dishevelment, muddle. And, as a consequence, the drama of life in time is felt to have the form of tragedy: for time itself is sheer anguish: it is servitude and captivity, it is hopelessness and homesickness, and abandonment. T. S. Eliot in "The Dry Salvages" summarizes the modern sense of time; in this "drifting wreckage," it appears that

> the way up is the way down, the way forward is the way back.
> You cannot face it steadily, but this thing is sure,
> That time is no healer.

15. See Arnold Hauser, *The Social History of Art* (New York, Vintage Books, 1958), 4, Ch. 8, and p. 241.

It is not surprising, therefore, that modern literature tacitly records a recession of the kind of concern that was generally expressed in earlier periods whenever time was the subject of reflection. The Psalmist often thought, for example, how

> our years come to an end like a sigh.
> The years of our life are three score years and ten,
> or even by reason of strength four score;
> yet their span is but toil and trouble;
> they are soon gone, and we fly away.
> (Ps. 90; RSV trans.)

This is in line with the reminder in Shakespeare's *Cymbeline*:

> Golden lads and girls all must,
> As chimney-sweepers, come to dust

and with Wordsworth's reflection in the "Immortality" ode that

> The Clouds that gather round the setting sun
> Do take a sober colouring from any eye
> That hath kept watch o'er man's mortality

and with Tennyson's regret in "Break, Break, Break" that

> the tender grace of a day that is dead
> Will never come back to me.

But though this traditional dirge on time as "the fire in which we burn" still persists in the literature of our period, it has long ceased being a characteristic emphasis. For the attitude of the modern imagination toward time is no longer that of a melancholy composure but is rather one that more nearly approaches a stifled panic. "Time surely would scatter all," reflects Joyce in *Ulysses*: and Stephen Dedalus says, "History is a nightmare from which I am trying to awake." And this young Dublin aesthete brings to a nice point the baffled anguish that is everywhere so much a part of the sensibility expressed in the most representative literature of the past fifty or seventy-five years when it confronts the mystery of time.

in Modern Literature

T. S. Eliot tells us in "Burnt Norton" that "Only through time time is conquered." But the late poems of Yeats present an important case of the line that the resistance to this ancient wisdom has often taken in the literature of this century. In the work of, roughly, his last twenty years (particularly in *The Tower*, 1928, and *The Winding Stair*, 1933), the sentimental reveries of the Celtic twilight had long since given way to a sternly tragic vision, and Yeats was deeply preoccupied not only with the special anxieties brought by his own decline into old age but also with what he felt to be the exhaustion that had overtaken the whole of Western civilization. The elaborately mythologic philosophy of history that he worked out in *A Vision* need not concern us here in all its thorny detail; suffice it to say, in Yeats's view, we had arrived at the twenty-third phase of our historical cycle—which meant:

Things fall apart; the centre cannot hold. . . .

And, as he contemplated the progress of his own decrepitude and the demise of traditions that had once held civilization together and given it unity, it was borne in upon him ever more depressingly that in the realm of nature and history no achievement is ever decisive, that human life itself and all the monuments of culture are subject to iron laws of cyclical process that bring everything inevitably to dissolution and decay. But from this malaise he sought relief in a dream, the dream of that "moment when Byzantium . . . substituted for formal Roman magnificence, with its glorification of physical power, an architecture that suggests the Sacred City in the Apocalypse of St. John." Here, he felt—"a little before Justinian opened St. Sophia and closed the Academy of Plato"— "religious, aesthetic, and practical life were one" as "never before or since in recorded history," and "architect and artificers . . . spoke to the multitude and the few alike. The painter, the mosaic worker, the worker in gold and silver, the illuminator of sacred books, were almost impersonal, almost perhaps without the consciousness of individual design, absorbed in their subject-matter and that the vision of a whole people."[16] Byzantium became for Yeats not so much a place as an image of a Heaven to which one could flee from "this filthy modern tide": its "Monuments of unageing intellect" came to symbolize for him the "artifice of eternity" to which the soul aspires, in its discontent with the flux and mutation of the natural world. And thus, even in the midst of his busy life in Ireland, after a time he felt himself to be most truly in Byzantium, whose

> starlit . . . dome disdains
> All that man is,
> All mere complexities,
> The fury and the mire of human veins.

The great "Byzantium" poems present a major statement, then, of what became a dominant aspiration of Yeats's last years—to find a better City for the human spirit than this "gong-tormented sea," to find a place on whose pavements at midnight flit

> Flames that no faggot feeds, nor steel has lit,
> Nor storm disturbs, flames begotten of flame,
> Where blood-begotten spirits come
> And all complexities of fury leave.

It was "a City which hath foundations" that he wanted, a City above and outside of time altogether, for man's prevailing depended finally on "time's filthy load" being sloughed off utterly. And the great thing about Byzantium was that, through the alchemy of his imagination, it became a City with no "antinomies/Of day and night." Indeed, to get to the top of "the winding stair," to be "beyond the curtain/Of distorting days"—this is what, in many of its phases, Yeats's later poetry is aiming at; and it is natural, therefore, that at last he should have found his Vergil in the Plotinus of the *Enneads*.

Now it is just such a negation of time, such a quest of a

16. William Butler Yeats, *A Vision* (London, Macmillan, 1937), pp. 279–80.

timeless eternity, that constitutes a principal effort of the literary imagination of our period. And most especially is this the case in the novel, since of all literary forms it is perhaps the one least "dominated by any indispensable formal pattern which might interfere with or superimpose a difficulty on the pattern of events in time with which it deals."[17] "We must get rid of our superstition of chronology," said Simone Weil, "in order to find eternity." And hers is a remark that offers a remarkably apt epigraph for many of the great books that must be considered in an effort to clarify the main movement of the modern novel. For this is generally a literature that places itself most insistently *sub specie aeternitatis*. And its rebellion against time may be regarded as having two principal philosophic guides and patron saints, the one being the eighteenth-century Neapolitan Giovanni Battista Vico and the other, Henri Bergson.

The *Scienza Nuova* (1725)—the modern discovery of which was made by the French historian Jules Michelet in the 1820s —was the product of a loyal Roman Catholic intelligence, but Vico so consistently interpreted the providential element in history in terms of a *lumen naturale* operative in human decision that any genuinely transcendent dimension was wellnigh completely obscured. Though he derived the basic direction of history from its ultimate source in God, the actualization of this nisus was so much an affair of the inner necessities arising out of the dynamism of the human drama itself that he ended in a virtually secular historicism. But Vico's significance in the history of thought is largely a result of his having elaborated this prevenient Hegelianism in the terms of a cyclical theory of time. Since he envisaged no likelihood of any direct or drastic ingression of the divine into the natural order, he conceived the movement of history to be a cyclical rhythm of *corso* and *ricorso*, of course and recurrence. His version of "the eternal return" does not, however, entail such a brutal fatalism as would destroy the possibility of any kind of sig-

17. David Paul, "Time and the Novelist," *Partisan Review*, 21 (1954), 639.

nificant novelty in history, for the cycles of *corso* and *ricorso*, in his view, are not endlessly identical. Yet the cyclical motion of time is itself sufficiently rigorous to preclude the possibility of the temporal process ever reaching any definitive fulfillment.

There are, of course, numerous figures in modern intellectual tradition—from Nietzsche to Toynbee—in whom the cyclical interpretation of history has won various kinds of restatement. But it is this remarkably independent Italian thinker on the threshold of the Enlightenment who makes perhaps the best claim to be regarded as the presiding genius behind the very considerable renascence of the cyclical imagination in our time: and that he should have been a direct and primary influence on James Joyce, one of the major exemplars of cyclical thinking in the modern novel, is perhaps sufficient proof that there is no historical whimsicality involved in discerning his shadow to fall across a large phase of twentieth-century literature.

The historian of religion, Mircea Eliade, has given us perhaps the best insight that recent scholarship affords into the essential meaning of "the myth of the eternal return." In his remarkably brilliant book that bears this title, Professor Eliade is not, of course, immediately concerned with any particular aspect of modern spirituality: his theme instead bears on the world of archaic man and how he renders that world imaginatively tolerable. However, in his analysis of archaic ideologies of archetypes and repetition, he has notably illumined a form of thought which man has perennially employed in interpreting his experience and whose inner logic is disclosed with especial clarity in pre-modern or "traditional" cultures. These are the cultures that "include both the world usually known as 'primitive' and the ancient cultures of Asia, Europe, and America." Professor Eliade finds ontological speculation in all these various systems of life to reveal an exceedingly low tolerance of history and a profound desire to apprehend structures of reality that may offer man some defense against the virulence of time. Indeed, archaic man feels so threatened by concrete, historical time that his aim is to abolish it: this is partly achieved by regarding every reality in the phenomenal world as modeled on an extraterrestrial archetype and by regarding all the significant patterns of human action (which are, of course, ritual actions) as imitations or repetitions of archetypal gestures primordially performed by the gods: and in this way "profane time and duration are suspended." But, more decisively even, time is abolished by its continuous regeneration through New Year festivals and through periodic purification rites that expel demons and disease and sin. And nowhere is the regeneration of time more fully proved for the primitive than in lunar rhythms, for the phases of the moon not only provide a convenient method of measuring profane time but also reveal the eternal return, reveal "an ontology uncontaminated by time and becoming" which,

> by conferring a cyclic direction upon time, annuls its irreversibility. Everything begins over again at its commencement every instant. The past is but a prefiguration of the future. No event is irreversible and no transformation is final. In a certain sense, it is even possible to say that nothing new happens in the world, for everything is but the repetition of the same primordial archetypes; this repetition, by actualizing the mythical moment when the archetypal gesture was revealed, constantly maintains the world in the same auroral instant of the beginnings. Time but makes possible the appearance and existence of things. It has no final influence upon their existence, since it is itself constantly regenerated.[18]

For archaic man, as Hegel declared, there is nothing new under the sun: for him things repeat themselves for ever and ever: but this is not an altogether unprofitable repetition, for it accomplishes the suspension, as it were, of time, and permits him therefore to refuse history and to rescue himself from the meaninglessness of profane time.

18. Mircea Eliade, *The Myth of the Eternal Return*, trans. Willard R. Trask (London, Routledge, 1955), pp. 3, 35, 89–90.

Now it is the powerful reassertion of just such a vision of the world in terms of cyclical periodicity that is noticeable in much of the literature of this century—and most especially so in its tendency to mythicize experience. For the myth is that form in which the imagination undertakes to grasp the eternal present, the Time which is above and outside of time, the Great Time, in which all the concrete times and seasons of life eternally return to the same. T. S. Eliot was perhaps the first to suggest the essential clue to what is at stake here when, in his early review of James Joyce's *Ulysses,* he remarked Joyce's derivation of his narrative order from Homer's *Odyssey* and stated that, "in using the myth, in manipulating a continuous parallel between contemporaneity and antiquity, Mr. Joyce is pursuing a method which others must pursue after him." This, said Eliot, is Joyce's way of "making the modern world possible for art." One suspects that at this point, as on so many other occasions in his criticism, he may really have been talking also about the affairs that were closest to his heart— namely, the affairs of poetry, and even of his own poetry: for in *The Waste Land* he had himself just attempted to make the modern world possible for art by manipulating mythical parallels between contemporaneity and antiquity. And this is the stratagem that many of his contemporaries in poetry (Yeats, for example, or, in another way, the Greek poet Constantine Cavafy, or, in still another way, the Frenchman St.-John Perse) were also employing. Nor can the force of his observation, simply as it stands, be questioned, for Joyce's *Ulysses* furnishes one of the richest examples in modern literature of the mythical imagination at work on the recalcitrant stuff of twentieth-century life. Indeed, as we follow Leopold Bloom through all the adventures and misadventures of a day in his life in Dublin, and as we contemplate all the cunning parallels with the career of Homer's Odysseus, from Bloom's encounter with his Telemachus in young Stephen Dedalus to his return to his disingenuous Penelope in the person of Molly Bloom, we feel that here is Vico all over again.

But Joyce (in *Ulysses* and *Finnegans Wake*) provides only one of many other significant examples that our fiction presents of the modern artist making his art possible by way of the mythical method. Just two years after the appearance of *Ulysses*, Thomas Mann was already realizing in *The Magic Mountain* that, since the motion of time is circular, it "might almost equally well be described as rest, as cessation of movement—for the there repeats itself constantly in the here, the past in the present."[19] In other words, at least as early as 1924 Schopenhauer's *nunc stans*—the Eternal Now, which is at the heart of all the illusory flux of time—had prepared Mann for the direction which he was to begin to pursue a few years later in the *Joseph* saga, whose major premise is that, since "it *is*, always *is*, however much we may say It was," the "timeless schema" of the myth is therefore the aptest instrument for story-telling, for it is the myth that plunges us down through the deep well of the past to the essential timelessness that engulfs the human story. And Joyce and Mann provide only the most distinguished examples of a tendency exhibited by many other writers of our period, in both fiction and drama (the Lawrence of *The Plumed Serpent*, the Gide of *Oedipus* and *Theseus*, the Giraudoux of *Tiger at the Gates* [*La Guerre de Troie*], the Sartre of *The Flies*), to find the enabling principle of their art in the primordial world of myth.

Professor Eliade has prepared us to discern what lies behind this whole style of imagination, for the mythical manipulation of parallels between contemporaneity and antiquity is a way of moving beyond, or of getting on top of, this uncongenial present. The attempt to recover through the myth what is timelessly archetypal in the complex history of man surely represents in part a reinstatement of the traditional vision of the eternal return and, as such, it is at one with that most ancient metaphysic—the real *philosophia perennis*—whose purpose, as Professor Eliade has taught us to understand, is not

19. Thomas Mann, *The Magic Mountain*, trans. H. T. Lowe-Porter (New York, Knopf, 1944), p. 344.

only to defend us against time but also effectively to abolish time in the interests of a timeless eternity. The dying Hotspur, in the final act of *Henry IV*, Part I, says to Harry Monmouth:

> But thought's the slave of life, and life's time's fool,
> And time, that takes survey of all the world,
> Must have a stop.

And it is Hotspur's third clause, "time . . . must have a stop," which summarizes, with a beautiful concision, a major part of the testimony of modern literature.

The way of Vico, then, is one way in which the modern rebellion against time proceeds. The other is the way of Bergson, whose theory of time is perhaps the more widely advertised and the one (popularly) most likely to be thought of as distinctively representing modern sensibility, for the author of *Time and Free Will* (1889) and of *Matter and Memory* (1896) is generally considered in the modern period to be the philosopher *par excellence* of time.

Bergson's initial preoccupation would seem to have been with the question as to what kind of unity constitutes the essential ground of selfhood. That is to say, man is beckoned toward the world by a thousand different interests and is engaged in innumerable transactions with his environment—all of which leave their residue in the mind in the form of the myriad impressions that furnish the self with a basis for the conduct of the daily business of life. But surely man is more than merely the bundle of discontinuous states of consciousness of which Hume spoke, and that this is so is indicated, Bergson felt, by the recurrent experiences that we do in fact have of the unity of our personal existence. These are experiences of which the catalyst is memory, for it is through the creative act of memory, he argued, that human interiority becomes something more than merely an aggregate of discontinuous impressions and achieves the unity of selfhood. The self constitutes itself, in other words, through a process of

> deep introspection, which leads us to grasp our inner states as living things, constantly becoming, as states not amena-

ble to measure, which permeate one another and of which the succession in duration has nothing in common with juxtaposition in homogeneous space. But the moments at which we thus grasp ourselves are rare, and that is just why we are rarely free. The greater part of the time we live outside ourselves, hardly perceiving anything of ourselves but our own ghost, a colorless shadow which pure duration projects into homogeneous space. Hence our life unfolds in space rather than in time; we live for the external world rather than for ourselves; we speak rather than think; we "are acted" rather than act ourselves. To act freely is to recover possession of oneself, and to get back into pure duration.[20]

So, in order to enter deeply into its personal identity, the self must cultivate a profound attentiveness to its own inner history, the kind of attentiveness that so integrates experiences of the past with those of the present that they cease to be a heterogeneous continuum and begin to flow into one another, to re-enter the stream of pure duration.

Simultanéité des états d'âmes is, then, the hallmark of the Bergsonian *durée*. And the preeminence Bergson is generally felt to have in modern reflection on the meaning of time is doubtless in part a result of the recognition that it is the actual experience of "simultaneity" that in fact largely defines the special situation of the men and women of our age. We fly from one continent to another in a few hours; a transatlantic telephone can connect a New York merchant with the office of an associate in Antwerp in virtually a matter of seconds; the miracle of television now brings into a living-room in Indianapolis events that transpired only a few hours earlier in South Viet Nam; and the enormous growth of historical consciousness gives to the average educated man of our time a knowledge of the past unimaginable a century ago, and not only of one segment of the past but of the total experience of the race. It is just this boundlessness of the modern horizon

20. Henri Bergson, *Time and Free Will*, trans. Pogson (London, Allen, 1912), pp. 23 ff.

that induces the feeling that everything is happening at once, that everything is dovetailing into everything else, and that the whole of reality is engulfed by the stream of interrelation.

Simultaneity is, therefore, the name of the time that men are given by modern civilization: so it is not surprising that modern literature should, in one of its aspects, express a sense of time that so closely resembles the *simultanéité* of Bergsonian *durée*. For what might be called Newtonian time is no longer a part of the time-sense of the age, and—to paraphrase a remark of Gertrude Stein—the composition in which we live makes for an art in which time takes on a new kind of imprecision and ambiguousness.[21] This is why so many of the great story-tellers of this century—Virginia Woolf and William Faulkner and André Malraux and Malcolm Lowry—do not any longer, as it were, begin at one end and end at another. Instead, they are concerned to express the shiftiness and the dynamism of time, and this often entails a kind of re-orchestration of empirical time that, in form, has a very striking affinity with the cinematic technique of *montage*. Indeed, much of twentieth-century fiction—Gide's *The Counterfeiters*, Joyce's *Ulysses*, Dos Passos' *U.S.A.* trilogy, Faulkner's *The Sound and the Fury*, Malraux' *Man's Hope*—makes us feel that it perhaps has more in common with the art of the cinema than with any other contemporary art-form.

The art of the cinema was very largely the invention of the American director D. W. Griffith, in the years between 1908 and 1916 (which culminated in his great films *The Birth of a Nation* and *Intolerance*). But it is to the Germans and the Russians that we are chiefly indebted for the formal elaboration of film aesthetic, and this was a development of the twenties, when German and Russian studios were producing such early masterpieces as Robert Wiene's *The Cabinet of Dr. Caligari* and Eisenstein's *Potemkin*, and were providing centers for the most creative film work being done anywhere. The basic theoretical work was mainly the accomplishment of three

---

21. See Gertrude Stein, *Picasso* (New York, Scribner's, 1946), p. 11.

men—the Russian directors Vsevolod I. Pudovkin and Sergei Eisenstein, and the German Rudolf Arnheim.[22] By the thirties, when theorists in the English-speaking world like John Grierson and Raymond Spottiswoode and John Howard Lawson began to take hold of the new medium, what Pudovkin and Eisenstein had helped to make clear was that a film aesthetic is very largely an aesthetic of *montage*. The full meaning of this French term eludes transmission through any English rendering of it, but Eisenstein, at least, offers us a fairly simple working definition when he says that by *montage* he means simply that "*representation A* and *representation B* must be so selected from all the possible features within the theme that is being developed . . . that their *juxtaposition* . . . shall evoke in the perception and feelings of the spectator the most complete *image of the theme itself*."[23] Here the implication is clear: the creation of a film is a process of editing whereby the director, when finally faced with a great mass of celluloid rushes, so puts together or *mounts* a series of visual images as to build a coherent work of dramatic art. But the special kind of *montage* that Eisenstein was experimenting with in films like *Potemkin* and *Ten Days That Shook the World* tended to alter somewhat the primary meaning of the term, for "as first *Potemkin*, then *Ten Days* swept through the Western world taking film makers and critics by storm, the word *montage* came to identify not cutting in general, but specifically the rapid, shock cutting that Eisenstein employed in his films."[24] And it is this secondary meaning of the term that we often have in mind today and that makes us think most immediately of the convention (deriving from Eisenstein's early experiments) of those sequences of blurred double exposures in

22. See V. I. Pudovkin, *Film Technique* (London, Gollancz, 1929); Sergei M. Eisenstein, *The Film Sense*, trans. Jay Leyda (London, Faber and Faber, 1943); also Eisenstein's *Film Form*, trans. Jay Leyda (New York, Harcourt, Brace, 1949); Rudolf Arnheim, *Film* (London, Faber and Faber, 1933).
23. Eisenstein, *The Film Sense*, p. 19.
24. Arthur Knight, *The Liveliest Art* (New York, New American Library, 1959), p. 80.

which a large span of clock-time is drastically condensed in such a way as to make the elements of an extended process— say, the hero's journey by plane from one city to another— simultaneously present.

Now it is precisely the kind of synchronization involved in cinematic *montage* that has become a staple of modern narrative art, giving it a remarkable adeptness in breaking up concrete, empirical time, so that different periods of time may coalesce and flow into one another to form a time that has been decontaminated of temporality. In thus presenting us with snapshots of long, complicated sequences of action, the modern novel has tended to spatialize time: indeed, in Joyce's *Ulysses,* in Virginia Woolf's *To the Lighthouse,* in Dos Passos' *The 42nd Parallel,* in Djuna Barnes' *Nightwood,* in Philip Toynbee's *Tea With Mrs. Goodman,* its form can be said often to be a "spatial form," insofar as it has tended to make temporal passage an instantaneous phenomenon that could be directly viewed in its entirety as though it were in front of us —in space.[25] Faulkner's *The Sound and the Fury,* for example, presents a typical case, where the actual time covered by the narrative is only four days but where these four days in fact hurtle us through the entire tragic history of the Compson family which is, itself, the history of the whole South in microcosm. The first major part of the book is dated, April 7, 1928, and the perspective is that of the idiot, Benjy. The section which follows is dated eighteen years earlier and is devoted to the day of Quentin's suicide, June 2, 1910. Then, in the third section, April 6, 1928, things are seen from the point of view of Jason Compson. And the day which dawns "bleak and chill" in the final section is April 8, 1928, on which Dilsey, having "seed de beginnin," now "sees de endin." The novel's refusal to accommodate itself to the sequences of empirical time finds a major symbolic image in Quentin Compson, who despises the "round stupid assertion of the clock"

25. This issue has been most profoundly studied in Joseph Frank's brilliant and now classic essay, "Spatial Form in Modern Literature," *The Sewanee Review,* 53 (Spring, Summer, Autumn 1945).

and who, in a rage against the bulging obscenity of time, rips the hands off his father's watch: he suspects that "Christ was not crucified," but "was worn away by a minute clicking of little wheels," and he tells himself that time is his "misfortune." The novel is *almost* persuaded to annihilate time altogether—as it is annihilated in much of the representative literature of the modern period—by *montage*, in pure "duration." But, in this particular case, it must be acknowledged that the drive of the narrative in this direction is, finally, brought to a halt by the reparative power that is incarnate in Dilsey and which does at last make manifest the possibility of a significant redemption of human time—through *agape*.

Though the techniques for the spatialization of time in the novel have grown more radical since the period of Proust, he presents what is still the most truly classic case and the one which offers perhaps the clearest clue to the final intent of that whole tradition in modern literature whose philosophic master is Bergson.[26] Superficially viewed, *Remembrance of Things Past* may, of course, seem to exist outside that ambiance designated by the term spatial form, for it is bent not so much on immobilizing the flow of time as on recovering "all the hours of days gone by": but the essential thing is its invocation of *simultanéité des états d'âmes*, and, in this, it joins in quite the same kind of effort at the abolition of time that is undertaken more radically, say, in Virginia Woolf's *Mrs. Dalloway* or Djuna Barnes' *Nightwood*.

The drama that is at the heart of Proust's fiction is the drama of what Jacques Maritain, in his discussions of Descartes,[27] has called "angelism," the refusal of the creature to

26. It is, of course, in a way ironical that in the literature of "spatial form" we should find the Bergsonian *durée*, since the achievement of the pure time of "duration" was, for Bergson, precisely contingent on our reaching *beneath* the spatialized self of discontinuous impressions and "homogeneous time"—the self that conducts the banal, mundane business of everyday—to that more fundamental core of selfhood which is the seat of "pure duration."

27. See Jacques Maritain, *Three Reformers* (New York, Scribner's, 1937); *The Dream of Descartes*, trans. Mabelle L. Andison (New York, Philosophical Library, 1944).

submit to or be ruled by any of the exigencies of the created natural order. The angel is angelic precisely because, despite its creatureliness, it undertakes the ambitious program of finding a habitation outside the natural order: it will not accept any commitment to the natural world, for its goal is a realm of pure spirit, where all the scattered leaves of life are into one volume bound, where substance and accidents, and their various modes, are all fused together into one blazing flame: this is the object of the angelic quest. And it is just toward such a goal that all the motions of Proust's long novel are launched. He, too, viewed the spectacle of man's life in history as one of sheer futility and indigence, since it is dominated by Time, which allows permanence to nothing under the sun, which, "like an ever-rolling stream,/Bears all its sons away." So, he reasoned, man's dignity requires that he get outside of time, and the seven volumes of *Remembrance of Things Past* comprise his account of how this may be done.

The vehicle of the Proustian transcendence of time is memory, involuntary memory, which is, he says, "the better part of our memory," the part that "exists outside ourselves, in a patter of rain, in the smell of an unaired room or of the crackling brushwood fire in a cold grate, wherever, in short, we happen upon what our minds, having no use for it, had rejected, the lost treasure that the past has in store, the richest, that which when all our flow of tears seems to have dried at the source can make us weep again." That is to say, the tinkle of a bell, the taste of a crumb of cake dipped in tea, the sudden rising of an odor, the sound of rain pounding on the roof of one's room in the middle of the night, the sight of the rays of the afternoon sun slanting across a garden, and a thousand other accidents of experience have the power instantly to bring flooding back, after the lapse of many years, large segments of the past that had been forgotten. In such moments, Proust believed, it is possible "to seize, isolate, immobilize for the duration of a lightning flash" a fragment of "pure time," a time that is altogether outside the scope of the ordinary fractures and discontinuities of historical time. And this is a time which, when it is rescued from the well of the past, is discovered never really to have been lost at all but to have been incorporated, to have been "incarnate," all along in the deepest part of the mind, indeed in the very body itself.

So it was in the phenomenon of involuntary memory that Proust found the formative idea for the great project of his career—namely, that of dramatizing a voyage in quest of *temps perdu*, of lost time.

At the end of his novel, his narrator, after having spent many years in a sanatorium, away from the aristocratic circles of high fashion in which he had formerly moved, comes out of his retirement one afternoon to pay his respects at the modish salon of the Princesse de Guermantes. There he meets again a host of old friends and former associates, but they have been so transformed by the ravages of time as at first to be virtually unidentifiable. He is dizzied a little by the contradictory images that flood his mind, of this person and that, as he used to be and is now. Gradually he begins to realize that just through such disparate images as these may time be transcended, for to have vividly present in one's mind two pictures of some significant reality that record a previous stage of its history as well as its present formation is no longer to be submerged in the flux of time: it is to have risen above it, and to be able to grasp the past and the present in the simultaneity of pure time. So the narrator decides to write a novel whose controlling idea will be this newly won insight. But, of course, such a novel as this is precisely the novel that is now drawing to a close. And what we begin to realize at this late stage is that, through discarding the "superstition of chronology," through the swift juxtaposition of incidents separated by large spans of time, and through various subtle and complicated techniques of *montage*, Proust has been inducing in us the same experience that his narrator had had that afternoon at the reception of the Princesse de Guermantes. The reading of *Remembrance of Things Past* itself is intended to be for us a practice-exercise in the negation of time and the quest of eternity.

The essentially duplicitous position of modern literature with respect to the matter of time takes, then, a dual form: one of two ways may be chosen, that of Vico or of Bergson. Whether through the eternal return in myth or through the simultaneity of *montage* and spatial form, the intent is to perform an act of assassination, to abolish the structures of concrete historical time with such effectiveness that the impurity of their finitude may be utterly escaped and access may be won to a timeless Eternity, to a Great Time, which is beyond anything resembling empirical temporality.

Now it is one of the interesting ironies of contemporary intellectual life, in a period when a profound nostalgia for a vanished Eternity is leading the literary imagination to regard time as a great embarrassment and inconvenience, as the Great Enemy, that the Christian theological community is steadily moving toward a position that refuses to envisage the relation between time and eternity as one of radical antinomy. Forty years ago Karl Barth, for example, was declaring that, "if I have a system, it is limited to what Kierkegaard called the 'infinite qualitative distinction' between time and eternity."[28] However, in more recent years, he has been eager to declare that "God does not live without time. He is supremely temporal. For His eternity is authentic temporality, and therefore the source of all time"—and also, "God would not be my God if He were only eternal in Himself, if He had no time for me."[29] Dr. Barth represents, of course, one of the extremest types of eschatological rigorism in Christian theology of the modern period, and that he should be moving now toward a refusal of any absolute disjunction between time and eternity is something that, against the background of much recent theological

28. Karl Barth, Preface to 2nd ed. (included in 6th ed.), *The Epistle to the Romans*, trans. Edwyn C. Hoskyns (London, Oxford University Press, 1933), p. 10.
29. Karl Barth, *Church Dogmatics*, 3, Pt. 2 ("The Doctrine of Creation"), trans. Harold Knight *et al.* (Edinburgh, T. & T. Clark, 1960), 437, 522.

ferment, appears to be a significant indication of basic realignment. It is indeed a kind of revolution in Christian sensibility that recent theology is achieving in the whole area of reflection on the relationship between time and eternity. In his Gifford Lectures, back in the early thirties, the late William Temple was already resisting the whole concept of time as a moving image of the static changelessness of eternity, as a realm ontologically inferior (by reason of its secondariness) to the absolute sufficiency of eternity—for, said he, "If there were no History, or if History were other than in fact it is, the Eternal would not be what the Eternal is. . . . The historical is . . . a necessary self-expression of a Being whose essential activity is at once self-communication and self-discovery in that to which He communicates Himself."[30] Today, the residual Hegelianism in Temple's thought, of course, gives to his idiom a certain air of remoteness; but the general direction in which he was driving is apparent, and it is now made much more fully manifest by two thinkers, as distant from Temple as they are divergent from each other, Rudolf Bultmann and Emil Brunner. In an essay written a few years prior to Temple's Gifford Lectures but now given a fresh importance by his *Entmythologisierung* phase, Dr. Bultmann, for example, declares:

> Belief in God is no more a mysticism rising superior to the world and imagining it will find God in timelessness, than it is a *Weltanschauung*, interpreting everything in the world on the basis of one principle. God is the mysterious, enigmatic power that meets us *in* the world and *in* time. . . . Belief implies an awareness that the human soul is not a special something in which man can free himself from involvement in the affairs of the world in order to fling himself into the arms of eternity. . . . It implies that what man

30. William Temple, *Nature, Man and God* (London, Macmillan, 1934), pp. 447–48.

has *done* and *does*—his decisions—constitute him in his true nature, that he is *essentially* a temporal being, and that wishing to escape from the temporal simply means wishing to escape from his own reality, and therefore from God, who is to be found by him no where else but in this temporal reality.[31]

And just a few years ago, in quite a similar tone, Emil Brunner was declaring that, from the perspective of the Christian faith, eternity must be seen to be not merely a

negation of temporality but its fulfilment. Since God Himself has come into time, He has united time with His own eternity. God has, so to speak, pledged Himself to time inasmuch as He has pledged Himself to temporal man. The Incarnation of the eternal Son of God means also His *Intemporation.* . . . When we say that Eternity is the end or the goal, that is not a negation of time, but merely the negation of its negations. Eternal life is not Platonic timelessness, but fulfilled time.[32]

The general movement in contemporary Christian thought represented by these and numerous other writers who could be cited is one which involves, at bottom, a profound discomfort with the kind of radical distinction between time and eternity that has persistently figured in theological tradition. This is a discomfort that is consequent upon a repossession in our period of "the strange new world within the Bible"—a world to which we have begun to see how utterly alien is the essentially Hellenic way in which Christian theology has traditionally approached the problem of time. Indeed, Dr. Brunner, in the passage quoted above, still reveals a remnant of this mode of thought when he speaks of the Incarnation as having involved Eternity coming *"into* time." For it is precisely the conception of eternity as irrupting into time, with

31. Rudolf Bultmann, "The Crisis in Belief" (1931), in *Essays*, trans. James C. G. Greig (New York, Macmillan, 1955), p. 9.
32. Emil Brunner, "The Christian Understanding of Time," *Scottish Journal of Theology*, 4 (1951), 8.

the prior conception of a fundamental difference *in kind* between time and eternity, that has been persistently determinative of Christian theism from the patristic period on into the quite recent past. However, what is now beginning to be discovered is that the whole notion of time and eternity as radically disjunctive descends not from the distinctively Biblical sources of Christian tradition but rather from the Hellenic (and, more specifically, Platonist) background of patristic thought. For the New Testament consistently proposes that that lambent point at which the meaning of human existence is most fully disclosed is located not outside time but within the historical continuum. It is not untrue to say, therefore, that for the Biblical community time is not so much to be understood *sub specie aeternitatis* as eternity is to be understood *sub specie temporalitatis*. Karl Barth even goes so far as to define God's eternity as His "readiness for time." For, he says, "in Jesus Christ it comes about that God . . . is present for us in the form of our own existence and our own world, not simply embracing our time and ruling it, but submitting Himself to it, and permitting created time to become and be the form of His eternity." Eternity as a divine attribute means, for Dr. Barth, that "the defects of our time, its fleetingness and its separations, are alien to [God] and disappear, and in Him all beginning, continuation and ending form a unique Now, steadfast yet moving, moving yet steadfast. He is temporal in that our time with its defects is not so alien to Him that He cannot take it to Himself in His grace, mercy and patience, Himself rectifying and healing it and lifting it up to the time of eternal life." And he asserts that, unless God's eternity does in fact have such temporality as this, the Christian message is nothing more than a pious myth. "For the content of this message depends on the fact that God was and is and is to be, that our existence stands under the sign of a divine past, present, and future, that in its differentiation this sign does not point away into space, to a God who, in fact, is neither past, present nor future. Without God's complete temporality the content of the Christian message has no shape. Its proclamation is only an inarticulate mumbling. Therefore everything depends on whether God's temporality is the simple truth which cannot be attacked from any quarter because it has its basis in God Himself."[33]

The testimony of the Biblical literature on this whole issue is being actively canvassed today by many scholars,[34] but perhaps only by the Professor of New Testament Studies at Basel, Oscar Cullmann, with such radicalism as characterizes his brilliant, controversial work, *Christ and Time*. What is most emphatically distinctive about Professor Cullmann's argument is that it flatly asserts that for primitive Christianity there is no difference at all between time and eternity, that eternity, far from being viewed as any kind of static timelessness, is simply time without limit—"or, to put it better, what we call 'time' is nothing but a part, defined and delimited by God, of this same unending duration of God's time."

In Professor Cullmann's rendering, time proceeds in the Biblical view along a consistently rectilinear line, "which is unlimited in both the backward and the forward direction." This line has a threefold division: 1) the age before the Creation; 2) the present age which lies between the Creation and the End; and 3) the age to come in which the eschatological drama will be enacted. For this whole pageant, the time framework is one that moves continuously forward, and it involves no dualism between time and a timeless eternity. Instead of the characteristically Hellenic preoccupation with time (whose movement is cyclical rather than linear) and a supra-temporal eternity, the polarity that is basic to Hebraic thought involves a contrast between this age (*aion*) and the *aion* to come, and

33. Barth, *Church Dogmatics*, 2, Pt. 1 ("The Doctrine of God"), trans. T. H. L. Parker et al. (Edinburgh, T. & T. Clark, 1957), 616, 617–18, 620.

34. See Marsh, *The Fulness of Time*; Minear, *Eyes of Faith*, especially Chs. 6, 16; also Minear, "The Time of Hope in the New Testament," *Scottish Journal of Theology*, 6 (1953), 337–61; Thorlief Boman, *Hebrew Thought Compared with Greek* (London, S.C.M. Press, 1960), Ch. 3; J. A. T. Robinson, *In the End, God* (Naperville, Alec Allenson, 1950); James Barr, *Biblical Words for Time*, Studies in Biblical Theology, 33 (London, S.C.M. Press, 1962); and James Muilenburg, "The Biblical View of Time," *The Harvard Theological Review*, 54 (1961), 226–52.

both are conceived temporally. And, insofar as the New Testament approaches any concept of eternity at all, it is not a dimension of life that can ever be hellenized into something qualitatively incommensurable with concrete historical time: on the contrary, the New Testament understanding of eternity embraces nothing more than "the endless succession of the ages (*aiōnes*)."[35]

Nor does the advent of Christ entail the emergence of a fundamentally new kind of time: the new thing that Christ brought to the Biblical community, Professor Cullmann suggests, was redemption from a purely futurist orientation to time. For Jewish Messianism had conceived of time in terms of a twofold division—into the present age and the coming age which would be the Messianic time of salvation. For Israel the center of history lay in the future, in the expected coming of the Messiah, and it was this great miracle that was counted on to establish a decisive mid-point between the ages. But the advent of Christ brought that mid-point out of the future and into the present age, for in Him the primitive Christian community found the meaning of all time to be revealed: the center of history is no longer the Parousia but the Cross and Resurrection of Christ: in these events the age to come does in fact already supervene upon this present age, and the joy of D-Day brings with it the assurance of the ultimate triumph of V-Day. It is, in short, says Cullmann, in the story of Jesus that the earliest Christians find the absolute norm that gives the full clue to the meaning of all time, for He is the One who is believed to have been appointed of God to represent the whole of creation, and through Him all times and all seasons are reconciled with God: "having made peace through the blood of His cross" (Colossians 1:20), all things through Him, "whether they be things in earth, or things in heaven," are brought into solidarity with God. In Jesus Christ God establishes His Lordship over time, and through Him the days of our years are set in order.

35. Oscar Cullmann, *Christ and Time*, trans. Floyd V. Filson (London, S.C.M. Press, 1951), pp. 62, 48.

Cullmann insists, however, that, for primitive Christianity, time (that is, time as redemptive time) does not come to a standstill with Jesus Christ. And this is why he feels that Kierkegaard's notion of "contemporaneity" is in error, in so far as it implies that the present cannot be the scene of *Heilsgeschichte*. Kierkegaard believed that the Christian man, by the power of his faith, is translated back into the time of the Incarnation and made contemporaneous with the original witnesses; but, as Cullmann argues, to see things in this way is to suppose that the history of redemption came to a stop with Jesus Christ and that, in order to enter the realm of salvation, we must somehow escape out of our own moment in time back into an earlier period. It is indeed to deny that in "the post-Easter present" the redemptive process continues, and it is insufficiently to estimate the eschatological urgency of the mission of the Church in the time between the Resurrection and the Parousia, as this is underlined in the injunction of Our Lord in Matthew 28: "Go ye . . . and make disciples of all nations . . . and, lo, I am with you alway, even unto the end." The present age, so far as the history of redemption is concerned, is not, in other words, a time of impoverishment, as the Kierkegaardian doctrine of "contemporaneity" would seem to imply: it is, on the contrary, *the final time before the end,* and it is filled with the dialectical tension that results from its being poised between the decisive deed of God in Jesus Christ and the *aion* that is to come. But the dialectic here is not a "dialectic between this world and the Beyond . . . not that between time and eternity; it is rather *the dialectic of present and future,*"[36] the future when every knee shall bow in acknowledgment of the reign of God and when "the glory . . . shall be revealed in us" (Romans 8:18). This coming age "has in the so-called eschatological drama its beginning and so a limit; but in the forward direction it is unlimited, unending, and only in this sense is it eternal." For Biblical religion, in short, "salvation is bound to a *continuous time process* which

36. Ibid., p. 146.

embraces past, present, and future,"[37] and every event in the entire drama of redemption is understood by the people of the New Testament in terms of its relation to the *one historical fact* at the midpoint. Nor is the event of Jesus Christ which constitutes this midpoint understood as an *invasion* of time by eternity. "We must rather say that in Christ time has reached its mid-point, and that at the same time the moment has thereby come in which this is preached to men, so that with the establishment of the new division of time they are able to believe in it and in this faith to understand time 'in a Christian way,' that is, by taking Christ as the center." Nowhere does the New Testament know anything that genuinely approximates the Greek contrast between time and eternity: it "knows only the linear time concept of Today, Yesterday, and Tomorrow; [and] all philosophical reinterpretation and dissolution into timeless metaphysics is foreign to it."[38]

This entire thesis has, of course, in many of its details, been submitted to the most drastic criticism, and most notably perhaps by John Marsh of Mansfield College, Oxford, and James Barr of the University of Manchester.[39] But what is primarily significant in this context is not the particular valuation that is to be placed upon this or that aspect of Professor Cullmann's total argument but rather the whole style of thought in recent theology of which it is so brusque an expression. For, however the lexical method, scriptural exegesis, and systematic theological orientation of *Christ and Time* may be assessed in all their particulars, its vigorous denial that other-worldliness is an *organic* part of New Testament faith is in essential harmony with a general testimony that is being made today with increasing force. Indeed, many of the most important Christian thinkers of our period, as a result both of reexamination of the Biblical material and of systematic theological reconstruction, are by various routes reaching the

37. Ibid., pp. 48, 32.
38. Ibid., pp. 93, 53.
39. See Marsh, pp. 174–81; and Barr, Ch. 3 (page 80 lists a number of the major critiques of Cullmann's work).

conclusion that Christian theology, far from being any kind of metaphysic, is (as it was put by the late Théo Preiss) "essentially a *commentary*, a reminder, an interpretation and declaration of a series of events, of an *oikonomia*, an *ordo salutis*."[40] Or, if the theologian's denial of any metaphysical pretension is unacceptable, then, it is being said, he must at least be understood to write metaphysics only in the sense in which the Bible writes it, "as though metaphysics were history."[41] For time and history are not only the medium in which the revelatory events occurred to which the Bible witnesses: they are also, and inevitably, the single medium in which all of man's transactions with reality take place and by which those transactions are qualified at every point. To contemplate the ultimate meaning of human existence is, therefore, to face an historical question, for history is the medium in which man has whatever is real for him. And, as a consequence, Christian faith is not metaphysical, not ontological, but radically historical and eschatological, for its message is addressed to questions about the meaning of existence arising out of the restlessly disruptive motions of history. But not only do the *questions* to which it is an *answer* arise out of history: it is also the case—and this is really the major premise of a thinker like Cullmann—that the only absolute norm which the Christian faith knows how to invoke for the settling of these questions is a norm that is discovered in time, in history: it is not any sort of transcendent datum lying beyond all time. "The Primitive Christian norm . . . consists not only in a single historical fact, but in a temporally connected historical series of a special kind, namely, the Biblical history."[42]

Indeed, something like this constitutes a newly emerging consensus in the theological conversation of the present time.

40. Théo Preiss, *Life in Christ*, trans. Harold Knight, Studies in Biblical Theology, 13 (London, S.C.M. Press, 1954), p. 66.

41. J. V. Langmead Casserley, *The Christian in Philosophy* (London, Faber and Faber, 1949), p. 66: "The Bible writes metaphysics as though metaphysics were history."

42. Cullmann, p. 21.

in Modern Literature

It is the impulse to accord a new dignity in the Christian dispensation to time; it is the determination to discover anew the profound truth enunciated by Schleiermacher in his speeches *On Religion,* when he said that "religion begins and ends with history"; it is this that one feels to lie behind the thought of such Europeans as the late Dietrich Bonhoeffer, Karl Barth (in his more recent work), Rudolf Bultmann, Friedrich Gogarten, Ernst Fuchs, and Gerhard Ebeling; and it is also most noticeably a chief motive in the recent work of such thinkers in the English-speaking world as Richard Niebuhr of Harvard, the late Carl Michalson of Drew, and the Bishop of Woolwich, J. A. T. Robinson, in England. Wherever one turns today on the map of current theological thought, the general tendency, it seems, is toward something like "an historical critique of the theological reason."[43]

We are confronting, then, as a major phenomenon of contemporary cultural life, a sharply reversive movement: for, whereas the literary imagination often wants very much to escape from time altogether and to find a timeless eternity, the theological imagination—to the perplexed astonishment, one imagines, of an old-fashioned secularism relying on its conventional critiques of other-worldliness—begins to be most ardently committed to the timescape of history and begins to regard the eternity of the traditional Christian vision as largely misconceived, if not chimerical. "The Christian faith," says Carl Michalson, "is an essentially historical reality embracing acts of faith as historical responses to God's self-manifestation in history."[44] And this is the testimony of virtually every major theologian of our period.

Now if it is true, as I believe it to be, that man steps into maturity and comes of age when he consents to accept his temporality as a permanent and undisposable part of the hu-

43. The phrase, with its allusive echo of Wilhelm Dilthey, is Carl Michalson's and forms the subtitle of his book, *The Rationality of Faith* (New York, Scribner's, 1963).
44. Ibid., p. 108.

man state as such, then—given the profound mistrust of time
that is expressed in modern literature—the question must
inevitably arise as to what may be the Christian mission to the
literary imagination of our age and how the theological community may assist the artist in learning something of the
same lesson in his sphere that it has already learned in its
own. Is there, in other words, any possibility of dispelling the
wistfulness in modern literature for an eternity which may
have had to disappear before a really tough and authentic historical maturity could be achieved?

Of course, to raise any question at all about how, in the
realm of belief and fundamental outlook, the literary imagination may be moved from one point to another may be to risk
seeming to take a bullying position. And if bullying it really
be, it is surely bound to be the most fruitless kind of intimi-
datory effort, for only the stupidest sort of henchman of Agit-
Prop could suppose that the life of high art can be tricked into
permitting itself to be managed in any way at all. The notion
of *l'art engagé* attempts in fact to give a heavy dignity to what
is, after all, fundamentally dishonest, the sort of dishonesty
that is enshrined in the dreary old slogans about "Art for the
Masses' Sake" or "Art for Politics' Sake." And the same dishonesty would be contained in anything like the formula "Art
for Religion's Sake." For the province of aesthetics is properly
controlled by its own inner necessities; and, when painting
or poetry answers to the beckoning of this commissar or that
divine with prompt obedience, she has simply become a whore.

Yet the slogans of nihilist aestheticism are quite as dreary
and quite as deceiving as those of political or religious zealous-
ness. And, however skillful and even magisterial may have
been the finest artists nourished by the modern mystique of
"Art for Art's Sake" (Mallarmé, Valéry, Rilke, Stevens), theirs
is an art that does finally strike us as having a certain unreality
at its very center. For whenever art has *added* wealth of the
richest kind to the life of the human spirit, it has done so because it has fed and fattened on something other than art itself. And the greatest literature of the Western tradition (say,

Dante's *Divine Comedy* and Shakespeare's *Lear* and Goethe's *Faust* and Melville's *Moby Dick* and Mann's *Doctor Faustus*) —the literature that gives us what Matthew Arnold called our "touchstones"—is a literature that is a *response* to the interpreted world.[45]

But, in the particular case of the dialogue that, hopefully, can arise from time to time between literature and the Christian theological community, how may the theological mind go about offering an *interpretation* of the world to the literary imagination, and do so with such manifest respect for the integrity of art as will persuade the writer to give his attention to what is being conveyed? Doubtless, no one is wise enough about the politics of culture to give a final and definitive answer, though at least we can be certain that the right procedure will not involve gathering poets and novelists around a conference table to discuss the kinds of issues which occupy Oscar Cullmann and Rudolf Bultmann. For, if there is to be a conference table, the talk that goes on around it must surely have as its immediate subject not theology but literature. Yet it may well be, if the right models are contemplated there with intelligence and liveliness of imagination, that this may be a dialogue that does at last *move* its participants from one point to another.

Into such a dialogue as is here being imagined one could not, of course, import the assumption that what is defective in the modern sense of time has utterly disabled our literature, for that would be patently nonsensical, since much of the writing that one has to cite as exemplifying the problem—Proust's *Remembrance of Things Past*, Joyce's *Ulysses*, Rilke's *Duino Elegies*—is (to paraphrase a line of Yeats on Dante, in "Ego Dominus Tuus") chiseling on the hardest stone and must, in the splendor of its art, evoke astonishment at the sheer magnificence of its lordship over language. But surely it is permis-

45. I have in mind the passage in Erich Heller's *The Disinherited Mind* (Philadelphia, Dufour and Saifer, 1952), 136, in which he says, "In the great poetry of the European tradition the emotions do not interpret; they respond to the interpreted world."

sible to believe that, other things being equal, the artist in whom there is a profound acceptance of *temporalitas* may have a better chance of winning "surprises of grace" than he who rebelliously refuses the human condition. It may therefore be an important part of the Christian's vocation toward the literature of our period to cherish and to admire, and thus indirectly to commend, some of the great examples, wherever they can be found, of the modern imagination reckoning with the world out of an acceptance of the fact that human life is irrevocably committed to time and to history.

In this connection, there is perhaps no modern text that asks to be studied so deeply as that great tetrad of poems which T. S. Eliot completed in the early forties, the *Four Quartets*. Here the decisive consideration is that, for Eliot, the problem of time is not a problem of metaphysics but a problem of charity, since, as he leads us to see, what we confront is not any ontological deficiency inhering in time as such but rather the moral necessity and obligation of making love the mode of our temporal orientation—"not less of love but expanding/ Of love beyond desire," and this in order to "redeem the time."[46]

Eliot does not take the high position of denying the actuality of flux or of claiming that time is somehow finally unreal. "Burnt Norton" says in its opening passage:

> What might have been and what has been
> Point to one end, which is always present.
> Footfalls echo in the memory
> Down the passage which we did not take
> Towards the door we never opened
> Into the rose-garden.

46. In the field of systematic theological thought, no one has explored the problem of time as a problem of charity and love so sensitively as the distinguished Japanese thinker, the late Seiichi Hatano, in his profound and moving book, *Time and Eternity*, trans. Ichiro Suzuki (Japanese National Commission for UNESCO, 1963). This is also the direction taken by Fr. Robert Johann, S.J., in his fine essay "Charity and Time," *Cross Currents*, 9 (1959), 140–49.

In this remorseful glance back at the unhappy decisions of the past and at the opportunities that were thereby lost, the fateful irreversibility of time is hinted at. We do not live above time or outside of time, in a timeless eternity: our human condition commits us to a world that passes ceaselessly. But, though time is not illusory, it can on occasion be lost. This may indeed be at the heart of the pathos of modern spirituality —in an age of extreme secularity in which the world has been emptied of all radical significance, time is often lost, in this "place of disaffection," where there is

> Only a flicker
> Over the strained time-ridden faces
> Distracted from distraction by distraction
> Filled with fancies and empty of meaning
> Tumid apathy with no concentration
> Men and bits of paper, whirled by the cold wind
> That blows before and after time,
> Wind in and out of unwholesome lungs
> Time before and time after.

The images of lost time in "Burnt Norton" are matched by similar images in "The Dry Salvages," where "the river" of time "is almost forgotten/By the dwellers in cities. . . . By worshippers of the machine" and where, as a consequence, time is

> counted by anxious worried women
> Lying awake, calculating the future,
> Trying to unweave, unwind, unravel
> And piece together the past and the future,
> Between midnight and dawn, when the past is all deception,
> The future futureless, before the morning watch.

Man recurrently supposes, of course, when his time has been lost, that it can be recovered through some wizardry of calculation, of science or of pseudo-science; and most especially does the rationalist technicalism of the modern consciousness make the men of our age susceptible to such a superstition.

To communicate with Mars, converse with spirits,
To report the behaviour of the sea monster,
Describe the horoscope, haruspicate or scry,
Observe disease in signatures, evoke
Biography from the wrinkles of the palm
And tragedy from fingers; release omens
By sortilege, or tea leaves, riddle the inevitable
With playing cards, fiddle with pentagrams
Or barbituric acids, or dissect
The recurrent image into pre-conscious terrors—
To explore the womb, or tomb, or dreams; all these are usual
Pastimes and drugs, and features of the press:
And always will be, some of them especially
When there is distress of nations and perplexity
Whether on the shores of Asia, or in the Edgware Road.
Men's curiosity searches past and future
And clings to that dimension.

But "The Dry Salvages" wants to remind us that redeeming
the time is not the work of the astrophysicist or the psycho-
analyst; it is, rather, says Eliot:

> an occupation for the saint—
> No occupation either, but something given
> And taken, in a lifetime's death in love,
> Ardour and selflessness and self-surrender.

And "a lifetime's death in love" brings us immediately to
the center of the *Quartets*, for what all these poems are proposing is a kind of death, an act of *kenosis*, a true emptying
—but not for the sake of annihilating time: for this is an
existential discipline whose goal is moral, not metaphysical:

> In order to arrive at what you are not
> You must go through the way in which you are not.

The *via negativa* that is being recommended here is not conceived to be an *askésis* that will enable us to slough off our
time-ridden finitude: it is, on the contrary, a discipline de-

signed for right action "in the meantime," in the concrete Now
in which we work and worship and hope, for, as the poet says
in "Burnt Norton," "Only through time time is conquered."
There is much talk of descent into "darkness, deprivation/And
destitution of all property" and of "abstention from movement." But it is not indifference to the happenings of historical
time that is being advocated, not the attainment of some point
outside of time, some point of "fixity,/Where past and future
are gathered": it is not detachment from responsible involvement in the human community that is sought, but from the
tyrannizing power of concupiscence, of self-will, of rampant
egoism. As Mr. Eliot says in the opening lines of the third section of "Little Gidding":

There are three conditions which often look alike
Yet differ completely, flourish in the same hedgrow:
Attachment to self and to things and to persons, detachment
From self and from things and from persons; and, growing
    between them, indifference
Which resembles the others as death resembles life,
Being between two lives—unflowering, between
The live and the dead nettle.

The practicing of this discipline of detachment, of submis-
sion to the will of God, is not, however, as we are told in "East
Coker," an affair of "the intense moment/Isolated, with no
before and after,/But a lifetime burning in every moment"—
"a lifetime's death in love." And, as "The Dry Salvages" reminds us, "the time of death is every moment." As for the
rest: it "is prayer, observance, discipline, thought and action"
—and, "East Coker" says, "if we do well, we shall/Die of the
absolute paternal care." The alternative is clear: we either
lose our time or we redeem it; that is, take hold of it again
and restore it to "a condition of complete simplicity" which is
the condition of love, so that

    all shall be well and
    All manner of thing shall be well . . .
    And the fire and the rose are one.

But, now, a quite different kind of example of commitment to the timescape of history and to the work of redeeming the time can be adduced in one of the most remarkable playwrights of our period, the German Bertolt Brecht. The harshly secular and brutally protestant character of Brecht's Marxist vision will, of course, make his work seem to many of his readers a particularly strident expression of what is *désacralisé* in modern life. Yet surely it can be said that here was a brilliantly gifted artist who spent himself in passionately announcing what life begins to be like in that abandoned and beleaguered City in which the people of our age can no longer find any access to the still half-remembered mercies of a Providence of long ago. And, in the conviction expressed in many of his finest works for the theatre that man's most essential and arduous task is that of transmuting the manifold contradictions and inequities of history into new patterns of order and justice and freedom, his is a secularity that is at least inclined toward the Christian vision of the redemptive power of the spirit amid the structures of historical time.

Brecht's theatre, with its "non-Aristotelian" or "epic" bias, does not, of course, conduce towards the usual dramatic catharsis. It is not a theatre of the-fourth-wall-removed, and every last illusion of naturalistic actuality is ruthlessly expunged. For Brecht believed that, when drama devotes itself to the gradual exposition of a realistic plot and invites the audience to identify with the protagonist, the result is merely a kind of hypnosis that may involve a purging of the emotions and a certain consequent refreshment of spirit but that cannot lead to what ought to be the final effect of a socially dedicated theatre—namely, the energizing of the audience to go back into the world to enter into the class struggle and to engage in social revolution. So, he undertook to rule out of his plays all the "illusionism" of the bourgeois naturalist theatre, in order that, instead of creating a specious present, they might simply register as accounts of happenings in the past from which a lesson may be learned about the meaning of contemporary life.

He wanted his audiences to think, not to enjoy an emotional binge. To this end, he forbade the actors working under his direction to identify sympathetically with the characters of the play, who were to be "shown," not impersonated; and all the various devices of his dramaturgy—the actors' addressing the audience, the advance tips that are given the spectator on how things will end, the episodic character of the action, the use of décor as a commentary on the dramatic situation—were intended to be a part of this campaign of "anti-drama." In his own summary:

> *The audience in the dramatic theatre says:*
> Yes, I have felt that too.—That's how I am.—That
> is only natural.—That will always be so. . . .
> *The audience in the epic theatre says:*
> I wouldn't have thought that.—People shouldn't do
> things like that.—That's extremely odd, almost un-
> believable.—This has to stop.

And he conceived it to be the purpose of a truly modern theatre not to be a "moral institution," not to moralize about the hurts and dislocations of twentieth-century life, but simply "to make visible the means by which those onerous conditions could be done away with."[47]

As Martin Esslin has observed, however, in his excellent book on Brecht, the bitter ironies of many of his finest plays are turned not merely against human nature under capitalism but against human nature itself, and

> only occasionally is there a qualifying clause: "man in these circumstances," "the world under this system," etc. Even then the truth of the proposition that the world can be changed for the better is never demonstrated. "Change the world: it needs to be changed!" is an exhortation that runs through Brecht's plays like a refrain. But he never succeeded

47. Bertolt Brecht, "Theatre for Learning," *Tulane Drama Review*, 6 (1961), 20, 24.

in convincingly demonstrating *what* he wanted the world to be changed into and *how* it could be changed.[48]

Yet, despite the pervasively corrosive pessimism which Mr. Esslin justly remarks, Brecht's genius as an artist was such as to make it impossible for his vision to be contained within the tight Marxian dogma of the class struggle or within his metaphysical nihilism. He was, as Cleanth Brooks said of Ernest Hemingway in *The Hidden God*, "too thoroughly committed to naturalism and too honest a man to try to delude himself into thinking that one can ever get outside the dimension of time." In play after play he gives us some of the most memorable portrayals that modern drama has anywhere produced of man launching his full stature into the task of making the world give way before his demand for accommodation: the Joan Dark of *Saint Joan of the Stockyards*, the Shen Te of *The Good Woman of Setzuan*, the Grusche of *The Caucasian Chalk Circle*, and the great old woman who claims the center of the stage in *Mother Courage* are all exemplars of what Paul Tillich calls the courage to be, and their purpose is to redeem the time.[49]

The circle of definition, then, that needs to be drawn about how the literary imagination and the Christian faith are related to time has now been finished. We have noticed how great the divide is at this point between authentic Christian belief and the crypto-Gnosticism that informs so much of the literature of the modern period. For Christianity has a deep and unbreakable commitment to the temporal order: it recog-

48. Martin Esslin, *Brecht: The Man and His Work* (Garden City, Doubleday Anchor, 1961), p. 260.

49. When the Pauline phrase is used at this point, the intention, as at all previous points where it has occurred, is that the term "redeem" should be thought of not in the sense of making good something that is bad but rather in terms of its most primitive meaning, of regaining or of recovering that of which possession had been lost. It is only in this sense, certainly according to the perspective of Christian theology, that time can ever be thought of as needing to be redeemed: for it never needs to be made good, since there is nothing at all intrinsically evil about it.

nizes time to be a fundamental structure of Creation, and since it is therefore of God, it is declared to be essentially good; and, being the basic category or dimension of man's finitude, it is also recognized to be inescapable. And, says Fr. William Lynch, though "the men of the infinite would have us believe that at least in prayer, at least at the moment of union with God, time is transcended and . . . some kind of quasi-eternity is reached," the Christian man knows that time itself "*is* a kind of ontological prayer," and that "there is no other form of union with God." This is the testimony that is recorded in the canonical literature of the primitive Christian community, as it is also again the testimony that is being made with increasing force by many of the major theologians of our period. So the profound lack of faith in time and the great craving for a timeless eternity that are so noticeable in our literature do not represent even a rough approximation of any distinctively Christian impulse: indeed, Fr. Lynch goes so far as to say that this modern impulse to forsake the temporal order "represents a disease of the feelings and a collapse of the true metaphysical mind": it is, he declares, "a fraudulent aping of religion and Christianity."[50]

Two radically different writers of our age, however, T. S. Eliot and Bertolt Brecht, have been submitted as evidencing the possibility of the literary imagination's reconstituting itself and rediscovering grace and glory not in infinites and eternities but

> in the moderate Aristotelian city
> Of darning and the Eight-Fifteen, where Euclid's geometry
> And Newton's mechanics would account for our experience,
> And the kitchen table exists because I scrub it.[51]

That city may not be so "moderate" for a writer like Brecht, but the important consideration is that—like the O'Casey of

50. William F. Lynch, S. J., *Christ and Apollo* (New York, Sheed and Ward, 1960), pp. 50, 44.

51. W. H. Auden, "For the Time Being: A Christmas Oratorio," in his *Collected Poetry.*

The Plough and the Stars, the Carlos Williams of *Paterson*, the Joyce Cary of *The Horse's Mouth*, the Silone of *Bread and Wine*, the Hemingway of *The Old Man and the Sea*, the Camus of *The Plague*, the Auden of *New Year Letter*—he knows man has no other place except the place that he is granted in his time, in his moment of history. This is, of course, an extremely heterogeneous group of writers—Eliot, O'Casey, Brecht, Joyce Cary, William Carlos Williams, Hemingway, Silone, Camus, Auden—and they are not all of equal rank; but, in their unquerulous acceptance of the irrevocable temporality of the human condition, they all in various ways furnish examples of that apart from which any greatness in the things of literary art must be very unstable indeed: and, for this reason, it is to such artists as these that the Christian critic of modern literature ought perhaps to turn for his proximate models of health and sanity of spirit.

Chapter Three THE BIAS
OF COMEDY AND
THE NARROW ESCAPE INTO FAITH

In one of his brilliant *Partisan Review* essays back in the forties, Clement Greenberg attempted to define "our period style" in the visual arts, the style that is fundamentally characteristic of all the painting, sculpture, decoration, and design of our time, and that furnishes the basic norm which underlies all the shifts and changes that have occurred in twentieth-century vision and taste. In a similar vein, the student of modern literature will be led to search, in this area too, for that which constitutes our period style. What is the modality of vision and belief, or of disbelief, of affirmation or of denial, of faith or of scepticism that furnishes the literature we recognize to be "ours" with its essential spiritual structure? In what particular accents and stresses do we discern that special style or signature that proves itself upon our own sensibilities to be a true expression of the age? This is a major question that must face contemporary criticism whenever it attempts to move beyond the trees to get a view of the forest and of the general terrain.

And I think we have lived long enough with the literature of the age of Joyce and Kafka to be certain that, insofar as it proceeds from any *mal du siècle*, this is a debility rooted in that same ontological crisis which Nietzsche made into a kind of scandal by his announcement in 1882 of the death of God. It is true, of course, that ultimate explanations of this sort may in their very ultimacy appear to sweep the critic away from all the interesting particularities of literary actuality, into the nebulousness of the metaphysical ether. But the fact of the matter is that even the most cautious commentators in contemporary criticism are increasingly recognizing that the truly significant particularities that characterize modern literature all speak in various ways of tragic losses, and of losses ultimately rooted in the loss of God.

We were, however, reminded in 1959 by R. W. B. Lewis that we live today under the immediate pressure not of the generation of Joyce and Kafka but of Moravia and Camus and Silone, and that these are writers who have foregone the metaphysical radicalism of the classic modern generation for a quieter kind of humanism, a humanism which commits them not to the practice of the presence (or absence) of God but to the practice of the presence of man.[1] I have no doubt that Mr. Lewis is right in contending that the avant-garde tradition of this century has already thus begun to periodize itself and that the dominant vision of those writers who have followed the great pioneers has this essentially anthropocentric focus. However, it is also to be asserted that the effort by the generation of Camus and Silone to redeem the time by sacramentalizing the relation between man and man is conceived to be the one remaining way of shoring up the human enterprise in this late, bad time of our abandonment. "In the sacred history of man on earth," says Silone, "it is still, alas, Good Friday." And, in *The Rebel*, the greatest testament of his career, Camus declared that "only two possible worlds can exist for the human mind: the sacred (or, to speak in Christian terms, the world of grace) and the world of rebellion. The disappearance of one is equivalent to the appearance of the other. . . . [And today] we live in an unsacrosanct moment in history. . . . [So] rebellion is one of the essential dimensions of man. It is our historic reality." And many similar testimonies could be drawn from the work of such writers of the present time as Samuel Beckett

1. See R. W. B. Lewis, *The Picaresque Saint* (Philadelphia, Lippincott, 1959), Ch. 1.

and the Escape into Faith

and Friedrich Duerrenmatt and Jean Genet and Alberto Moravia and Tennessee Williams.

So the cosmic homelessness and the strenuous metaphysics of the generation of Joyce and Kafka, though perhaps they assert themselves less stridently today, have yet not been put aside, and their basic premise continues to be the unquestioned axiom of the modern imagination—that what we ultimately face is a Silence, an Absence, a threatening Emptiness at the center. The grime and grit and seediness that we encounter in so many of Graham Greene's novels; the glum, dispirited ennui and acedia of Moravia's Roman world; the nasty, viscous disintegration of the phenomena of daily life in Sartre's *Nausea;* or, even among younger writers, the arid, cheerless, chromium world of Norman Mailer's *The Deer Park,* the dingy bleakness of the landscape we sometimes meet in the fiction of Britain's young rebels (reminiscent of early Orwell), and the curiously abstract violence of Kerouac's *On the Road* are among the characteristic and most frequently encountered qualities of recent literature. Our dominant metaphors are still metaphors of dearth and deprivation. The world that is explored and rendered in contemporary fiction is very often, like that presented by earlier literature of this century, a world that has been evacuated of radical significance. Beckett and Moravia and Alain Robbe-Grillet and Nathalie Sarraute and Norman Mailer are writers who live under a spiritual dispensation essentially the same as that classically emblematized by such earlier modern texts as *Hugh Selwyn Mauberley* and *The Waste Land* and *The Magic Mountain* and *The Castle* and *The Sun Also Rises.* That is, our period style, despite the numerous elaborations of it that are added by each successive decade of this century, continues in its deepest aspect to be the one forged by Dostoievski and Conrad and Hardy and Kafka and Hemingway—by those in whom was born the characteristically modern vision of a world with nothing at the center.

When Melville, at a central point in *Moby Dick,* remarks

that "though in many of its aspects this visible world seems formed in love, the invisible spheres were formed in fright," he seems almost, with a remarkable prescience, to be anticipating what was to become a tacit assumption in the twentieth century. For many of our writers—the Elias Canetti of *Auto da Fé*, the Malcolm Lowry of *Under the Volcano*, the Camus of *The Stranger*, the Penn Warren of *Brother to Dragons*— have made us feel that the world for them was very nearly a kind of nightmare—as Henry James phrased it in his last years, "a nightmare from which there is no waking save by sleep." And it is not surprising that James should have called his last novel *The Ivory Tower*, for, when the earth has become "merely a planet in the company of planets," when it is no longer "the center of divine attention,"[2] when human thought is no longer steadied by any Incarnational principle, when Meaning and Reality are sundered, and when poetic art seems fated to be only a desperate

> raid on the inarticulate
> With shabby equipment always deteriorating,
> In the general mess of imprecision of feeling,
> Undisciplined squads of emotion.[3]

then the writer will indeed seek out some barely tolerable *tour d'ivoire*. Or else, being given a kind of courage by his very despair, he will simply plunge into the whirling vortex of the world's disorder and make a kind of Absolute out of the sheer absurdity of existence itself. For all of James's greatness, the fact that he more nearly inclines to the former than to the latter course establishes his distance from what we recognize as the characteristic style and stance of the modern imagination. As Hannah Arendt has remarked, for the modern intelligence "to yield to the mere process of disintegration has become an irresistible temptation, not only because it has assumed the spurious grandeur of 'historical necessity' but also

2. Erich Heller, *The Hazard of Modern Poetry* (Cambridge, Bowes and Bowes, 1953), pp. 13, 17.
3. Eliot, "East Coker."

because everything outside it has begun to appear lifeless, bloodless, meaningless, and unreal."[4] And, in the things of the imagination, this fascination with the Abyss is perhaps the chief characteristic of our time.

In much of the great literature of our period, then, the world is perceived as opaque, as undependable, and strange. The English critic J. Isaacs says, "The topography of Hell and its interior decoration is a very great concern of the modern dramatist and the modern novelist."[5] And it is, indeed, in terms of the image of man amidst the dilapidation and ruins of modern existence that Hell is conceived in Pound's *Hugh Selwyn Mauberley* and Eliot's *The Waste Land*, in Ford's *The Good Soldier* and Fitzgerald's *The Great Gatsby*, in Faulkner's *Sanctuary* and Nathanael West's *The Day of the Locust*, in Cocteau's *The Infernal Machine* and Sartre's *No Exit*. Even time itself is very often experienced as a kind of captivity to what is deficient and oppressive: one might say perhaps that the soteriology of modern fiction often involves either some attempt to obliterate time in the interests of a mystical simultaneity, as in the most characteristic novels of Virginia Woolf, or some stratagem of rebellion, as in the novels of Camus. That is, even in our most secularized literature there is a central core of eschatological passion, or, at least, as Lionel Trilling puts it, a certain "resistance to history," a "secret hope" that "man's life in history shall come to an end."[6] What Henri-Charles Puech says of the Salvation envisaged in the ancient texts of primitive Gnosticism does, in fact, describe with a most startling exactness the controlling vision in many of the most representative literary expressions of the modern sensibility; it was, he says, a Salvation which "takes place in time, but the act on which it is founded is intrinsically atemporal. It is an interior and individual illumination, a revelation of oneself to oneself, a sudden gratuitous act which is

4. Hannah Arendt, *The Origins of Totalitarianism* (New York, Harcourt, Brace, 1951), p. viii.

5. J. Isaacs, *The Assessment of Twentieth-Century Literature* (London, Secker & Warburg, 1951), p. 59.

6. Trilling, *The Liberal Imagination*, p. 195.

accomplished by a predestined individual and which presupposes no previous condition or preparation in time."[7] And precisely the same extreme impatience with our life in time lies behind all those emotions of apathy and nausea, of vertigo and anguish, of terror and despair that make up the staple in the literature that has become for the modern imagination a kind of scripture.

Nor is it at all gratuitous to recall in this context the witness of ancient Gnosticism, for there we get a kind of elaboration into metaphysical system of what has comprised many of the formative attitudes in modern literature. The disquiet, the sense of insecurity, the metaphysical radicalism that the French associate with *littérature problématique*—these attitudes which we meet in the books of Hardy, Kafka, Camus, and Beckett are all based upon a fundamental mistrust of the created orders of finitude, upon a suspicion either that they are not stout enough to withstand the invading pressures of the Abyss or that they are not reliable enough to be "a glass of vision" into ultimate reality. And it was just this breakdown and resignation of courage in the presence of the limited, concrete actualities of historical existence that constituted what was the essential heresy of Basilides, Valentinus, Marcion, and those others who brought into being that dissident movement of the second century which we call Gnosticism. These ancient heresiarchs and *gnostikoi* postulated an absolute seclusion of that which is Radically Significant from all the provisional and proximate meanings of historical experience, and they conceived the world of finite existence to be a delusive and fraudulent imposture. Theirs, in other words, was a God unknowable by nature (*naturaliter ignotus*) and utterly incommensurable with the created order; and man's involvement in time and history was, therefore, felt to be a crushing burden and the ultimate disaster from which man was to be rescued. Henri-Charles Puech summarizes their position in this way:

7. Henri-Charles Puech, "Gnosis and Time," in *Man and Time*, ed. Joseph Campbell (New York, Pantheon, 1957), p. 76.

and the Escape into Faith

Present life with its infinite sufferings is not true Life. Still more, time, whose instants engender and destroy one another, in which each moment arises only to be engulfed in the next moment, in which all things appear, disappear, and reappear in a twinkling, without order, without aim or cessation or end—time contains within it a rhythm of death beneath an appearance of life.[8]

So, far from being any kind of *paidagogia* whereby man is formed and educated by God into an adequate maturity, time itself for these *pneumatikoi* was anguish, and they understood the human situation to be one of abandonment in a treacherous and indifferent world.

Now this same profound scepticism about the possibility of any commerce between the two spheres of time and eternity distinguishes our own period style and makes it a variant of an ancient heresy. But a despairing rejection of time is hardly calculated to yield any fruitful advance in human affairs, since it is only by moving deeply into the exigent realities of our human condition that there is any good chance of that condition being reconstituted in ways that are more promising and hopeful. And, in searching for that stratagem of the literary imagination that is most likely to assist us in redeeming the time, it may well be that, instead of relying on some yet-to-be-developed mutation within the terms of modern Gnosticism, we ought rather to explore the resources of another kind of radicalism altogether—namely, the radicalism of comedy.

And no sooner have we turned to the problem of comedy than we are given what may be still another measure of the propensity of the modern mind toward the various Gnostic and proto-Gnostic forms of tragedy, for, apart from Bergson's essay on *Laughter*, there is no indispensable treatise by any modern theorist on the comic imagination. We have George Meredith's *Essay on Comedy*, which has something of the dusty status of a school classic, and, in many ways, it is a genuinely useful guide; but, in the special attention that it

8. Ibid., pp. 65–66.

gives to those "volleys of silvery laughter" that will be provoked by the vanities and pretensions of men in society, it limits itself rather closely to comedy of manners. There are also other, less well-known formulations of more recent date by James Feibleman and Albert Cook and Northrop Frye and Arthur Koestler; but even the most recent literature on the subject has no very high interest, and it is neither rich nor various. So, an approach to the subject at present will inevitably entail some reconnoitering in order to discover a preliminary point of departure, and it may not be, therefore, improper simply to return to the very beginning of the tradition and to consider the cues that may be found in Aristotle.

Of course, it will not be forgotten that the central subject of the *Poetics* is tragedy: but it has long been thought that Aristotle at some point in his career also produced a treatise on comedy, his interest in the subject being clearly attested to by several passages in the *Poetics*. And since in Chapter 18 of Book III of the *Rhetoric* he speaks of having already classified "Jests" in the *Poetics*, many scholars (Bywater among them), taking this to be a reference to a discussion of comedy, have even concluded that this material, which does not appear in the existing *Poetics*, must have made up the second part of a work of which the extant *Poetics* constituted Book I. But, however this particular issue will be disposed of, judging from internal evidence within the *Poetics*, it would seem by no means implausible to suppose that Aristotle did produce an analysis of comedy that in its comprehensiveness and systematic rigor was comparable to his analysis of tragedy; and it also seems likely that much of his generalization in this area was based on the comedies of Aristophanes.

The basic consistencies of the *Poetics* suggest that Aristotle regarded all forms of literary art as subject to the executive principle of *mimesis,* and he doubtless made as much of a point of this in whatever treatise he devoted to comedy as he did in his discussion of tragedy. The poet, he insisted, imitates the action of human beings, men and women who are doing something. These personages are to be differentiated from one another in terms of their moral qualities: they are either better or worse than we are. Indeed, it is just at this point that Aristotle does explicitly distinguish in the extant *Poetics* between comedy and tragedy, for, as he says at the close of Chapter 2, "Comedy aims at representing men as worse, Tragedy as better than in actual life": or, as he says more systematically at the beginning of Chapter 5, comedy is "an imitation of persons inferior—not, however, in the full sense of the word bad, the Ludicrous being merely a subdivision of the ugly. It consists in some defect or ugliness which is not painful or destructive." And this defect, presumably, consists in one, or in some combination, of the vices enumerated in the *Nicomachaean Ethics*, such as vulgarity or buffoonery or foolhardiness.

This much may be said, then, about the object of the comic poet's imitation in Aristotle's probable understanding of the matter: it is an action which is ludicrous or mirthful, the action being rendered in the several media of language and rhythm and harmony. But what is the end of comedy: what function does it perform? If Aristotle's way of dealing with the problem of tragedy is at all to be taken as indicative of the way in which he wanted to deal with drama generally, it would seem that he very probably conceived it to be the function of comedy (as of all the various forms of mimetic art) to conduce to a special sort of pleasure. And, in Chapter 11 of Book I of the *Rhetoric*, he tells us what he means by "pleasure": it is "a movement by which the soul as a whole is consciously brought into its normal state of being."

Tragedy, of course, has its distinctive way of bringing the soul into its normal state of being—that is, of rendering it efficient for the conduct of the affairs of life. For, since the presence in the self to any excessive degree of the emotions of pity and fear would render it incompetent, tragedy arouses these emotions in order that they may be worked off and expelled, or purged: tragic pleasure comes about by the *katharsis* of the tragic emotions: it is something essentially medical and therapeutic.

Similarly, it seems reasonable to suppose, Aristotle very probably also conceived the ultimate effect of comedy to involve a special sort of pleasure, a pleasure partaking of a comic katharsis. Of this there is no indubitable proof, but it seems to be at least a good guess. We cannot, of course, at this point rely too heavily upon the *Tractatus Coislinianus*, and yet its testimony is significant. This document is generally referred to by this title because it is a part of the De Coislin Collection in the Bibliothèque Nationale in Paris. It is a manuscript of the tenth century A.D. whose contents date apparently from about the first century B.C., and, though it is only a brief fragment, it is, apart from the *Poetics* and Plato's *Philebus*, the only other important vestige of a theory of comedy that we have from the Greek tradition. And what is significant is that it very definitely embraces a theory of comic katharsis; indeed, it says, "Comedy is an imitation of an action that is ludicrous and imperfect . . . through pleasure and laughter effecting the purgation of the like emotions." Now this is patently a gloss on Aristotle; but, whether or not it truly reflects Aristotle's position, it seems at least to be a plausible guess as to what that position may have been. For Aristotle believed that comedy properly deals with the ludicrous and arouses in the spectator the sense of the ridiculous. "But," as John Crowe Ransom has observed, "this sense is analogous to pity and terror, in that it unfits a man for this duty: for there is implied in the citizen, if he goes about finding everything ridiculous, the belief that he is witnessing an irrational universe."[9] So it seems likely that Aristotle concluded that, just as there must be katharsis in tragedy, so too must comic drama effectuate a genuinely cathartic experience in which potentially disabling emotions are harmlessly discharged.

Here, then, are what were probably the main elements of Aristotle's conception of comedy, and, when taken all together, they amount to an exact transposition of his definition

9. John Crowe Ransom, *The World's Body* (New York, Scribner's, 1938), p. 189.

86

of tragedy; formally phrased, it would go like this: Comedy, then, is an organically complete imitation of an action which is ludicrous; in language embellished with each kind of artistic ornament, the several kinds being found in separate parts of the play; in the form of action, not of narrative; with incidents arousing pleasure and laughter, wherewith to accomplish its katharsis of such emotion.

So now, despite the unhelpful tenuity of modern criticism, we have at last, through Aristotle, a way into our subject. And, though the concepts we derive from him may require very considerable recasting, they do, if only in providing us with something to resist or to negate, enable us to begin to draw a circle of definition about the fundamental issues. And, indeed, perhaps our very first response to Aristotle ought to be sceptical. "Comedy," he tells us, "aims at representing men as worse, Tragedy as better than in actual life." But is this really so? It is true, of course, that tragedy and comedy represent men differently, but is the difference quite of the sort which Aristotle suggests?

Let us approach the matter in this way. We may say, I think, that true tragedy has always thrust us into those acute situations of crisis in which man's unhappy consciousness of the contradictions of human existence impels him to perform an act of radical self-transcendence. He is led to ask himself what it means to be a man, what it means to-be rather than not-to-be, and how dependable is the essentially human thing in himself. And when a man thus becomes a problem to himself, it is because in some critical moment life, in its fundamental axiological structure, has appeared to be at cross-purposes with itself, ultimately and irremediably. He discovers that what he believes to be most valid and authentic in himself is somehow radically contradicted or threatened by the objective order that constitutes the theatre of the human enterprise. So he begins to wonder how he can "choose" himself, or if perhaps, in a universe in which man, as such, is fundamentally defective, his having already "chosen" himself is not the cause of his present embarrassments. In this "boundary-situation," the tragic man is not simply a passive agonizer: he is committed to a course of action, and this is why it is proper to refer, as we do, to the great tragedies in literature as "tragic actions," for in them the central figure is one who not only suffers but who actively resists whatever it is that would destroy his dignity and bring to naught his highest purposes. What we see, in Richard Sewall's summary of the matter, is "man at the limits of his sovereignty—Job on the ash-heap, Prometheus on the crag, Oedipus in his moment of self-discovery, Lear on the heath, Ahab on his lonely quarter-deck." And here, "with all the protective covering ripped off,"[10] the hero, facing into the utter insecurity of his situation, is led to muster all his resources in one great effort to transcend the fundamental limitations of his creaturehood. It is not, as Aristotle says, that he is better than we are: it is rather that he is, as Henry Myers puts it, more of an extremist than most of us are. "To reach his goal, whatever it may be, he is always willing to sacrifice everything else, including his life. Oedipus will press the search for the unknown murderer, although he is warned of the consequences; Hamlet will prove the King's guilt and attempt to execute perfect justice, whatever the cost may be to his mother, to Laertes, to Ophelia, and to himself; Ibsen's Solness will climb the tower he has built, at the risk of falling into the quarry; Ahab will kill Moby Dick or die in the attempt."[11] It is precisely with this kind of intensity that the protagonists of the great tragic actions live in the world; and it is, therefore, not surprising that most of them die early and never enjoy the felicity of a long and complete life. For they soon exhaust themselves in the effort to gain release from the restrictions that are a consequence of their finitude: this is an essential part of what we are to include in the "tragic rhythm of action," which is the rhythm that man's life has

10. Richard B. Sewall, *The Vision of Tragedy* (New Haven, Yale University Press, 1959), p. 5.

11. Henry Alonzo Myers, *Tragedy: A View of Life* (Ithaca, Cornell University Press, 1956), p. 45.

when it is lived at the difficult and perilous limits of human capability.[12]

However, the systole and diastole of the "comic rhythm of action" are altogether different, and the best way of measuring the difference is to consider the personage who has always been the presiding genius of comedy—namely, the clown. The particular clown I want to recall is Charlie Chaplin, whose art places him, I believe, among the few great comic geniuses of the modern period. It is not, however, the Chaplin image of the late films—*Monsieur Verdoux,* or *Limelight,* or even *The Great Dictator*—that I have in mind, but rather the Tramp of the early and middle films, *The Kid* and *The Gold Rush* and *City Lights:* the little, downtrodden, but urbane and chivalrous man in big, baggy trousers and wrinkled, out-of-size shoes, who has an expression of amazement and alarm written into the innocence of his face. This is the Chaplin who has provided us with an image more memorable than any other in cinema history of the lonely, unprotected individual clinging to his humanity amid the horrible impersonality and dehumanization of the modern world. Charlie's Tramp represented the little man, the *homunculus,* who, amid the dreary facelessness of men completely involved in the rituals of a money culture, insisted on behaving as though his fellow human beings were still human. And he was, of course, as a result, to them a scandal, an utterly absurd little scandal. But he was never regarded as a serious threat, for the society's dedication to its materialism was so complete that no one ever really took the trouble to consider his eccentricity for the profoundly subversive thing it was: in film after film he was simply regarded by the sober fools with whom he collided as a charming, though utterly irrelevant, little scapegrace.

Yet, erratic and unpredictable as the Tramp's behavior was, he was never ridiculous. One wants instead to say that he was touching, for everything that he did was so utterly human,

12. See Francis Fergusson, *The Idea of a Theatre* (Princeton, Princeton University Press, 1949), Ch. 1.

even his pranks and his mischief. And when one occasionally sees these old films again in little art-cinema houses, one feels that here is a man, that here is a richly particularized and wonderfully eccentric human being living out his life—a little hobo whose every gesture somehow manages to redeem the human image by revealing how beautifully mysterious it would be were it unencumbered by the mechanical reflexes which it has learned in an unpropitious time. When, in *The Kid*, he dreams that all men are angels, when he topples over the bannisters in *His Favorite Pastime*, when he shares his last sausage with a bulldog in *The Champion*, when he sets out to walk to the horizon in *The Tramp*, we feel that here is the real human thing itself—clothed not in the unearthly magnificence of tragic heroism but in the awkward innocence of essential humanity.

A particularly memorable film is *City Lights*, in which Charlie strikes up a relation with a rich man on a drunken spree who, taking a fancy to him, domiciles him in his great mansion. But when his host recovers his sobriety, he is so repelled by the little man that he flings him out of the house. And the fun of the movie arises out of the alternations that ensue between inebriate acceptance and sober rejection and that continue, to Charlie's utter bafflement. In the allegory of the film, the rich man is a representative of that bourgeois mentality which is completely captive to the materialistic ethic of "the skin game." When he is half intoxicated, he cannot resist the charming gaiety and insouciance of the little fellow who regards material affluence as too ephemeral and as requiring altogether too much trouble to make it worth scrambling after. One suspects that the rich man embraces Charlie in his drunkenness because the lackadaisical little tramp is in some way his own deeper self which he has submerged and repressed and for which he yearns. But in his moments of sobriety he rejects Charlie, expels him from his house. Again, one suspects that he does so because the tramp, with his languid, smiling irony, engenders in him the remembrance that to be a man and to be a great material success are not one and the same thing, and this is a fact which he has not the courage to face. So he finally drives the clown out of his life, since Charlie evokes memories with which he has not the spiritual resources to deal.[13]

Here we come upon what is perhaps the basic function of the comic man, and it is, I believe, simply to be a kind of icon of the human actuality. It is not, as Aristotle says, that the tragic man is better than we are: no, what differentiates him from the rest of us is that he is more of an extremist than most of us are; and, in the resistance he offers to whatever he feels ultimately to threaten the human enterprise, he is, by seeking to transcend the limitations that attach to our creatureliness, always in danger of forgetting that he is not an angel and only a man. Moreover, the comic man is not, as Aristotle says, worse than we are: on the contrary, it is his function simply to be an example of the contingent, imperfect, earth-bound creatures that in truth we all really are, and it is also his function to awaken in us a lively recognition of what in fact our true status is. He asks us not to be afraid to acknowledge that we are only human and that our residence is not in the heavens. And he asks us to examine critically all the spurious stratagems we employ to evade a frank acceptance of our finitude, whether they be those of bourgeois worldliness or of philosophical and religious mysticism. What the comic man cannot abide is the man who will not consent to be simply a man, who cannot tolerate the thought of himself as an incomplete and conditioned creature of a particular time and a particular place.

The great difference between the tragic man and the comic man is something that arises out of their different ways of dealing with the burden of human finitude. For the tragic man it is a profound embarrassment and perhaps even a curse, for he would rather be pure intellect or pure will or pure something-or-other, and nothing wounds him more deeply than to be reminded that his life is a conditioned thing and that there is nothing absolute at all in the human stuff out of which he is

13. See Parker Tyler, *Magic and Myth of the Movies* (New York, Henry Holt, 1947), pp. 36–38.

made. But the comic man is unembarrassed by even the grossest expressions of his creatureliness: though the world may not be all dandy, he has no sense of being under any cruel condemnation; nor does he have any sense of desperate entrapment within a prison. He can say, without ironic bitterness, "I'm only human," in full recognition of the fact that making this admission is itself the condition of his life's being tolerable and of his being able to address to God an appropriate *Confiteor*. He does not insist upon life's conforming to his own special requirements but consents to take it on the terms of its own created actuality, and the art of comedy is devoted to an exhibition of his deep involvement in the world: so it shirks nothing—none of the irrelevant absurdities, none of the vexatious inconveniences that are the lot of such finite creatures as ourselves.

An incisive essay by Aldous Huxley, "Tragedy and the Whole Truth," begins by recalling that famous Twelfth Book of Homer's *Odyssey*, in which Odysseus and his men, in the course of their journey back to Ithaca, encounter the monster Scylla and the whirlpool Charybdis. And in this story, Odysseus relives that dreadful day and sadly remembers the poor, hapless souls whom Scylla had devoured. He again sees them being lifted, struggling, into the air: he hears their screams and the despairing cries for help. He recalls how he and the other survivors could only look helplessly on at the awful struggle, and adds that it was the most pitiable sight he had ever seen in all his "explorings of the passes of the sea." But, then, once the danger that night had been passed, Odysseus and his men went ashore to prepare their dinner on the Sicilian beach—and prepared it, Homer says, "expertly." The entire episode is concluded by the poet's telling us that "when they had satisfied their thirst and hunger, they thought of their dear companions and wept, and in the midst of their tears sleep came gently upon them."

Now this, Mr. Huxley tells us, is "the truth, the whole truth and nothing but the truth."

In any other poem but the *Odyssey*, what would the survivors have done? They would, of course, have wept, even as Homer made them weep. But would they previously have cooked their supper, and cooked it, what's more, in a masterly fashion? Would they previously have drunk and eaten to satiety? And after weeping, or actually while weeping, would they have dropped quietly off to sleep? No, they most certainly would not have done any of these things. They would simply have wept, lamenting their own misfortune and the horrible fate of their companions, and the canto would have ended tragically on their tears.

Homer, however, preferred to tell the Whole Truth. He knew that even the most cruelly bereaved must eat; that hunger is stronger than sorrow and that its satisfaction takes precedence even of tears. He knew that experts continue to act expertly and to find satisfaction in their accomplishment, even when friends have just been eaten, even when the accomplishment is only cooking the supper. He knew that, when the belly is full (and only when the belly is full) men can afford to grieve, and that sorrow after supper is almost a luxury. And finally he knew that, even as hunger takes precedence of grief, so fatigue, supervening, cuts short its career and drowns it in a sleep all the sweeter for bringing forgetfulness of bereavement. In a word, Homer refused to treat the theme tragically. He preferred to tell the Whole Truth.[14]

Now Mr. Huxley does not go on to say that the Whole Truth is the truth of comedy, but this is a line that he might very well have taken. Indeed, if I may propose at this point another amendment of the Aristotelian formulation, I should say that the art of comedy is not an art that is dedicated to the ludicrous, but is rather an art that is dedicated to the telling of the Whole Truth: this is what it is that comedy "imi-

14. Aldous Huxley, *Collected Essays* (New York, Bantam Books, 1960), p. 98.

93

tates"—not the ludicrous, but the Whole Truth. Surely Mr. Huxley is luminously right in finding Homer to be a poet of the Whole Truth, for Homer knew that, however grief-stricken men may be by the loss of dearly beloved companions, they will remember to weep only after they have satisfied their hunger, and that they will then forget their tears in slumber. In other words, the point made in the Scylla-Charybis episode is that men are not pure sensibility, that they also have bodies which must be fed and which, when overcome by fatigue, must relax in sleep. And this is, in a way, the point that comedy is always making: we are not pure, disembodied essences; indeed, we are not pure anything-at-all, but we are men, and our health and happiness are contingent upon our facing into the fact that we are finite and conditioned, and therefore subject to all sorts of absurdities, interruptions, inconveniences, embarrassments—and weaknesses. This is, we might say, the courage that the comic vision requires of us.

But to turn from this poet of ancient Hellas to a modern novelist such as Virginia Woolf is immediately to have a splendid example in our own time of what the comic writer is most emphatically not like.

To recall Mrs. Woolf's achievement in the novel is, of course, at some point or other in the course of one's reflections to be put in mind of her much-quoted essay of 1919, "Modern Fiction," for in this early statement she summarized the aims to which the whole of her subsequent career as an artist was devoted. Here she was attempting to set forth the reasons for her dissatisfaction with the realism of the generation of Galsworthy and Wells and Bennett, whose books, however many of the journeyman virtues of the professional novelist they might occasionally reflect, did not, she felt, plunge beneath the merest surface of life. The spirit of this manifesto shows itself in the following passage:

> Examine for a moment an ordinary mind on an ordinary day. The mind receives a myriad of impressions—trivial, fantastic, evanescent, or engraved with the sharpness of

steel. From all sides they come, an incessant shower of innumerable atoms; and as they fall, as they shape themselves into the life of Monday or Tuesday, the accent falls differently from of old; the moment of importance came not here but there; so that, if a writer were a free man and not a slave, if he could write what he chose, not what he must, if he could base his work upon his own feeling and not upon convention, there would be no plot, no comedy, no tragedy, no love interest or catastrophe in the accented style, and perhaps not a single button sewn on as the Bond Street tailors would have it. Life is not a series of gig lamps symmetrically arranged; but a luminous halo, a semi-transparent envelope surrounding us from the beginning of consciousness to the end. Is it not the task of the novelist to convey this varying, this unknown and uncircumscribed spirit, whatever aberration or complexity it may display, with as little mixture of the alien and external as possible?

"Let us record," said Mrs. Woolf, "the atoms as they fall upon the mind in the order in which they fall, let us trace the pattern, however disconnected and incoherent in appearance, which each sight or incident scores upon the consciousness."[15] And this was precisely what she undertook to do. As she said in an essay written five years later, "Mr. Bennett and Mrs. Brown," she felt that the Wellses and the Bennetts and the Galsworthys had "laid an enormous stress upon the fabric of things." They, in their old-fashioned naturalism, were preoccupied with the literalities and the surfaces of life: so she proposed that they be called "materialists." Were all three, for example, to be traveling in the same compartment from Richmond to Waterloo with a frayed, timid, little old lady named Mrs. Brown, Wells, in his account of the trip, "would instantly project upon the windowpane a vision of a better, breezier, jollier, happier, more adventurous and gallant world, where these musty railway carriages and fusty old

15. Virginia Woolf, *The Common Reader* (New York, Harcourt, Brace, 1925), pp. 212–13.

women do not exist." Galsworthy, "burning with indignation, stuffed with information, arraigning civilization . . . would only see in Mrs. Brown a pot broken on the wheel and thrown into the corner." And Bennett would proceed to make meticulously accurate notations on the appointments of the carriage and on the details of Mrs. Brown's attire and appearance—on everything, indeed, except whatever it is that constitutes Mrs. Brown's human identity. And so it was, Mrs. Woolf was contending, with the Edwardians generally: their vision was superficial: they entirely neglected Mrs. Brown. "In order to complete them," she said, "it seems necessary to do something—to join a society, or, more desperately, to write a cheque."[16] But Mrs. Brown, she was insisting, is the proper focus and subject of literature, and had you asked her who Mrs. Brown was, she would, one imagines, have referred you back to her earlier statement of 1919 and said that Mrs. Brown is just, quite simply, "the atoms as they fall upon the mind in the order in which they fall."

This was the reality that Mrs. Woolf—like Joyce and other writers who were to follow—wanted to get into her books. So it is no wonder that she could say, "When I write I am merely a sensibility." And thus it is also no wonder that one of her critics, intending to be complimentary, has said her characters "are not characters," but are, "like her incidents and her intuitions," "unfinished, spreading as the ripples of a lake spread in the sunlight."[17]

Though her first novel, *The Voyage Out*, is by far exceeded in importance by some of her later books, it is, nevertheless, a good case in point and beautifully illustrates the method and the manner. The central character is Rachel Vinrace, whose twenty-four years of life in Richmond have been sheltered by her father and two maiden aunts from everything that might

16. Virginia Woolf, *The Hogarth Essays* (Garden City, Doubleday, 1928), p. 14.
17. Bernard Blackstone, *Virginia Woolf: A Commentary* (London, Hogarth Press, 1949), p. 10.

have deepened and sophisticated her moral sensibilities. But now, on her father's boat, the *Euphrosyne,* she is going to the Villa San Gervasio in Santa Marina for a South American holiday with her uncle and aunt, the Ambroses, and Helen Ambrose intends to take her education in hand. This purpose is somewhat forwarded by the boarding of Mr. and Mrs. Richard Dalloway when the steamer drops anchor in the mouth of the Tagus, for Dalloway—"a rather dull, kindly, plausible" gentleman recently a Member of Parliament—soon begins a flirtation with Rachel. But when he kisses her one stormy afternoon, amid the lurchings of the ship, she trembles: "a chill of body and mind" creeps over her, and she is struck by the insignificance of the event. Then, at the Villa San Gervasio, she meets young Terence Hewet, who is writing a novel about "Silence, or the Things People don't Say," because he wants his characters to be "more abstract than people who live as we do." After a time, the two become engaged, but nothing is to come of it, for a few weeks later Rachel contracts a severe headache after a picnic-expedition, takes to her bed with a fever, and in a short time is dead. But, in the brief period that these two young people have together, we are often in their company on afternoon strolls through the hot forests of the place, and, one day, as they are out together, they come upon two young people who are also living at the hotel, Susan Warrington and Arthur Venning: "They lay in each other's arms and had no notion that they were observed."

"Here's shade," began Hewet, when Rachel suddenly stopped dead. They saw a man and woman lying on the ground beneath them, rolling slightly this way and that as the embrace tightened and slackened. The man then sat upright and the woman, who now appeared to be Susan Warrington, lay back upon the ground, with her eyes shut and an absorbed look upon her face, as though she were not altogether conscious. Nor could you tell from her expression whether she was happy, or had suffered something. When

Arthur again turned to her, butting her as a lamb butts a ewe, Hewet and Rachel retreated without a word. Hewet felt uncomfortably shy.

"I don't like that," said Rachel after a moment.

And Hewet says, "It's so enormously important, you see. Their lives are now changed for ever." Rachel agrees, saying that she could almost burst into tears. And after a moment's consideration Hewet answers, "Yes, there's something horribly pathetic about it, I agree." On another occasion, Rachel, with an inspired breathlessness, asks Hewet, "Does it ever seem to you, Terence, that the world is composed entirely of vast blocks of matter and that we're nothing but patches of light?" Or, again, we are told that one day "They stood together in front of the looking-glass, and with a brush tried to make themselves look as if they had been feeling nothing all the morning, neither pain nor happiness. But it chilled them to see themselves in the glass, for instead of being vast and indivisible they were really very small and separate, the size of the glass leaving a large space for the reflection of other things."

This is the tone of the book, and it is not surprising that one of Mrs. Woolf's admirers should have found it "vague and universal," for everything is fleeting deliquescence and vague, shadowy mistiness: indeed, many of the characters themselves, amidst the hallucinatory flashes of significance that punctuate the story, are often wondering what it all comes to. The vagueness and universality of *The Voyage Out* were to become even more emphatically characteristic of Mrs. Woolf's later books, of *Jacob's Room* and *To the Lighthouse* and *Mrs. Dalloway*. She was bent on dissolving the substantialities of character and event into that luminous halo which, in her understanding of the novelist's art, was the great thing to be striven for. And finally, as her famous delicacy and sensitivity operate on experience, we begin to feel amid the tenuous and fragile little epiphanies that the hegemony of the objective world has been completely broken and that we are flapping about in a void.

Indeed, what is most impressive in Mrs. Woolf's most characteristic novels—particularly in *Mrs. Dalloway, To the Light-house*, and *The Waves*—is the profound distaste for, and the deep fear of, the conditioned and limited world that is actually the scene of human life. Hers is an intelligence (and in this she is like so many of the artists of our time) which has neither the courage nor the patience to temporize with the concrete, sub-stantial stuff that constitutes the occasion and the circumstance of man's actual career in time. It is an intelligence that cannot dive into the thick, coarse realities of the human condition, for these are not realities that are regarded as leading anywhere or as associable with what is Radically Significant in life. There is no deep faith or confidence in the realm of human finitude and in the possibility of its being a glass of vision into the ul-timate. So an effort is made to flee into the safe and impreg-nable citadel of pure consciousness, and this is surely what ac-counts for the vulgarity that we may sometimes feel in the very refinement and delicacy and exquisiteness of sensibility that Mrs. Woolf's most ardent admirers like so much to praise. That is to say, we find vulgarity in the delicacy and the elegant sen-sitiveness, because it is all so bloodless and so far removed from the elemental things of human life. In her works there is so much impatience with the clumsy grossness of the human creature and with the rough, ragged edges of life, and there is so much in the daily round of human living that Mrs. Woolf will not deign to bring within her orbit that, paradoxically, we feel finally that a kind of dirt is being done on life. She will never allow us to wallow about in the rucky mire of our hu-manness, and no one in her books ever howls or moans or really laughs over the human fate. There is no passion because the characters in her novels have all been abstracted by her preciousness into fragile, gossamerlike states of mind: it seems that only in this way could the human reality become for her just barely tolerable.

The recoil into sensibility is but one of many detours away from the human actuality to be encountered in modern litera-ture, and principal among the others is the recoil into disgust which is archetypally expressed in Jean-Paul Sartre's novel of

1938, *Nausea*. The hero, Antoine Roquentin, is a young intellectual who takes up residence in the provincial town of Bou-
ville-sur-Mer to finish a biography of an obscure eighteenth-
century nobleman, the Marquis de Rollebon. The novel is
written in the form of his journal, which is devoted to the record that he keeps of his experience during his sojourn in this
place. As he lives alone in his squalid roominghouse and works
amid the dreariness of the town's public library, Roquentin's
spirits are soon depressed to the point of utter distraction by
the drabness and monotony of life in this little coastal village,
and, after a time, his restlessness making sustained scholarly
labor impossible, his thinking becomes solely a matter of in-
trospection and self-analysis. What is borne in upon him ever
more deeply in the vacant, joyless days that ensue is his own
isolation and the unshakeable indifference of the world to the
human spirit. So intense does this vision become that he is
stricken by first one and then another attack of sheer physical
wretchedness: he is positively sickened by the amorphous factuality of the phenomenal world, by the obscene stubbornness
with which things persist in retaining a *thereness* that seems to
have no link with his own existence and that seems, therefore,
to that extent to oppose his own inward being. Indeed, his inner exacerbation becomes so acute that even the most commonplace objects in his environment at last prove capable of
throwing him into a spasm of retching or into utter gloom—a
pebble on the beach, a glass of beer, his own face in a mirror,
the knob of a door. The whole of existence becomes for him
simply one vast, obscene, bulging pile of junk, and his fundamental sensations come to be those of nausea and disgust. It is
the very arbitrariness with which events occur and things exist
that fills him with distress, for it deepens his sense of the
contingency and finitude of his own being. Everything seems
to be fragmentary and disheveled and messy—and the obscenity of it all makes him twitch with fury.

There is only one diversion that lights up the gray tedium of
his days: it is to hear a gramophone record of a Negro song-

stress singing the jazz melody "Some of These Days." At the end of the novel, after having given up his research and completed preparations for his departure, he sits in a dingy little cafe listening to the song and its saxophone accompaniment for the last time. Suddenly, what he has really wanted all his life dawns on him: it has been, he says, "to chase existence out of me, empty the moments of their fat, wring them out, dry them, purify myself, harden myself, so as to give out finally the clean, precise note of a saxophone."

It is clear that what fills Roquentin with horror is simply the sheer untidiness of existence: he is oppressed by the messiness of things, the bedragglement of the world; and his imagination is fixed upon images of *le visqueux*, because the opaqueness of things reveals to him how ultimate is the ontological discontinuity between himself as a discrete, finite creature and everything else that exists. Every object and every event he experiences seem, in the sheer arbitrariness and contingency of their reality, to imply that the kind of metaphysical order he craves is an impossibility. His sense of justice is outraged, and, in his consuming disgust, he desires to be disembodied into the purity of sound made by a blues-saxophonist: he would live the incorporeal life of the angels, being no longer a man but a mere breath of music.

This deep shudder of Sartre's hero before the phenomenal world presents us with an excellent example of the response that is made to existence by him who is the antithesis of the comic man. What Antoine Roquentin reveals in the violence of his distaste for the created order is precisely that profound distrust of creation which the comedian always calls into question, in effect, at least, if not by intention. For the comic man, characteristically, grapples with the thickness and the density of the concrete world of human experience, delighting in all its smells, sounds, sights, and tactilities. The comedian is not generally an aviator: he does not journey away from this familiar world of earth; he refuses the experiment of angelism; he will not forget that we are made out of dust; and, when his wrath is aroused, as it sometimes is, it is not because man is bound to the things of earth but rather because man sometimes foolishly supposes that he can simply fly away from them.

This is, indeed, always the lesson of Comedy: we are creatures whose nature it is to form an earthly City and who become ridiculous when we commit ourselves to some abortive venture beyond the precincts within which alone we can hope to win some proper understanding of our true human stature. It is not, of course, the purpose of the comedian to enforce a simple Sunday school lesson: all he wants to do is to give his suffrage to the Whole Truth and, as Susanne Langer says, to "reincarnate for our perception . . . the motion and rhythm of living" in the world. "Real comedy," says Mrs. Langer, "sets up in the audience a sense of general exhilaration, because it presents the very image of 'livingness'."[18] Because, we might add, it tells us what Homer tells us in the Twelfth Book of the *Odyssey*, what Shakespeare tells us through Falstaff in the *Henry IV* plays when he takes us to Gad's Hill or into Eastcheap, or what Charlie Chaplin in *City Lights* tells us. This means, of course, that, when men decide that they are pure mind or pure will or pure sensibility, it is natural for the comic imagination to take on a critical, even polemical, aspect. It is appropriate, for example, that the Socrates of *The Clouds*, in his contempt for the common world of human experience and in his consuming passion for the clear and distinct idea, lives ridiculously suspended in a basket high up in the air. It is further appropriate that Aristophanes brings this philosopher down from the clouds, does not allow him to get away with his pretense that he lives above the relativities of history, and makes him confront some of the elemental facts of life. Or, again, we feel the justice of comedy to be operative in Molière's *Le Misanthrope*, when the outrageous pharisaism of Alceste finally has the consequence of relegating him to an essentially

18. Susanne K. Langer, *Feeling and Form: A Theory of Art* (New York, Scribner's, 1953), pp. 344, 348.

private universe between which and the actual world there ceases to be any connection at all. And, had an Antoine Roquentin entered the orbit of so superb a modern comedian as Joyce Cary, he would have been reminded that he is not really a pure breath of music but a man who eats, sleeps, defecates, catches colds in winter when he doesn't wear his long drawers, and that he had better remember these undignified facts if he wants to retain any dignity as a man.

The major purpose of the comedian is to remind us of how deeply rooted we are in all the tangible things of this world; he is not, like Shelley or the author of *To the Lighthouse*, a poet of an "unbodied joy." The motions of comedy, to be sure, finally lead to joy, but it is a joy that we win only after we have consented to journey through this familiar, actual world of earth which is our home and, by doing so, have had our faith in its stability and permanence restored. The joy of comedy is a great joy, but it is a joy that can sometimes come only after humiliation—the humiliation the arrogant millionaire suffers when, walking down the street fully concentrated on his dignity and importance, he suddenly slips on the banana peeling he had failed to notice, and is thus reminded that he is, after all, only a man and as much subject to the law of gravitation as the rest of humankind. The event may not at first bring joy to the man himself, if his capacity for self-transcendence has been so long unused that he cannot immediately regard with wry amusement the spectacle that he has created before the gaping schoolchildren. But, even if he is not the comic hero but rather merely the comic butt of the event, we who are also looking on grasp the meaning of what has occurred, and it brings us joy because it reminds us again how inescapable our humanity is, how established and permanent and indestructible it really is. To be sure, the man's backside is bruised as a result of the fall —yet what is really hurt in him is his pride. The essentially human thing in him is not bruised: indeed, it is the lesson of comedy that this does somehow manage, again and again, to remain intact. True, it is often challenged, and men sometimes become ashamed of it and tamper with it and even reject it, but this stuff that is constitutive of what is human in them does, nevertheless, prevail—and its reassertion of itself is the central moment of comedy.

The comic way, then, descends into the mundane, conditioned world of the human creature, moving confidently into all the diverse corners of man's habitation. The difference between this way and the tragic way is not that the latter leads into suffering and agony and the former into rollicking mirth and jollity, for the men and women of comedy sometimes suffer too. Indeed, one of the most heart-rending moments in all Shakespearean drama is that in *Henry IV*, Pt. II, V. 5, when Falstaff, hearing his beloved master, Prince Hal, declare, "I know thee not, old man," turns to Justice Shallow a moment later and says "Master Shallow, I owe you a thousand pound." In this moment, his anguish is hardly less than that of Lear when he moans, "How sharper than a serpent's tooth it is/To have a thankless child!" But the agonies of the comic protagonist never have the kind of distilled purity that belongs to the sufferings of the tragic hero: the comic man, when he becomes involved in real difficulty, is no more pure-suffering than he is pure-anything-else: Odysseus and his men, when they finally stumbled upon the Sicilian beach that night, first ate their supper before weeping for their lost comrades, and then, being exhausted, their tears ceased to flow, and they fell off to sleep.

So the art of comedy reminds us, however far we may venture into the strange corridors of the world or however high we may climb the treacherous mountains of the mind, that we are of the earth and earthy—that we are creatures whose finitude is ineluctable. Kafka, in one of his Parables, says:

> [Man] is a free and secure citizen of the world, for he is fettered to a chain which is long enough to give him the freedom of all earthly space, and yet only so long that nothing can drag him past the frontiers of the world. But simultaneously he is a free and secure citizen of Heaven as well, for he is also fettered by a similarly designed heavenly chain.

and the Escape into Faith

So that if he heads, say, for the earth, his heavenly collar throttles him, and if he heads for Heaven, his earthly one does the same.[19]

And though it may be the office of tragedy to be the heavenly collar that throttles us when we head for earth, it is certainly the office of comedy to be the collar that throttles us when we make up our minds to expatriate ourselves from the conditioned realm of historical existence. For what comedy never gives up insisting upon is that we are not angels and that we belong, therefore, not to any unhistorical heaven of pure essences but to the moving, restless, dynamic world of time and space.

Now, at last, a tentative definition of the comic may be proposed, and it will be a gloss on the definition offered by W. H. Auden a few years ago in his "Notes on the Comic," in which he said that it is "a contradiction in the relation of the individual or personal to the universal or impersonal which does not involve the spectator in suffering or pity."[20] I should, however, prefer to put the matter a little differently and to say that the comic is a contradiction in the relation of the human individual to the created orders of existence; this contradiction arises out of an over-specialization of some instinct or faculty of the self, or out of an inordinate inclination of the self in some special direction, to the neglect of the other avenues through which it ought also to gain expression. This predilection of the self to identify too completely with some special interest or project (cf. Aristophanes' Socrates or Jonson's Volpone or Molière's Tartuffe or Sterne's Walter Shandy or Shaw's Professor Higgins) blinds the self to the integral character of its humanity and thus throws it out of gear with the fundamental norms and orders of human existence. However, in the comic action, this contradiction in the individual's relation to the created orders of life does not involve the spectator in suffering or pity,

19. Franz Kafka, "Paradise" (trans. Willa and Edwin Muir), *Parables* (New York, Schocken Books, 1947), p. 27.
20. W. H. Auden, "Notes on the Comic," *Thought*, 27 (Spring 1952), 57.

for he is not led to identify with the protagonist who, indeed, in the course of the action becomes the butt of his laughter.

But, this definition of the comic is not yet complicated enough, for it suggests what is not quite the case, namely, that the comic protagonist is always the butt of laughter, and of laughter that is untempered with love or sympathy. This is, of course, very often the case, but not always. It is most certainly not true of the figure who must centrally be taken into account in any theory of comedy—Sir John Falstaff. This "swoll'n parcel of dropsies," this "huge bombard of sack," this "stuff'd cloakbag of guts," is—let us admit it—a rogue and a cheat, a braggart and a sensualist. Yet he is the most lovable rogue in all literature. He is old and fat and broken-winded, and yet there is in him a kind of fresh, prelapsarian innocence that makes us think of him always as youthful and even boyish. Like many of the boys in American literature from Mark Twain's Huck Finn to J. D. Salinger's Holden Caulfield, Falstaff is a great liar—he lies, however, like Huck and Holden, in order to protect himself against the conventional dishonesty of other men. Falstaff has traveled throughout the world, has met all types of people, suffered all sorts of hard knocks, and pinched ladies' buttocks in every corner of England: yet there is in him no fatigue, no world-weariness, and he retains a remarkable zest and enthusiasm for adventure. Above all else, he has a great capacity for living intensely in the present moment: one might say that he is the original existentialist hero, if one means by "existentialist hero" not the fastidious and disgusted man of Sartre's *Nausea* but rather the man who is *engagé,* who is intensely committed to the present moment and the present task: indeed, in this latter sense, Falstaff is perhaps the prototype of the existentialist man. And this may be why he is so impatient with the restraints of conventional moral codes and laws, for, however relevant they may be to the general circumstances of life, he always finds them ineffective and irrelevant to the uniqueness and contingency of the immediate occasion. Yet, despite his outrageous improvisation in morality, it is his passionate commitment to the present moment and to concrete reality that makes Falstaff so wonderfully and richly human.

Sir John's great scenes are, of course, in the two parts of *Henry IV* (rather than in *The Merry Wives of Windsor*), and it is no wonder that here his role becomes finally that of victim. These are plays whose whole drama is stirred into being by the anarchy that has overtaken the English realm; and since, in the world of Shakespearean experience, civil anarchy in every form is most "unnatural," the drama of *Henry IV* must, therefore, move toward the recovery of order in the body politic. Prince Hal is the one destined to be the agent through whom order will be restored; and, since he finds in plump Jack a symbol of everything that would endanger or subvert decorum and order, he drives him off. And that is precisely what Falstaff stands for. In the boldness, enterprise, vivacity, and wit of this fat old rascal we have the most brilliant image that the literary tradition affords of that zest, spontaneity, and independence in the human creature that makes him an intractable nuisance for every order that defines itself so constrictively as to leave no room for a man to move about in and stretch himself. So, despite all his faults, there is greatness in Sir John. He has vices, it is true, but, as Mark Van Doren says, "they have not the sound of vices. None of them is an end in itself—that is their secret. . . . He does not live to drink or steal or lie or foin o'nights. He even does not live in order that he may be the cause of wit in other men."[21] He simply lives for the joy of the adventure itself—and we must say, I think, to the glory of God. There is in him nothing of the protestant (small *p*): he has no quarrel with life: he is not a romantic: he is engaged in no cosmic debate: he is content simply to be a man. And though he is not a very virtuous, not a very good man, though he is a rascal and a scalawag, he *is* a man, always and intensely human—and this, I take it, is why he is the great saint of Western comedy. We laugh at old Jack, but we also admire him and love him; and, when we laugh at him, it is simply be-

21. Mark Van Doren, *Shakespeare* (Garden City, Doubleday Anchor, 1953), p. 114.

cause he is so different from the rest of us—different because he is so deeply rooted in the human condition that he restores our confidence in its resilience, in its essential stoutness and vitality. This is simply to say that he is the archetypal instance of the comic *hero*.

And now I am able to widen my definition of comedy to the extent of providing for two types of protagonist. That is to say, he may, on the one hand, like Volpone or Tartuffe or Dostoievski's "Underground" man, be the target of a fundamentally unsympathetic laughter because of his deviation from some accepted human norm. Or, on the other hand, like Don Quixote or Falstaff or Joyce Cary's Gulley Jimson, he may be a figure of heroic proportions whom we laugh at and yet admire. And the presence in a given action of the one or the other type determines the character of the resulting katharsis.

The comic katharsis does, I think, essentially involve such a restoration of our confidence in the realm of finitude as enables us to see the daily occasions of our earth-bound career as being not irrelevant inconveniences but as possible roads into what is ultimately significant in life. This restoration of our confidence in the conditioned realities of historical existence may be managed by the comic author in either of two ways, depending on which type of protagonist he has placed at the center of his action. If his central personage is one whose eccentricity arises out of some willfully maintained imbalance of character which is not of the sort that excites pity or fear, our awareness of the validity of the human norm from which he has deviated will be renewed and deepened as we see him rendered incompetent by this eccentricity. The Socrates of Aristophanes' *The Clouds* is an example of this kind of comic figure. But if the protagonist is, like Falstaff, a man whose eccentricity is a consequence not of his deviateness but of the very depth of his rootedness in our common humanity, then the experience of katharsis grows out of the joy we take in the discovery of how stout and gamy the human creature really is. And this is, of course, the discovery that the comic hero enables us to make. He is, Mrs. Langer says, the indomitable living creature fending for itself, tumbling and stumbling . . . from one situation into another, getting into scrape after scrape and getting out again, with or without a thrashing. He is the personified *élan vital*; his chance adventures and misadventures, without much plot, though often with bizarre complications, his absurd expectations and disappointments, in fact his whole improvised existence has the rhythm of primitive . . . life coping with a world that is forever taking new uncalculated turns, frustrating, but exciting. He is . . . now triumphant, now worsted and rueful, but in his ruefulness and dismay he is funny, because his energy is really unimpaired and each failure prepares the situation for a new fantastic move.[22]

This is the comic man *par excellence*, and this is the rhythm of action that, in its greatest moments, his life exemplifies.

Now it seems that the great sympathy which the Christian imagination may feel for the testimony of the comedian is, in large part, a consequence of the extent to which it is governed by the same robust materialism in which comedy is so deeply rooted. This is a characteristic of Christianity that, among its recent interpreters, the late Archbishop Temple often liked to remark: indeed, one of the most striking sentences in his Gifford Lectures asserts that, "One ground for the hope of Christianity that it may make good its claim to be the true faith lies in the fact that it is the most avowedly materialist of all the great religions."[23] I assume that when Temple spoke of the materialistic character of Christianity he meant that the Christian belief in the Creation and the Incarnation makes for a profound respect for nature and time and history which is not easily to be found elsewhere in the history of religion. And this means that the Christian imagination is enabled to rejoice in the quiddities and haecceities of existence in a way that accords very closely with the path taken by the comic vision.

22. Langer, *Feeling and Form*, p. 342.
23. Temple, *Nature, Man and God*, p. 478.

That which first guarantees the Christian's confidence in the realm of the finite is his belief in the doctrine of Creation. This is not, of course, a doctrine that purports to be a scientifically accurate account of a dateable beginning of the cosmic process. It is, rather, a mytho-religious way of asserting that, though man and his world are in all respects enmeshed in relativity and contingency, creation is neither illusory nor evil nor a mere concretion of some universal World Spirit. To say, as the Bible does, that God created the world out of nothing is to assert that He is the sole Ground and Source of everything that exists, and it is to assert the utter dependence of the world upon Him; but it is also, against all the various forms of Idealism and Gnosticism, to emphasize the genuine reality of finite existence: for it was *made* by God. And though this world of ours has been injured by man's sin, it is, despite its distinctness from God, *essentially* good, because it proceeds from Him and exists by His design. Nor can the doctrine of Creation be reconciled to any form of Pantheism, for in effect this doctrine denies both that the world is identical with God and that it is in some way an emanation of the "World Soul": it says that "every creature in [the world] possesses a true self which, however much perfected," "is never swallowed up or lost in God. Therefore, all God's creatures are images of Him in the same way, and to the same limited extent, as a work of art is an image of its maker—his, yet in a manner distinct from him."[24]

The crucial Biblical word here is a very simple word: it falls at the very beginning of the story, in the great first chapter of Genesis—"And God saw everything that he had made, and behold, it was very good." And upon what is implicit in this single sentence rests the whole Biblical interpretation of life and history: a view fundamentally premised upon the assumption that the world of finite and contingent existence is not essentially defective simply by reason of its finiteness. Indeed, when the Christian faith has been true to itself, it has never quite forgotten that its genius in large part consists in its un-

24. Dorothy L. Sayers, *Further Papers on Dante* (New York, Harper, 1957), p. 187.

derstanding that the finitude and particularization of created existence are not in themselves evil, since they are a part of God's plan for the world.

There are, of course, many passages in Biblical literature that dwell upon the discrepancy between the Creator and the created world. "All flesh is grass and all the goodliness thereof is as the flower of the field; The grass withereth, the flower fadeth: . . . but the word of our God shall stand forever." "Thou, Lord, in the beginning hast laid the foundation of the earth; and the heavens are the work of thy hands: They shall perish; but Thou remainest; and they all shall wax old as doth a garment; and as a vesture shalt thou fold them up, and they shall be changed: but Thou art the same, and thy years shall not fail." "Behold, the nations are as a drop of a bucket, and are counted as the small dust of the balance: . . . all nations before him are as nothing; and they are counted to him less than nothing." One could go on to cite many other passages which point to the incommensurability between the created world and its Creator, but what is significant is that this kind of testimony never has it as its purpose to suggest that the transiency and fragmentariness are in themselves evil. On the contrary, as Reinhold Niebuhr remarks in his Gifford Lectures:

> The fragmentary character of human life is not regarded as evil in Biblical faith because it is seen from the perspective of a centre of life and meaning in which each fragment is related to the plan of the whole, to the will of God. The evil arises when the fragment seeks by its own wisdom to comprehend the whole or attempts by its own power to realize it.[25]

There is in the Biblical doctrine of Creation a sober realism and sanity that prompts the Hebraic imagination simply to accept the insufficiency and the incompleteness of human life as a part of God's design. And when the transiency and finiteness of human existence are dwelt upon in Biblical literature, they

25. Reinhold Niebuhr, *The Nature and Destiny of Man*, 1 (New York, Scribner's, 1943), p. 168.

are stressed only in contrast to and as proof of the glory and majesty of God, and there is no suggestion that this discrepancy bears any moral connotation. On the contrary, what is robustly affirmed is that the created world is good, because it is the work of God.

The finiteness of the human condition is, of course, never minimized; our human nature remains creatural, even in the highest reaches of its freedom and self-transcendence, and we never cease to be involved in the relativities of historical existence. But always in Christian history, when the full implications of the doctrine of Creation have been understood, the Biblical insights into the essential goodness of finite existence have been preserved. "And God saw everything that he had made, and behold, it was very good."

Perhaps an even more crucial doctrine for the Christian estimate of the essential character of finitude is the doctrine of the Incarnation, wherein it is declared that the glory of God Himself dwelt in our mortal flesh and became manifest to the eyes of men. Even the distinguished Protestant theologian Karl Barth, who is closely associated with the contemporary reaction against the "Jesus of history" movement of nineteenth-century Liberalism, insists in his *Church Dogmatics* that the central passage of the New Testament is John 1:14, "The word became flesh and dwelt among us." And the Christian community has from time immemorial perceived that what is of the essence in the Gospel is a divine act of Condescension to our low estate—whereby, as the Nicene Creed puts it, "God the Father Almighty, Maker of heaven and earth . . . for us men and for our salvation came down from heaven, And was incarnate by the Holy Ghost of the Virgin Mary, And was made man." This is unquestionably the heart of the Gospel and the central miracle of Christian experience.

Now when, in its worship, the Church recites these words, its intention is to assert that "in the fullness of time" God did really become man without ceasing to be God. It does not merely assert that through the life of Jesus the carpenter of Galilee we may come to discern what God is like: it says, rather, that Jesus Christ *is* God Himself incarnate. We have not in Christ merely a religious genius or hero of some sort; nor are we dealing in the New Testament with a God who, like the gods of pagan Greece, merely disguised Himself as a man. On the contrary, as Langmead Casserley robustly puts it:

> His was a real babyhood and youth, a real growth in mind and stature, a desperately human hunger, an exquisitely human pain, an agonizingly human death. In His thirty years of incarnate existence, God was touched and harrowed by all that is most menacing in the lot of man—physical pain, economic insecurity, subtle temptation, a tragic death foreseen and awaited, the frustration of noble purposes, intellectual misunderstanding, the wearisome, disillusioning absence of sympathy, slander, unpopularity, injustice, persecution, rejected love. All that most easily overcomes the spirit of man He faced without defeat, all that is most prone to embitter and distort the human character He absorbed without bitterness or spiritual loss, smiled kindly through the endless frustrations which so often cynicize and disillusion romantic and idealistic men, loved unwearyingly through the rejection of love with a love which not even hatred could remould in its own image, confronted temptation with an invincible perfection of character and purpose against which the hitherto victorious powers of evil were powerless, and finally placed in the hands of death a life so intense and concentrated on its destiny that death's age-old mastery over life was revealed as a broken thing.[26]

It is the Christian faith that a tremendous phenomenon occurred in this astonishing series of events, that in the unique segment of history that is constituted by our Lord's earthly career we were, in effect, "delivered from the woe of being alive," as Denis de Rougemont says in *Passion and Society*. And I assume this is in part what Paul Tillich meant when he spoke, as he so often did, of Christ as "the center" of history,

26. J. V. Langmead Casserley, *No Faith of My Own* (New York, Longmans, Green, 1952), pp. 35–36.

the center round which the entire human story arranges itself. For, in the event of Jesus Christ, the whole of human existence, contaminated though it had been by the poisons of sin, was made valid and put right again, when God Himself entered the sphere of our life and brought grace and truth into our very midst.

Emil Brunner is, of course, altogether right in contending in his little book, *The Divine-Human Encounter,* that the ultimate significance of the Incarnation is misunderstood if it is supposed that Jesus Christ came merely to come. No, says Dr. Brunner, He "did not come merely to come, but He came to redeem. To be sure, only the Incarnate Lord—very God, very man—can be the Redeemer. But the Bible guides us to ponder less the secret of the Person of Jesus than the mystery of His work."[27] And I do not myself want to suggest here that the full significance of the doctrine of the Incarnation is properly construed in terms merely of the *Person* of Christ or in terms of how it illumines the true relation of the finite and the infinite. But, at the same time, I am eager to avoid the imbalance that so much of Protestant theology often represents today, of interpreting the Incarnation in such a way that, as the Lutheran theologian Joseph Sittler has noticed, it receives "only that light which can be reflected backward upon it from Calvary. While, to be sure, these events cannot be separated without the impoverishment of the majesty of the history of redemption, it is nevertheless proper to suggest," says Dr. Sittler, "that our theological tendency to declare them only in their concerted meaning *at the point of fusion* tends to disqualify us to listen to the ontological-revelational overtones of the Incarnation."[28] And surely it is not to do violence to the true import of Biblical faith to insist that God's having condescended to "tabernacle amongst us," to assume a human body, a human

27. Emil Brunner, *The Divine-Human Encounter* (Philadelphia, Westminster Press, 1943), p. 142.

28. Joseph Sittler, "A Theology for Earth," *The Christian Scholar,* 37 (1954), 374.

mind, a human soul, and to submit Himself to all the conditions of our life in the natural order—surely it is not improper to insist that His having deigned to do this has the effect of giving a new value to all the finite vehicles and instrumentalities which He thus employed. And the consequence is that the Christian's fundamental attitude toward existence must always be profoundly affirmative: the particularity and fragmentariness of existence can never be, for him, the offense that they are to more fastidious men: nor can he ever in any way impugn the validity of the natural and the temporal order, since for approximately thirty years this was the home of God Himself.

This, then, is what I assume Temple had in mind when he spoke of the materialism of Christianity—the attitude of respect, of esteem, of love even, for the actual, specific, concrete things of this world which belong to the order created by God and which formed an adequate theatre for the drama in which His Son took the leading part. The Christian imagination does not shrink from the tangibility and gross concreteness of our life in time, and it is not afraid to face the limited, conditioned nature of human existence. It is, indeed, affirmative—radically affirmative—in its attitude toward nature and time and history. It does not spend its time looking about for an elevator that will whisk it up out of the world into eternity, for it is committed to the world, and it wants the world to confront itself, not to run away from itself. It believes that God's way of dealing with us is by and through the things and creatures of this world, and that He is Himself to be met not *in* Himself but in His works and in His gifts. And it believes that in the Incarnation God Himself affirmed the world, affirmed the realm of finitude, the realms of nature and history. Therefore, the religion which finds its main fulcrum in the Incarnational event is one which does not take us out of this world: it takes us, rather, deeper and deeper into it. This is to say that, unlike the kind of modern imagination represented by Virginia Woolf, the Christian mind has no desire to be an angel, but, rather, to the scandalization of idealists and angelists, it persists in wallowing about in all the temporal, creatural stuff of human life, for it was in this stuff that God Himself became Incarnate.

I earlier contended that the function of comedy is to enliven our sense of human actuality, to put us in touch with the Whole Truth, particularly when, in pursuit of some false and abstract image of ourselves, we have become embarrassed by the limitations of our creatureliness and undertaken to bring our life in history to an end, either by some violently conclusive action or by some disillusioned flight into the realm of pure idea. Forsaking all the meretricious forms of eschatology, comedy moves toward the actual: it asks us to be content with our human limitations and possibilities, and to accept our life in this world without the sentimentality either of smugness or of cynicism. And when we wish to be pure discarnate spirit or pure discarnate intellect, the comedian asks us to remember the objective, material conditions of life with which we must make our peace if we are to retain our sanity and survive. He will not let us forget that we are men, that we are finite and conditioned creatures—not angels. In its deeply affirmative attitude toward the created orders of existence, in the profound materialism of its outlook, the comic imagination, it seems to me, summarizes an important part of the Christian testimony about the meaning of human life.

Indeed, this profoundly affirmative quality in the comic vision makes the appreciation of it involve, in our time, a very strenuous effort of the moral imagination. For the kind of vision which has the most direct appeal for us is one which, in offering some radical and extremist conception of ourselves, promises to increase the psyche's temperature. The great heroes of our cultural life, as Lionel Trilling remarked in *The Opposing Self*, are "the tigers of wrath"—the Kafkas and the Sartres and the Becketts—and they are cherished as examples of a charismatic power, which we covet for ourselves, of being able to endure the stigmata of our Alienation with such fierceness and valor that the inconveniences and disadvantages of history might be left behind, and the spirit liberated from the conditioned character of our mundane existence. We are, in fact, as a people always on the verge of electing to bring our life in history to an end.

> [We] are discontented with the nature rather than with the use of the human faculty; deep in our assumption lies the hope and the belief that humanity will end its career by developing virtues which will be admirable exactly because we cannot now conceive them. The past has been a weary failure, the present cannot matter, for it is but a step forward to the final judgment; we look to the future when the best of the works of man will seem but the futile and slightly disgusting twitchings of primeval creatures.[29]

So the way of comedy which attempts to lead us into that special sort of truth which Aldous Huxley calls the Whole Truth is one of the most difficult ways which the modern imagination can be asked to take. Yet, if this way be taken, it may be a *preparatio* that will permit us once more to be brought to the point of being able, with both laughter and reverence in our hearts, to say with the Psalmist, "The earth is the Lord's and the fulness thereof, the world and those who dwell therein." This, I suspect, is a large part of what Christopher Fry means, when he tells us that "comedy is an escape, not from truth but from despair: a narrow escape into faith." It is, he suggests, the "angle of experience where the dark is distilled into light. . . . It says, in effect, that, groaning as we may be, we move in the figure of a dance, and, so moving, we trace the outline of the mystery."[30]

Fr. William Lynch tells us that "it would be unfair to tragedy to think that it is only to the tragic that comedy is addressing itself as semantic challenger, vocabulary against vocabulary."[31] And Mr. Fry says that he is always on "the verge of saying that

29. Lionel Trilling, *E. M. Forster* (New York, New Directions, 1943), p. 22.

30. Christopher Fry, "Comedy," *Tulane Drama Review*, 4 (March 1960), 77.

31. Lynch, *Christ and Apollo*, p. 95.

comedy is greater than tragedy." But, he says, "On the verge I stand and go no further." Nor have I wanted to put comedy into the kind of competition with tragedy that would necessitate our opting for one against the other: so to pose the issues would, of course, entail an impossibly narrow kind of scholasticism, since, as Mr. Fry has reminded us, "we find ourselves in [comedy or tragedy] by the turn of a thought,"[32] and the man who is unqualified for tragedy is also unqualified for comedy. But I have wanted to suggest that comedy affords the Christian student of modern literature a high and promising ground from within literature itself for a radical critique of the various Gnosticized forms of tragedy that constitute our period style. And, obversely, I have also wanted to suggest something of the kind of constructive theological insight (heretical as this may be within the forums of post-Arnoldian criticism) that the literary imagination itself, in its comic phase, proposes to the Christian intelligence—that, as Fr. Lynch states (and in all this he has been, as his readers will recognize, my fundamental guide):

a thing need not step out of the human to be all things, and to achieve the liberty of the children of God. The mud in man, the lowermost point in the subway, is nothing to be ashamed of. It can produce . . . the face of God. . . . To recall this, to recall this incredible relation between mud and God, is, in its own distant, adumbrating way, the function of comedy.[33]

32. Fry, p. 78.
33. Lynch, p. 109.

118

Chapter Four THE TRAGIC
VISION
AND THE CHRISTIAN FAITH

In the last decade or so there is perhaps no single issue that has more deeply engaged students of Western literary tradition than the problem of tragedy. Year after year the literature in this field continues to grow, and, since the early fifties, there has been an unremitting flow from publishing houses of books bearing such titles as *The Spirit of Tragedy* (by Herbert Muller), *The Tragic Vision* (by Murray Krieger), *Tragedy: A View of Life* (by Henry Alonso Myers), *The Vision of Tragedy* (by Richard Sewall), *The Harvest of Tragedy* (by T. R. Henn), *The Death of Tragedy* (by George Steiner), and *The Tragic Vision and the Christian Faith* (edited by Nathan A. Scott, Jr.). In part this is doubtless a development that results from a reaction among younger literary scholars and critics against what is felt to be the excessive formalism that has characterized the central tradition in literary criticism of our period. For, after a long period of having been taught that a work of literary art is or should be an absolutely self-contained and discrete set of mutually interrelated references, a new generation in criticism begins now to ask whether the mode of existence of imaginative literature is really characterized by such isolation from the other departments of experience. The direction which is now being aimed at was nicely suggested by Leslie Fiedler in one of his spirited essays:

> The "pure" literary critic, who pretends, in the cant phrase, to stay "inside" a work all of whose metaphors and mean-

ings are pressing outward, is only half-aware. And half-aware, he deceives; for he cannot help smuggling unexamined moral and metaphysical judgments into his "close analyses," any more than the "pure" literary historian can help bootlegging unconfessed aesthetic estimates into his chronicles. Literary criticism is always becoming "something else," for the simple reason that literature is always "something else."[1]

"Literary criticism is always becoming 'something else,' for the simple reason that literature is always 'something else.' " Mr. Fiedler is saying that the work of art is involved in the total human experience, the experience from which it issues and the experience upon which it is, in some way or other, a comment. And all the more interesting fresh tacks that criticism has taken in recent years have represented various attempts to pay a partial tribute to this fact and, more and more, to push literary analysis in the direction of a new philosophical (and, perhaps even, theological) criticism. It is being increasingly recognized that, though the literary work is a special sort of linguistic structure, what holds the highest interest for us is that this structure is instrumental toward a special seizure of reality. The very nature of literature, in other words, is felt to require the critic finally to move beyond the level of purely verbal and stylistic analysis to the level of metaphysical and theological valuation. Thus it is that such an issue as the nature of tragedy has come to be a central preoccupation among students of literature in our time.

Yet this preoccupation is not to be accounted for solely in terms of the inner dynamics of recent *literary* history. For ours is a century of bedlam and extreme peril—an age of anxiety. And since it is the peculiar office of the tragedian to be attentive to the inner and outer insecurities of man's lot and to the background of danger against which the human drama must be enacted, it is not surprising that our generation should have

1. Leslie Fiedler, "Toward an Amateur Criticism," *Kenyon Review,* 12 (1950), 564.

turned to him for assistance in discerning the signs of the time. Over the past two decades, the bite of events and the disorders in the days of our years have been the fundamental cause of the great reawakening of interest in the problem of tragedy. Man has become a question to himself and, in this icy aeon of perplexity, he feels the definitive category of his self-interpretation to be that of the tragic.

So the great literature of tragedy, from Sophocles to Shakespeare and from Melville to Faulkner, has today an unrivaled prestige, and a major critical effort on the contemporary intellectual scene involves an attempt to redefine the special insight into human experience that is made available by the tragedian.

This is, of course, a territory whose first occupant was Aristotle, for it is from him that the first great interpretation of tragedy in Western tradition descends. Even now, virtually every theorist in this area initiates his own enterprise, almost in the manner of an automatic reflex, by first tacking on footnotes and marginal glosses of various sorts to the *Poetics*. There are perhaps no pieties that exert a stronger claim to eminence than the pieties of academic scholarship: the dusty classics of the schoolroom are not easily put aside, and they continue to have an intimidating influence long after they have ceased to have anything more than a limited usefulness. In the field of literary theory, there is perhaps no better example of this than Aristotle's *Poetics*. It is unquestionably a treatise of very high importance, and this, to be sure, is the first word that it deserves to have said. In the consistency with which it follows inductive procedures, in the rigorous empiricism with which it analyzes its concrete specimens into their component parts, and, in the lucidity of its conclusions, it is one of the great models in theory of literature. But, in its concentration on such matters as imitation (*mimesis*) and discovery (*anagnorisis*) and reversal (*peripeteia*) and purgation (*katharsis*), the *Poetics* is so heavily committed to formalistic definition as to neglect very nearly altogether the question of what converts these categories into the stuff of tragedy; and it leaves quite untouched all the complex issues that we want to raise concerning the attitudes and perspectives and ideas that make up what Unamuno called "the tragic sense of life."

Although we shall not want to discard this ancient Greek text, it is well to recognize that it may not be the best starting-point for contemporary inquiry. For, what we need first to do is to reach some clarity about the general tenor and atmosphere and the basic issues that constitute the tragic experience; and, on this level, the Stagirite is not very helpful.

When one attempts to define the central story, the essential myth or fable, that underlies those great actions that most fully exemplify the tragic genre—as in *Oedipus, Lear, Moby Dick*—one must say, first of all, that tragedy is a story of collapse and of disintegration. In the tragic universe, life is experienced as having broken down: that congruence between the highest aspirations of the human spirit and its world-environment, apart from which existence seems utterly futile, is no longer discernible, and the protagonist finds himself adrift in a rudderless bark whose passage is through deeps uncharted and unconsoling.

Roger Hazelton has inveighed against what he calls "the toothache view of tragedy," and this is a very proper objection. For, in everyday speech, we are all incorrigibly habituated in designating as tragic those events and experiences that put us in mind of what Vergil called "the tears in things." We go through the evening newspaper and learn of a little girl mercilessly brutalized and murdered by some human beast of prey, or of a brilliant young artist whose life has been suddenly snuffed-out in an airplane crash, or of a dozen other sad and pitiful occurrences that have happened in the course of the day—and we say, "How tragic!" But thus to nominate the thousand natural shocks that flesh is heir to is so to rob the tragic fact of "its own specific gravity and point"[2] as to make all genuine discriminations in this area impossible. What is constantly to be kept in mind is that the primary literature of this subject is marked by certain consistencies which indicate

2. Hazelton, *God's Way with Man*, p. 138.

that a measure of preciseness belongs to the concept of tragedy; and, unless this preciseness is properly honored, we shall end by viewing tragedy as a seamless garment and as something coextensive with existence as such, the term thus ceasing to have any specific reference at all.

Keeping this cautionary word in mind as well as the great texts of tragic literature, when we undertake to define what characterizes the tragic experience, the first thing to be put aside, then, is the toothache view of the matter. For, with the tragic worlds of Sophocles and Shakespeare and Melville in view, it is apparent that not merely the sad and the pitiful shocks and ailments of life establish a particular situation as tragic. On the contrary: the first and the basic fact in the worlds of Job and Oedipus and Hamlet and Ahab is that "the time is out of joint." The tragic protagonist is overborne by a sense of shipwreck,[3] a sense of radical fissure or rift in the realm of ultimate reality.

This breakdown or wreckage of life registers with the tragic man as a discrepancy between the facts of his situation and what would appear to be the requirements of justice and right reason. Indeed, the tragic man is very close to Albert Camus' description of "the metaphysical rebel." The metaphysical rebel, said Camus:

attacks a shattered world in order to demand unity from it. He opposes the principle of justice which he finds in himself to the principle of injustice which he sees being applied in the world. . . . Metaphysical rebellion is a . . . protest against the human condition both for its incompleteness, thanks to death, and its wastefulness, thanks to evil. . . . [The] rebel refuses to recognize the power that compels him to live in this condition. The metaphysical rebel is therefore not definitely an atheist, as one might think him, but he is inevitably a blasphemer. Quite simply, he blasphemes primarily

3. See Karl Jaspers, *Tragedy Is Not Enough*, trans. H. A. T. Reiche, et al. (Boston, Beacon Press, 1952), p. 80.

in the name of order, denouncing God as the father of death and as the supreme outrage.[4]

And though, unlike this modern adventurer of Camus, the tragic man may not give himself to acts of sabotage against the world that threatens him, he is one in whom the slings and arrows of outrageous fortune are not merely suffered but become the occasion of a darkly sceptical brooding on the reliability of that fundamental order which constitutes the theatre of the human enterprise.

Indeed, at the heart of the tragic experience there is a certain sense of nausea and vertigo that is induced by the apparently complete collapse of the world's order. "Tragedy occurs," says Dr. Jaspers, "wherever the powers that collide are true independently of each other. That reality is split, that truth is divided, is a basic insight of tragic knowledge."[5] Therefore, the universe of tragedy is a universe direly strained by oppositions between irreconcilable forces, and forces whose impact is felt not externally but as part of the interiority of the human situation. Aeschylus' Orestes, for example, is enjoined by Apollo to avenge himself against his mother, Clytemnestra, for her murder of his father, Agamemnon. Though this would be for him to honor the bond between himself and his dead father, it would, at the same time, be for him to violate the other loyalty which is equally as sacred—namely, that which is owed by a son to his mother. And out of this irresolvable antimony Aeschylus weaves the various complex and bitter strands of his great play. Sophocles' Antigone is also beset by a similarly baffling quandary. Her brother, Polyneices, in leading a foreign army against their uncle, Creon, who is ruler of the city, has become guilty of treason. Thus, in accordance with the traditions of the time it was not unreasonable that, following Polyneices' death in the ensuing battle, Creon should ordain that his corpse be left to rot unburied outside the city

4. Albert Camus, *The Rebel: An Essay on Man in Revolt*, trans. Anthony Bower (New York, Vintage Books, 1956), pp. 23–24.
5. Jaspers, p. 57.

walls. Yet, for Antigone to obey this edict and to acquiesce in the denial to her dead brother of proper burial rites would be for her to commit an act of sacrilege against the gods of the dead. So she defies her uncle, and, as a consequence, is sentenced to the promised penalty of death. Though Antigone is thus punished for her refusal to accede to the valid claims of the state upon her, Creon does not go unscathed for his abrogation of the sanctity of the family. For his son, Haemon, who was affianced to Antigone, is maddened by grief after her death and dies a suicide—his death being followed by that of his mother whose grief over the loss of her son leads her to commit suicide also. Thus Creon's offense against the pieties of family life leads to the destruction of his own family. And thus, also, the action of the *Antigone* culminates in complete and utter waste. But, as A. C. Bradley remarked, "in this catastrophe neither the right of the family nor that of the state is denied; what is denied is the absoluteness of the claim of each."[6]

The world of tragic experience is a world presided over by clashing antimonies, by tensions and antagonisms that are ontological as well as moral: its people live under the dominance of powers which are veiled and therefore vaguely menacing. It is a world of mystery and insecurity, of anxiety and dread, for the executive powers to which man owes his loyalty are powers that are in opposition to one another. The human protagonist finds himself to be fundamentally uncertain as to the relation in which he stands to that which is transcendently real: the spheres of man's self-experience and of ultimate reality are sundered, and the commerce between them moves obscurely and unpredictably, in a way that eludes any conceptual chart.

These characteristic dissonances of tragic experience, the sensations of nausea and vertigo to which they give rise, and the sense of the time being out of joint are not alone sufficient to establish the full tragic situation. They figure indispensably, of course, in the general atmosphere which the tragedian in-

---

6. A. C. Bradley, "Hegel's Theory of Tragedy," in *Hegel on Tragedy*, ed. Anne and Henry Paolucci (Garden City, Doubleday Anchor, 1962), p. 371.

habits, but what is essential is that these incongruities should so shock a protagonist out of his normal and hitherto un-questioned prepossessions as to drive him toward some radical effort at their alleviation, or at least toward some defiant asser-tion (as Camus put it) of that "principle of justice which he finds in himself." And here we are put in mind of that *hybris* which has traditionally been held to be the dynamic, existential source of the tragic action. This term is customarily trans-lated into English as "pride"—which is doubtless a rendering that does a rough kind of justice to that insolent self-assertive-ness which the Greeks supposed it to be the divine office of Nemesis to punish. But since "pride" carries as perhaps its ma-jor connotation the notion of egotism, this disqualifies it as an adequate substitute for the Greek *hybris*. For it is not egotism which is the mainspring of the tragic action. The tragic hero does, to be sure, stand in a peculiar relation to himself. But what is at issue is not overweening vanity or superciliousness but, rather, the fact, as Kierkegaard would say, of his having "chosen himself": that is, he is a man who has taken upon himself the full burden of his own destiny; and he wants to speak out in his own behalf against whatever it is that threatens to humiliate or to baffle or to unhinge his humanity in some intolerable way. Indeed, we ought perhaps by *hybris*, or by any other term which we adopt in its place, to mean that ex-treme passion with which the tragic man hurls himself against the boundary-lines of his existence in an effort to summon out of the innermost depths of reality some promise of the possi-bility of his being finally accommodated. Though this "heroic" position of the tragic man is wrongly understood if its main-spring is regarded as being simply egotism, it remains to be said that it is by no means a position which is morally neutral. For the "pathetic" element in the tragic situation arises out of the fact that the protagonist's self-affirmation generally in-volves his championing some particular value which, however valid it may be in itself, remains only a partial and limited good. Thus the ardor of his commitment to what is only a limited and determinate good renders him insufficiently responsive to his total situation and has the effect of throwing his life out of gear with certain facets of reality which also have a valid claim upon him. So the choice of self becomes the occasion of guilt and of the protagonist's subjection to that retributive justice which the Greeks called Nemesis.

The whole slant and bias of authentically tragic drama, in other words, is humanistic.[7] In both ancient and modern tragedy, e.g. the *Eumenides* of Aeschylus and T. S. Eliot's *The Family Reunion*, divine personages are sometimes present, but the central emphasis always falls on the human protagonist who is exhibited as one interrogating the executive powers, protesting against the obscurity of their ordinances, and demanding that what is ambiguous in reality consent to clarify itself. "The tragic *agon*, unlike the ritual contest between divine powers, introduces a strictly human plane of reality and involves phases of reflection and decision that spring from man's individual autonomy."[8]

Yet what is bitter and ironic is that precisely in thus choosing himself and assuming the burden of his own destiny the tragic man becomes a guilty man. For his commitment to the truth as he sees it is, inevitably, a commitment to a truth that is something less than the Whole Truth: he is finite, his perspectives are limited, his standpoint can never in the nature of the case afford a sufficiently spacious view of his total situation: *finitum non capax infiniti*—that is to say, in the quest for meaning, man is at a fundamental disadvantage simply by reason of being human. This is the real crux of the tragic fatality. For what is defective and enervating in the tragic hero's situation is not such an egotistical propensity as is suggested when, after identifying the hero's central flaw or *hamartia* as *hybris*, we then proceed to translate *hybris* as pride. No, what is most fundamentally disabling in the situation of the tragic man is not any mere remediable defect of character, but, rather, it is

7. See Herbert J. Muller, *The Spirit of Tragedy* (New York, Knopf, 1956), p. 18.

8. Susan Taubes, "The Nature of Tragedy," *The Review of Metaphysics*, 7 (1953), 198.

his finitude—and this is without remedy. Once he "chooses" himself, he must then, in the course of life's adventures, make all sorts of further ambiguous choices to protect against the taciturn indifference of the world what he recognizes in himself to be distinctively human. These are choices that involve giving his suffrage to certain particular values—whether they be the cause of human enlightenment (as exemplified by Prometheus) or the redress of regicide (Oedipus) or the sanctity of the family (Antigone) or the penetration and mastery of "that intangible malignity which has been from the beginning" (Ahab). But no sooner does the tragic man affirm some particular value than he is caught in the ultimate axiological morass that awaits all men; for, whatever the commitment may be that he has undertaken, it proves to be one that renders him inattentive to other values that have an equally strong claim upon him. And thus it seems that to affirm value must at the same time be to negate value. But since there would be no guilt—and hence no suffering—had not the protagonist committed himself to some partial and limited good, and since this is a commitment he would not have undertaken had he not been attempting through it to affirm his humanity, it must be concluded that the fundamental cause of his guilt is that act of transcendence whereby he "chose" himself.

In other words, the ultimate offense of the tragic man is his very existence as a limited and conditioned creature. His *hybris* is not so much his pride as his presumptuousness in daring to speak out at all in his own behalf. His suffering is the inevitable concomitant of his equally inevitable wrongdoing,[9] which is inevitable because simply for him *to be* is for him to be guilty of trespass against the executive powers. The classic example is still that of Sophocles' Oedipus, who entangles himself ever more deeply in disaster with each step that he takes to resolve the difficulties that he and his fellow Thebans face: the more resolutely he searches out the murderer of Laius the more surely he brings about his own undoing: every effort

9. See R. J. Z. Werblowsky, *Lucifer and Prometheus* (London, Routledge, 1952), p. 60.

he makes to establish both his own identity and the well-being of his city is frustrated, and, at every stage of the action, he is the instrument whereby his own fate is worsened. Not only does he take the leading role in the search for Laius' murderer, but it is also he who pronounces the curse on the murderer, so that, most ironically, he initiates the whole chain of events which culminates in the final revelation that he is the murderer of the King. He pronounces the curse in his own capacity as King: this is a gesture whereby he seeks to express his sense of being responsible for the welfare of his city. And just this assumption of responsibility—the pronouncing of the curse—sets in motion the sequence of events that culminates in his own downfall. For when in assuming responsibility the human protagonist thus gives expression to the creative capacities that make him human, he becomes guilty of that which in the universe of tragedy is the primal offense, of choosing to be a man: his irredeemable crime, in other words, is his very existence, and his great woe is simply that of being alive.

However, our circle has not as yet been fully drawn, for the tragic action has a certain shape that has thus far been only partially indicated. And nowhere is the essential pattern defined with greater economy and precision than in Francis Fergusson's brilliant book *The Idea of a Theater*, in which he makes an adaptation of a schema first proposed by Kenneth Burke in *A Grammar of Motives*. Mr. Burke designated the central moments in "the dialectic of tragedy" as "*poiema, pathema,* [and] *mathema* (the act, the sufferance or state, the thing learned)": these, he said, "are at the very center of [tragedy's] dialectical motivation."[10] Now Mr. Fergusson very suggestively translates these traditional designations as *Purpose, Passion* or *Suffering,* and *Perception;* they are, he says, in their consecutive order, the beginning, the middle, and the end of the tragic action. In the *Oedipus,* for example, the first major moment of the drama is initiated by the protagonist's

10. See Kenneth Burke, *A Grammar of Motives* (New York, Prentice-Hall, 1952), pp. 38–41.

129

reasoned purpose of finding Laius' slayer. But this aim meets unforeseen difficulties, evidences which do not fit, and therefore shake the purpose as it was first understood; and so the characters suffer the piteous and terrible sense of the mystery of the human situation. From this suffering or passion, with its shifting visions, a new perception of the situation emerges.[11]

And, says Mr. Fergusson, in the kind of movement presented by Sophocles' play we have an archetypal instance of the tragic rhythm of action, a rhythm that moves from Purpose to Passion to Perception.

In describing the tragic man as one who wants to speak out in his own behalf, who chooses himself, and who assumes the burden of his own destiny, I have already treated that dimension which Mr. Fergusson designates as Purpose. And the tragic anguish (or Passion) has, of course, also been remarked. In addition, what needs to be emphasized now is that the dialectic of tragedy is a rhythm which drives finally towards Perception: the movement of the action always brings the tragic man through the worst that, under the circumstances, can be imagined; and at the end, on some chill boundary of the world where all certainties have collapsed and all hope disappeared, the hero *perceives* that the universe into which he has been thrown is divided against itself and askew: on some lonely crag or cliff of the mind he *sees* at last that human life is irremediably fated to shipwreck and defeat in a world where implicit in all human accomplishment is an "inescapable nexus of guilt and doom."[12] His last state is one of sober incredulity and utter disenchantment; and, though in this state Karl Jaspers descries a certain "deliverance," it turns out he means little more than that the tragic man stands fast in the end and, in refusing to flinch before what he sees, wins through to such a victory as is represented by the head that is bloody but unbowed. So, in Act V of *Hamlet* (Scene 2), the young prince

11. Fergusson, *The Idea of a Theater*, p. 18.
12. Jaspers, *Tragedy Is Not Enough*, p. 96.

says at last to Horatio, "Thou wouldst not think how ill all's here about my heart . . . the readiness is all." And Brutus speaks for many another when, almost at the end of *Caesar*, he says to Clitus:

> Night hangs upon mine eyes; my bones would rest,
> That have but labour'd to attain this hour.

The tragic story is, then, a story of man besieged by hazard and adversity, and of man standing at last amidst shipwreck and defeat: on some forsaken heath or ash-heap the tragic man comes finally to see himself as outmatched and overborne by the terrible, voiceless Mystery of the world. And, at this outer extremity of his existence, as he remembers the misery and ruin he has suffered and as he contemplates the irremediably tragic structure of reality, he cries out with Prometheus, "Behold me! I am wronged." Sophocles' Oedipus and Shakespeare's Hamlet, Racine's Athalie and Melville's Ahab, Hardy's Jude and Faulkner's Quentin Compson are all figures who suffer a terribly ultimate kind of cheat and who are finally overwhelmed by "powers and passions, elemental forces, and dark abysses of suffering"; by "the central fire, which breaks through the thin crust of civilization," and causes a great holocaustal glow "in the sky above the blackness of ruined homes."[13]

The tragic vision is, in short, an unpalliated vision of shock and crisis, and of man in the extremest possible situation where all guaranties of meaning and security in his pilgrimage on earth have disappeared.

Yet so to state the matter is very sharply to contradict much of the received testimony about the tragic perspective in the literature of modern criticism. For this literature is replete with proclamations of the great triumphs that are won by the tragic man. "Tragedy arises," says Joseph Wood Krutch, "when, as in Periclean Greece or Elizabethan England, a people fully aware of the calamities of life is nevertheless serenely confident

13. Walter Raleigh, *Shakespeare* (New York, Macmillan, 1907), p. 197.

of the greatness of man." And this is the tone and accent that modern theorists of tragedy characteristically like to take. They tell us about how "the sturdy soul of the tragic author," uses suffering "only as a means by which joy may be wrung out of existence."[14] And they enthrall themselves by imaginings of those great peaks of victory to which the tragic man is swept in the course of his brave battling with the dragons he encounters in his earthly journey. The tragic story is, on this accounting, a story of "heroic" adventure, in the sense of the term that is advertised by the Hollywood film studios: it ends in magnificence and exaltation. In some way or other "the human spirit" is validated and vindicated, and the final scene gives us a glimpse of an Eternal City wherein the sovereignty of man is enduring and indestructible. The frustrations, the ordeals, the disappointments that the tragic man encounters are *there*, as it were, only to provide him opportunities for revealing how resplendently valiant and invincible his humanity is. Spirit somehow wrests a victory from Nature, and at that great height where "ecstasy is not to be shunned," the tragic protagonist is to be beheld as "alone, unique and sufficient"— as a "star in the dark."[15]

There is, of course, a measure of truth in this kind of witness about the rhythms and cadences of tragedy, and it is a witness that can claim the immensely prestigious support of both Aristotle and Hegel. What Aristotle meant by the doctrine of *katharsis* poses, to be sure, a question that may be answered in various and contradictory ways; but, even if Aristotle's testimony is not unambiguous, there is Hegel's magisterial example to be cited as that of a great theorist of tragedy who clearly envisaged the tragic experience as moving finally towards "reconciliation." Yet merely to invoke, or to deprecate, time-honored authority is not effectively to adjudicate between the claims of a theory of tragedy whose central

14. Joseph Wood Krutch, *The Modern Temper* (New York, Harcourt, Brace, 1929), pp. 122, 126.
15. William Van O'Connor, *Climates of Tragedy* (Baton Rouge, Louisiana State University Press, 1943), pp. 44–45.

principle is the cathartic principle and a theory of the tragic situation which asserts that, in the end, great enterprise miscarries and all the energy and aspiration of man are threatened by nullification. In the tragic universe, is the end of things the glimpse of some "brave new world," is it some still point where there "is no unrest, no travel, no shipwreck"; or, is it all blackness, all defeat, a place where "all wilts and yields, as if loaded down"? Perhaps it is both—but in what sense, and how? This is the essential nub of an old and still baffling perplexity—which one sometimes feels it has been the precise purpose of modern theory to evade.

Here, however, we may be very greatly helped by the formulations of Murray Krieger, whose contribution to theory of tragedy is the freshest and most cogent in recent literature. What is perhaps most clarifying in Mr. Krieger's way of tackling our problem is his distinction between "tragedy" and "the tragic vision." The tragic vision, in his analysis, is "born *in*side tragedy, as a part of it: as a possession of the tragic hero," but it is distinct and separable from that formal arrangement of the hero's story which is properly named tragedy and whose very formality requires that "the fearsome chaotic necessities of the tragic vision" be soothed and palliated in the interests (if of nothing else) of aesthetic form itself. The vision of life as tragic, says Mr. Krieger, is something which comes about in a moment of "shock," when a man, as it were, all at once discovers himself to be "outside the universal." Like the hero of Kafka's *The Trial*,

> he can one day . . . wake up and find himself irrevocably arrested "without having done anything wrong." Or an Ahab, living until then by the proper laws of seamanship, can one day lose his leg to the leviathan; a Lord Jim, living until then by a schoolboy's code of honor, can one day be paralyzed into inaction and be made to play the coward's role. Melville's Pierre, having dedicated himself at all costs to absolute righteousness, can discover in his righteousness a lust that has led to incest; Conrad's Kurtz, having dedi-

cated himself through altruism to a missionary zeal, can discover in his zeal a worship of self and of gold that has led to blood-sacrifice.

And it is "this shattering seizure," however swiftly and un-expectedly it comes, which jars a man loose from his moorings and precipitates him into the sickness unto death, the despair which is, Krieger says, "the essence of the tragic vision."

What the tragic man beholds on this reading of his situation is "the existential absurdity" of human life and the fragility of its moral ground and meaning. He is a man who has been "seized from without by the hollowness" of a world "whose structure and meaning" had hitherto sustained him. In this terrible extremity, bereft of all consolations, he is under the dominance of that "underground" reality which Nietzsche named the Dionysian principle.

But the Dionysian principle, as we are again reminded by Mr. Krieger, is powerless to yield the coherences that make up aesthetic form. For it is "a product of crisis and of shock, is an expression of man only in an extreme situation, never in a normal or routine one." The peculiar function of the Dionysian principle, then, is to disclose life as "unalleviated, endlessly and unendurably dangerous, [as] finally destructive and [even] self-destructive." Although it belongs to the nature of tragedy to try to absorb and contain this kind of material, tragedy needs, simply by reason of the requirements of aesthetic form itself, to have the dissonances of the tragic vision exploded. Indeed, "even if there were no thematic elements of release for the passions aroused by the tragic performers, the disciplining and restricting demands upon aesthetic contemplation made by the rounded aesthetic whole would effect the catharsis demanded by Aristotle."[16] This is why, even when the final scene on the tragedian's stage is a scene of wreckage, woe, and utter defeat, the disaster and the doom are not alto-gether unbearable. For the very fact that tragedy is an aes-

16. Murray Krieger, "Tragedy and the Tragic Vision," *Kenyon Review*, 20 (1958), 283, 284, 291–92, 293, 294, 298, 289.

thetic form means that what is substantive—the tragic vision —has been *shaped,* has been *contained.* Thus, as Krieger rightly argues, tragedy becomes, through the sheer energy of its *formal* power, "a force for affirmation."

From this standpoint, then, it should be apparent that the old and often renewed debate about the possibility of "Christian tragedy" is a debate that is somewhat supererogatory. For if tragedy, by its very nature, must in some measure conciliate or resolve the dissonances of the tragic vision, it will achieve this transcendence only by invoking some principle of healing and redemption—which need not, of course, be a distinctively Christian principle but which is yet not, in the nature of the case, forbidden to be. And Preston Roberts—in his analysis of the beginning, middle, and end of a Christian play; of the nature of a Christian hero; of what must be involved in a Christian *peripeteia;* and of the effect upon us of a Christianly organized dramatic action—has given a most thorough specification of what the pattern will look like when it is an authentically Christian pattern.[17]

So the question that has been perennially fidgeted over, as to whether there can be such a thing as Christian tragedy, is a question easily answered in the affirmative. But whether there can be any modus vivendi between Christianity and what is *substantive* in tragedy, namely, the tragic vision, is an issue somewhat more complicated and less easily resolved. And the answers generally given in recent criticism are answers which, in flatly asserting an absolute contradiction between the two perspectives, have not tended to do full justice to the intricate subtleties present in the problem.[18]

Karl Jaspers gives us perhaps the most convenient summary of this line of argument. His contention is, quite simply, that

17. See Preston J. Roberts, Jr., "A Christian Theory of Dramatic Tragedy," in *The New Orpheus: Essays Toward a Christian Poetic,* ed. Nathan A. Scott, Jr. (New York, Sheed and Ward, 1964), pp. 255–85.

18. See, e.g., Jaspers, *Tragedy Is Not Enough;* Laurence Michel, "The Possibility of a Christian Tragedy," *Thought,* 31 (1956), 403–28; Sewall, *The Vision of Tragedy,* Ch. 5; and D. D. Raphael, *The Paradox of Tragedy* (London, Allen & Unwin, 1960).

"every one of man's basic experiences ceases to be tragic in a Christian context," that "tragic knowledge must escape the Christian," for the "darkness of [tragic] terror" is, in the soul-scape of Christian life, "pierced by the radiance of blessedness and grace." Under Christ's dispensation, all the fearful discrepancies and discordancies of human existence to which the tragedian gives expression are ultimately quelled; and the Christian's equanimity derives from his assurance that "the boon that is his through faith" guarantees him an exemption from any kind of final disaster: the substance of tragic knowledge must therefore escape him, for, in the event of Jesus Christ, things were once again made right and valid; and, henceforth, the world could be only a proving ground for the pilgrim's preparation for entrance into the Eternal City. According to Dr. Jaspers, the Christian lives within a firmanent of value in which "the world exists as a flow of events guided by Providence. Here all is but way and transition," and whatever threatens or imperils the human enterprise is believed, ultimately, to be set at naught by the sovereign purposes of God: no ache, no wound, no woe, can be beyond God's power to heal and save. Hence, for the Christian man there can be no "shipwreck" in the last act of man's earthly drama. For, in the deed of God in Christ, the sting of all misfortune, both actual and imaginable, is alleviated and subdued. So, in the perspective of Christian faith, what is tragic in existence has been overcome, has indeed been effectively annulled. And thus, says Dr. Jaspers, it should be no surprise that in writers like Dante and Calderón the tragic predicament undergoes so profound a transformation. For inevitably the Christian poet must include the tragic predicament "within the plan of Providence and the operation of Grace, a plan and an operation that deliver man from all the vast nothingness and self-destruction in this world."[19]

Now what ought perhaps to strike us as most remarkable in formulations of this problem that are of the sort exemplified

19. Jaspers, pp. 38–40, 82–83.

and the Christian Faith

by Karl Jaspers' is the complete extrusion from the world of Christian thought and experience of the vibrant eschatological tension that is so much a part of the Gospel. But surely any account either of the faith of the primitive Church (as we have it in the New Testament) or of the historic theological tradition must reckon with the dual vision that has been persistently characteristic of the Christian imagination. That is, the Church, on the one hand, has always wanted to declare (as Paul says) that "we have peace with God through our Lord Jesus Christ," that "through Him we have obtained access to this grace in which we stand" (Romans 5:1–2). The Church has, in short, wanted to speak of Christ's Lordship as a fact established and altogether immitigable, and its great dream has been that "every tongue [might] confess that Jesus Christ is Lord, to the glory of God the Father" (Philippians 2:11). But, then, on the other hand, always the Church's faith has also been an affair of anticipation, for it has been not only a response to a deed already done but also the hope of a great final victory which, when it is realized through God's mighty act, will definitively subdue everything in the world which resists His sovereignty.

This is the tension to which the Christian faith, in its great classical and historic forms, has always been committed. On the one hand, instructed by the New Testament proclamation, Christianity asserts that, the Word having become flesh and dwelt among us, the New Age has already arrived. The great dream of Hebraic prophecy of a time which would bring time to a halt, when all the moral ambiguities of history would be resolved, and God's purposes for the human community would be fully revealed has, Christianity declares, in fact been fulfilled in the event of Jesus Christ. For, in Him and through His miraculous ministry, man has at last been rescued from the dominion of the powers of darkness: that darkness has been pierced by new Light which makes it henceforward incapable of affording man any shelter against the Divine Imperative. In Christ the *Eschaton*, the End, has arrived, for in Him we have the first fruits of the Kingdom of God. And, therefore, the whole family of mankind now stands in a radically new relation both to time and to eternity: indeed, as Paul says, "if any one is in Christ, he is a new creation; the old has passed away, behold the new has come" (II Corinthians 5:17).

Yet the Christian imagination has always had to reckon with the unignorable fact that, though Eternity has given itself to Time in the advent of the Incarnate Word, human life continues to be stained by the improbities and corruptions of man's sin. Those who give themselves to Christ in faith are raised with Him to newness of life and are enabled to behold in Him the End; nevertheless, the End is "not yet," and the life that is lived "in Christ" is but a pledge and foretaste of the "last things" which shall be the absolutely decisive *finis*, when what are now the first fruits shall be the complete and final consummation.

The scene of man's historical existence has, in other words, always been understood in Christianity to be an interim period between that *disclosure* of history's meaning which occurred in the drama of the Incarnation and that final *fulfillment* of its meaning which is the Christian's ultimate hope and expectation and which, in the Biblical mythos, is expressed in the symbol of Christ's "second coming." And, when Dr. Jaspers posits a simple and absolute incommensurateness between "tragic knowledge" and Christian faith, what he does in effect is completely to elide from the soulscape of the Christian man the eschatological tension in which his life in fact has always been lived. For the Christian man belongs to the interim that history has become since the Incarnation: he belongs to "the age between the Ages": and, though Dr. Jaspers may forget it, the Christian man has always known, indeed could never help but know that

in the meantime, in the time between the resurrection and the end, whatever that may be, the world still hurts us, it still bears its demons that need to be exorcised, it still contains mammon, anxiety, and self-righteousness that need to be fought. . . . We are now the Lord's, to be sure, and this is our confidence, our peace, and our warrant for living gladly in this world; but we shall be the Lord's too, and this explains our loneliness, our suffering, our experience of the world as threat and as enemy.[20]

The kind of exemption from the qualms of tragic experience (on the basis of a stiffly undialectical over-interpretation of the doctrine of Providence) that Karl Jaspers claims for the Christian life is, in other words, simply untrue to its actuality. What is wrong in his analysis is a consequence of a drastic oversimplification of the full complexity of Christian existence.

There is, however, another angle from which it is possible to oversimplify or to attenuate what is many-sided and complicated in Christian experience, and it is one which in the English-speaking world arises in the so-called "realized eschatology" which the distinguished British scholar C. H. Dodd has developed from his exegetical studies in the New Testament.[21] This is a position which involves a very great emphasis on that aspect of the New Testament proclamation which speaks of the "End" as having already entered the historical process in Jesus Christ; and, though Dr. Dodd develops it with a most admirable tact, its extremer versions by some of his associates and disciples have sometimes had the effect of very considerably blunting what is genuinely radical in Christian eschatology. But, even if the extremest renderings of realized eschatology were wholly adequate and we did not have to reckon with the *tension* that has here been imputed to the Christian experience of life, it would still be impossible to maintain, as Dr. Jaspers does, that "tragic knowledge" is something utterly alien to the universe of Christian thought. For, if the Christian man knows nothing of the Christ who is to come and knows only the Christ who did come, what he surely cannot escape is the fact that this man of Galilee whom he calls Lord is one in whom lordship assumes the form not of

20. William Hamilton, *The New Essence of Christianity* (New York, Association Press, 1961), p. 113.
21. See C. H. Dodd, *The Apostolic Preaching* (Chicago, Willet, Clark, 1937); and *History and the Gospel* (New York, Scribner's, 1938).

pomp and power but of lowliness and suffering and humiliation. It is the irrefragable testimony of the New Testament record that

> though he was in the form of God, [he] did not count equality with God a thing to be grasped, but emptied himself, taking the form of a servant, being born in the likeness of men. And being found in human form he humbled himself and became obedient unto death, even death on a cross. Therefore God has highly exalted him and bestowed on him the name which is above every name, that at the name of Jesus every knee should bow, in heaven and on earth and under the earth, and every tongue confess that Jesus Christ is Lord, to the glory of God the Father. (Philippians 2:6–11)

And, when Paul speaks in this way, he is wanting to declare that God's way of being present to man is one which involves His "taking the form of a servant" and that the very extremity of the humiliation which Christ consented to endure proves His lordship, proves that at His name "every knee should bow." In Him, in other words, the Christian man beholds "very God of very God"—in *this* human life which is totally pledged in responsibility *for others,* and which is crucified.

But, then, to affirm that the Crucified One is Lord—that in the shape and pattern of His life the meaning of all life is revealed—is also to make a further affirmation that is even bolder and more radical. For, if the Christian's way of talking about God, about what is Radically Ultimate, involves his pointing first of all to the Cross, this is for him to declare that there is suffering in the life of God Himself and that He is moved and harrowed by everything that menaces or threatens the destiny which He has ordained for His creatures. "To say that Jesus is Lord is to say that humiliation, patience, and suffering are the ways God has dealt with man in the world, and thus are also the ways the Christian man is to deal with the world."[22] As Dietrich Bonhoeffer put it:

22. Hamilton, pp. 106–07.

140

Man is challenged to participate in the sufferings of God at the hands of a godless world.

He must therefore plunge himself into the life of a godless world, without attempting to gloss over its ungodliness with a veneer of religion or trying to transfigure it. He must live a "worldly" life and so participate in the suffering of God. . . . To be a Christian does not mean to be religious in a particular way, to cultivate some particular form of asceticism (as a sinner, a penitent or a saint), but to be a man. It is not some religious act which makes a Christian what he is, but participation in the suffering of God in the life of the world.[23]

There is, then, a central and very important sense in which a Christian perspective on human life may lead a man to say, as Ignazio Silone says, that "in the sacred history of man on earth, it is still, alas, Good Friday."[24] And, therefore, between this perspective and what Dr. Jaspers calls tragic knowledge there can be no simple and absolute antithesis.

But, though there is no simple and absolute antithesis between the tragic vision and the Christian faith, the relation is, nevertheless, always one of strain. Indeed, *finally,* it is one in which what is tragically broken in life is taken up and absorbed into the great Eucharistic action of offering, consecration, and communion, whereby the self-oblation of the Church becomes one with Christ's own oblation of Himself for our redemption. Here it is, in the celebration of the rich mystery of the Divine Liturgy, that time is

redeemed [and] brought back into the possession of its rightful owner. Time has become so limp, so lifeless; the *kairos,* the opportunity . . . so fragile and volatile . . . so easily swung this way and that. . . . Only God can recapture

23. Dietrich Bonhoeffer, *Letters and Papers from Prison* trans. Reginald Fuller and ed. Eberhard Bethge (London, Collins, "Fontana Books," 1959), pp. 122–3.
24. Ignazio Silone, *And He Hid Himself* (New York, Harper, 1946), p. vi.

it and nurse it back to life, so to speak—back to its own life, which is really His.[25]

And this, in what has always been the Christian testimony, is what He does in the Eucharist—which is the supremely efficacious form of the Divine action in the period of the interim.

The Eucharist is, to be sure, a fact about the Christian man, for he and his fellows in the Church are "the eucharistic people, the people who take their lives, and break them, and give them, in daily fulfillment of what our Lord did and does." Yet the ultimate truth is that the Eucharistic mystery springs out of the very life of God Himself, for the Eternal Son of God is not only the One who is offered but the One who offers. The sacrifice of the eucharistic people is in Him, and His sacrifice is in them; and thus *Eucharist* is not only the central fact about the Christian man, but, far more profoundly, it is, as Bishop Bayne says, "an eternal fact about God," and it "can only be understood in terms of an eternal offering, which indeed may be represented or re-enacted on every altar, every day, but which is, first of all, outside Time altogether."[26]

It is true, of course, to say (as Reinhold Niebuhr did in his brilliant and moving book *Beyond Tragedy*) that Christianity finds the resolution of tragedy in the Cross, that "here suffering is carried into the very life of God and overcome."[27] Yet, if nothing more than this is said, then the event of Calvary must itself be an essentially bootless thing which occurred in the first century A.D. and which may now produce mental and emotional reactions of various kinds but which does not, in any ontological way, enter into the living present. Of course in point of fact, Calvary, for the Christian man, is not simply past history, and is not so precisely because of the strange and

25. Martin Jarrett-Kerr, C. R., *The Atonement in Our Time* (New York, Morehouse-Gorham, 1953), pp. 155–56.

26. Stephen F. Bayne, "The Eucharist and the Church," in *The Eucharist and Liturgical Renewal*, ed. Massey H. Shepherd, Jr. (New York, Oxford University Press, 1960), pp. 17, 9.

27. Reinhold Niebuhr, *Beyond Tragedy* (New York, Scribner's, 1937), pp. 155–56.

wonderful relation to it which the Eucharist makes possible for him. For, though the sacrifice of Calvary was made two thousand years ago, it is yet also made

> by Christ, in us, every time we offer ourselves to Him. . . . And the Eucharist is Calvary. It is the taking and the breaking and the giving of His life, world without end, by us, in us, with Him, in Him, until the dying of the Lord Jesus in the lives of all His flock is accomplished, and His life reigns unchallenged and serene.[28]

Thus the Eucharist is not only Calvary but also the bridge between Calvary and the *Parousia* (the Second Coming), and in its strength the Christian man is empowered to live in the interim: here it is that, for him, the agitations of the tragic vision are overcome and laid to rest. It is not that in the Eucharist—which is, it need hardly be said, not merely a form of Church worship but the very shape and pattern of Christian existence—that man in this great drama of the Christian life is simply wafted above the rough weathers of history, as Karl Jaspers thinks. Indeed, it is just here that we are made most keenly aware that "our lives are lived on the boundary, the frontier between the Kingdom and this present world of sin, suffering, and death."[29] The antithesis between the tragic vision and the Eucharistic life is not, in short, a simple antithesis. But what is finally availing is the fact that, in this rich and fecund Mystery, "at every point we are met by [the risen] Christ whose grace is offered not as a means of escape from the world but as power to transform us and all [of] life."[30] Thus, in the full spectrum of Christian experience, Silone's words, "In the sacred history of man on earth, it is still, alas, Good Friday," finally have to give way before the majestic message of Easter morning:

28. Bayne, pp. 16–17.
29. Arthur C. Lichtenberger, "The Social Implications of the Liturgical Renewal," in *The Liturgical Renewal of the Church*, ed. Massey H. Shepherd, Jr. (New York, Oxford University Press, 1960), p. 110.
30. Ibid.

If God be for us, who can be against us? He that spared not his own Son, but delivered him up for us all, how shall he not with him also freely give us all things? . . . Who shall separate us from the love of Christ? shall tribulation, or distress, or persecution, or famine, or nakedness, or peril, or sword? . . . Nay, in all these things we are more than conquerors through him that loved us. For . . . neither death, nor life, nor angels, nor principalities, nor powers, nor things present, nor things to come, nor height, nor depth, nor any other creature, shall be able to separate us from the love of God, which is in Christ Jesus our Lord. (Romans 8:31–39)

Now, to be sure, this ultimately *eucharisto-centric*[31] character of the Christian faith may rarely, if ever, provide the Christian tragedian with the immediate materials of his art. But it does, nevertheless, stand as what most basically antecedes the distinctive mutations which he introduces into tragic literature. For, having heard

> Authentic tidings of invisible things,
> Of ebb and flow and ever-during power,
> And central peace subsisting at the heart
> Of endless agitation,

the poets of *Lear* and *Polyeucte*, of *Billy Budd* and *The Idiot*, of *Murder in the Cathedral* and *Requiem for a Nun* do verily (if sometimes obscurely) descry the horizons of a brave new world. And it is a world the bridge to which, far from bypassing what is tragic in human life, does indeed lead directly into the fields of anguish—but by way of a dialectical route through death-and-renewal that recapitulates the great central Mystery of Christian existence.

31. I am indebted to Martin Jarrett-Kerr for this phrase. See *Atonement*, p. 151.

Chapter Five THE CRISIS OF FAITH
IN THE NEW THEOLOGY
AND THE PROMISE OF GRACE
IN POETIC ART

—*for Erich Heller*

Among Nietzsche's epigones today there are perhaps none who have learned to pronounce his verdict of 1882 concerning the death of God more casually than certain younger Christian theologians. Indeed, the central message of *Zarathustra* and of the *Gay Science (Fröhliche Wissenschaft)* is sometimes, one feels, so much by way of being reduced to the status of cliché by the hucksters of what is modish and agitating that a special effort of imagination is required in order to recover some sense of the great terribleness of Nietzsche's verdict. And the judgment that he threw down like a gauntlet upon the European scene of the late nineteenth century was in truth an awesomely terrible and audacious one. For, said he in effect, that which has supported human life for centuries is no longer vital and efficacious, and ours is therefore a contention with a world in which there is nothing spiritually transcendent over man himself. The passage which, above all others in Nietzsche's canon, gives the most pungent publicity to this new crisis of human existence is the passage in his *Gay Science* that is entitled "The Madman":

> Have you not heard of that madman who lit a lantern in the bright morning hours, ran to the market place, and cried incessantly, 'I seek God! I seek God!' As many of those who do not believe in God were standing around just then, he provoked much laughter. Why, did he get lost? said one. Did he lose his way like a child? said another. Or is he hid-

145

ing? Is he afraid of us? Has he gone on a voyage? or emigrated? Thus they yelled and laughed. The madman jumped into their midst and pierced them with his glances. 'Whither is God,' he cried. 'I shall tell you. We *have killed him*—you and I. All of us are his murderers. But how have we done this? How were we able to drink up the sea? Who gave us the sponge to wipe away the entire horizon? What did we do when we unchained this earth from its sun? Whither is it moving now? Whither are we moving now? Away from all suns? Are we not plunging continually? Backward, sideward, forward, in all directions? Is there any up or down left? Are we not straying as through an infinite nothing? Do we not feel the breath of empty space? Has it not become colder? Is not night and more night coming on all the while? . . . God is dead. . . . And we have killed him. . . . What was holiest and most powerful of all that the world has yet owned has bled to death under our knives. . . .' Here the madman fell silent and looked again at his listeners; and they too were silent and stared at him in astonishment. At last he threw his lantern on the ground, and it broke and went out. 'I come too early,' he said then; 'my time has not come yet. This tremendous event is still on its way . . . it has not yet reached the ears of man. Lightning and thunder require time, the light of the stars requires time, deeds require time even after they are done, before they can be seen and heard. This deed is still more distant from them than the most distant stars—*and yet they have done it themselves.*' —It has been related further that on that same day the madman entered divers churches and there sang his *requiem aeternam deo.*[1]

"Quietly," says Karl Jaspers, "something enormous has happened in the reality of Western man."[2] And, in modern intel-

1. Friedrich Nietzsche, *The Gay Science*, Section 125, in *Existentialism from Dostoevsky to Sartre*, ed. Walter Kaufmann (New York, Meridian Books, 1956), pp. 105–06.
2. Karl Jaspers, *Reason and Existenz*, trans. William Earle (New York, Noonday Press, 1955), p. 23.

lectual history, it is the distinctive vocation of Friedrich Nietzsche to have been the first to perceive with absolute clarity the true import of this great happening, that the human universe in the modern age has become a kind of unlit and wintry vacuum from which the last vestige of any transcendent radiance has disappeared. "With him," as Camus said in *The Rebel*, "nihilism becomes conscious for the first time," and henceforward there was no possibility for the modern consciousness of escaping knowledge of what this Promethean-like Jacob[3] had discovered in his wrestling with the angel of the Lord, that a terrible collapse had occurred in the Courts of Heaven and that God Himself had disappeared.

It would doubtless be to mistake Nietzsche's intention, were his declaration that God is dead to be taken as a metaphysical doctrine. For, in this connection, it is significant surely that he never contended that there was no God, but said rather only that a deicide had been committed on this earth. It seems likely, in other words, that he was not intending to put forward a proposition about some supersensible event that had taken place in the realm of noumenal reality: he wanted rather to give us, in melodramatic fashion, a judgment about the direction and tonality of our culture. In short, when he asserted that God is dead, he was speaking not in the role of metaphysician but in his capacity as observer and diagnostician of modern civilization, and what he really wanted to announce was a "great refusal" which modern man himself had made.

But however Nietzsche's message is finally to be assessed, in its various minutiae, we do unquestionably face today an immense body of testimony, in philosophy and theology and imaginative literature of the last fifty years, whose purpose it is to suggest that behind the deep sense of loss in the twentieth century—of cultural order, even of what our psychologists call identity—is a sense of the loss of God. The long and complicated process that prepared for this development was

3. Erich Heller has noticed the mergence in Nietzsche of the figures of Jacob and Prometheus: see "The Importance of Nietzsche," *Encounter*, 22 (April 1964), 59–66.

summed up, with his characteristic concision, by the late
Dietrich Bonhoeffer in one of his letters from Tegel Prison (8th
June 1944) to a friend:

> The movement beginning about the thirteenth century (I
> am not going to get involved in any arguments about the
> exact date) towards the autonomy of man (under which
> head I place the discovery of the laws by which the world
> lives and manages in science, social and political affairs, art,
> ethics and religion) has in our time reached a certain com-
> pletion. Man has learned to cope with all questions of impor-
> tance without recourse to God as a working hypothesis. In
> questions concerning science, art, and even ethics, this has
> become an understood thing which one scarcely dares to tilt
> at any more . . . it is becoming evident that everything gets
> along without "God," and just as well as before. As in the
> scientific field, so in human affairs generally, what we call
> "God" is being more and more edged out of life, losing more
> and more ground.[4]

The great change that has taken place here does, at bottom,
doubtless involve a revolution in what the followers of Rudolf
Bultmann call our "self-understanding." For man most assuredly no longer normally thinks of himself as a point of in-
tersection between two spheres, the natural and the supernatural, and thus he no longer regards human personality as
open to penetration and influence by powers proceeding from
some "other" world. Indeed, the whole structure of "the mythical view of the world"[5] and of theistic supra-naturalism no
longer offers a viable schema for constructive thought, whether
at the level of anthropology or of cosmology. Except by way of
a *sacrificium intellectus*, reality can simply not be thought of
any longer as an affair of two realms, at least not by the men

4. Bonhoeffer, pp. 106–07.
5. See Rudolf Bultmann, "New Testament and Mythology," in *Ke-
rygma and Myth*, ed. Hans Werner Bartsch and trans. Reginald Fuller
(New York, Harper Torchbooks, 1961).

148

and women who breathe the cultural atmosphere of the Western world. For theirs is not a mythological mode of thought, and thus the extremity in which they find themselves is one in which it appears that no credence can now be given to what Bonhoeffer called "the religious premise." As he said in the Spring of 1944, "We are proceeding towards a time of no religion at all: men as they are now simply cannot be religious any more."[6] For "the linchpin" of the whole structure has been removed—namely, the notion of the *Deus ex machina*, of a supreme being to whose "existence" that of all other beings is subordinate, the notion of a *terra incognita* "above" or "beyond" the place that is occupied by man: this whole structure is now a shambles, an irreparable debris, and there seems to be no possibility of dressing it out anew in any sort of garment that will make it genuinely comprehensible to the modern mind.

Yet what is shaky and problematic in the present state of traditional theistic belief hardly constitutes the full extent of modern secularity. Howard Moody, the minister of the Judson Memorial Church in New York City, has recently spoken of the representative man of our period as "the fourth man," following three older types of man "already produced in Western culture, namely, Christian man, the Renaissance individualist, and the bourgeois moralist."[7] And Mr. Moody's formula, in the account that it gives of the isolation and the *anomie* that define human existence in the world of the fourth man, suggests something of the degree to which the profanization of life in our period surpasses and extends far beyond the mere collapse of formal theistic religion. For the desacralized character of life in the modern West is not simply an affair of pervasive agnosticism with respect to the creedal formularies of the received tradition: nor does it even proceed merely from the eclipse in our culture of the last vestige of any "pre-Kantian

6. Bonhoeffer, p. 91.
7. See Howard Moody, *The Fourth Man* (New York, Macmillan, 1964).

metaphysical faith," though a deep "distrust of *all* . . . categorical certainties"[8] is most assuredly an element of modern secularity. At the profoundest level, what is *désacralisé* in the predominant sensibility of our period stems from a cast of mind distinguished by an inability to descry in the world any reality that evokes a sense of ultimacy or of radical significance. This is a kind of total secularization of consciousness that is, to be sure, most sharply focalized in the collapse of theistic faith; but, in its deepest aspect, it entails not so much the loss of God as the loss of connection with anything resembling what Rudolf Otto in *The Idea of the Holy* called "the numinous": what is basically lost is the Sacred, and the great impoverishment of the human spirit consists in the death of all awareness of any animating power or *presence* amid and within the familiar realities of nature and history.

The chief result of this new mentality is a general banalization of the world and of experience—and this is something that can be felt with an especial vividness if we set against such an acount of "the fourth man" as Camus gave us in *The Stranger* an obscure Chinese treatise of the seventeenth century on the art of painting, the document that is called *The Mustard Seed Garden Manual.*[9] In this ancient handbook, the artist is advised so to compose his picture that, if, say, he is painting a man looking at a mountain, the man will appear to be bent in an attitude of homage and the mountain will itself appear to be slightly bent, in an attitude of acknowledgment. Or, if a lutist is playing his instrument under the moon, the painter is advised to make it appear that the lutist is listening to the moon and that the moon is listening to him. And, of course, the spiritual presupposition of this charming aesthetic is that man stands in a relation of reciprocity with the world, because the

8. Erich Heller, "Ludwig Wittgenstein," *Encounter*, 13 (September 1959), 43, 45.

9. Mai-Mai Sze, *The Tao of Painting*, 2 (New York, Pantheon Books, Bollingen Series, 49, 1956). I am indebted for my awareness of this treatise to Philip Wheelwright's fine book, *Metaphor and Reality* (Bloomington, Indiana University Press, 1962).

whole of reality is instinct with spirit and with presence, with the numinous and the Sacred.

But think now of how different is the world inhabited by that forlorn, dispirited little cipher who is the protagonist of Camus' novel of the early forties, *The Stranger*. In the very narrative procedures that were here guiding Camus' art we can sense the essential thrust of the testimony being made, for the basic *form* of the novel confirms the sense of absurdity it wants to convey. The narrative perspective is that of the central personage, Meursault: yet he appears quite incapable of the kind of ordering or evaluation of experience that the history of fiction, from Sterne's Tristram Shandy to Mann's Serenus Zeitblom, has taught us to expect from the first-person narrator; indeed, the novel begins on a note of utter confusion:

> Mother died today. Or, maybe, yesterday; I can't be sure. The telegram from the Home says: YOUR MOTHER PASSED AWAY. FUNERAL TOMORROW. DEEP SYMPATHY. Which leaves the matter doubtful; it could have been yesterday.

And the protagonist's indifference about the exact time of his mother's death is of a piece with the apathy of spirit and confusion of mind that generally define his presence in the novel. His perceptions are disjointed because he inhabits a world that is out of joint and in which a man cannot easily take possession of his life. Even the staccato rhythm of his speech—Mother died today. Or, maybe, yesterday; I can't be sure.—does itself suggest that the basic relationships of his experience are disconnected and askew. This is a man whose life is wholly enclosed within the tenuity of the present instant, and so, as Jean-Paul Sartre observed in his fine essay on *The Stranger*, Meursault's sentences are "islands": they are not "arranged in relation to each other; they are simply juxtaposed"—and they are all "equal to each other, just as all the absurd man's experiences are equal. Each one sets up for itself and sweeps the other into the void."[10] Nor does this little Algerian clerk have at his

10. Jean-Paul Sartre, "Camus' *The Outsider*," *Literary and Philosophical Essays*, trans. Annette Michelson (London, Rider, 1955), pp. 38–40.

command a vocabulary that is sufficiently rich and varied to permit its becoming a vehicle of any kind of analysis of his experience: as John Cruickshank has noticed in his book on Camus, the prose of *The Stranger* is a "verb-centered prose" which says in effect that the incoherences of human life make any sort of intellectual synthesis impossible. And the "slow, persistent breeze" that blows in upon Camus' protagonist from "the dark horizon of [his] future" has a great leveling effect on his life, giving an equal significance to all actions and all experiences. When a neighbor offers him friendship, when a girl offers him her love, when his employer offers him the chance for advancement, when a priest offers him the comforts and consolations of religious faith, his unvarying response is either indifferent acceptance or indifferent refusal, for nothing makes much difference, given "the cruel mathematics that command our condition." Things have fallen apart, the center no longer holds—as Yeats says, "mere anarchy is loosed upon the world." So this man is a "stranger," an "outsider": he faces the world with a stubborn taciturnity because—unlike the universe portrayed in that old Chinese treatise, *The Mustard Seed Garden Manual*—the world itself is silent: it is a gritty and mute, abandoned place. Here there is no "dialogue," no reciprocity between the human spirit and its world-environment, but only

> A heap of broken images, where the sun beats,
> And the dead tree gives no shelter, the cricket no relief,
> And the dry stone no sound of water
> Here is no water but only rock
> Rock and no water and the sandy road.
>
> (*The Waste Land*)

And here indeed, in the memorable anti-hero of *The Stranger*, we have one of the finest exemplars in modern literature of man living in an absolutely desacralized world and constituted of nothing but the brute "historicity" of his dereliction. Nor is this a creature bearing the glamor of that lonely grandeur which Nietzsche expected to distinguish the post-Christian man, the man whom he called the "Superman." Indeed, there is nothing at all *super*-human about Camus' protagonist: he is instead a man who strikes us as being defined primarily by emptiness and denudation: he is a hollow man, "headpiece filled with straw." He has no loyalties, no affiliations: nothing claims his reverence or elicits in him any piety. And his is a world without thresholds: he does not live on "the borderland of a something more"; time has no threshold, for the immediately experienced moment is all that Meursault has; it stands "in the same relation to future and past as Indiana to Ohio and Illinois"[11] and is in no way interpenetrated by these dimensions, so that he does not live on the threshold of an anticipated future to which his past is organically bound. Nor is he given a threshold by his relations with other persons, for he and they do not in any deep way interpenetrate one another. In a universe where "no man is an island," the *I* stands always on the verge of the *Thou*—but this is a threshold which Meursault knows nothing of, locked as he is in his icy solitariness. And, of course, the threshold of the Holy, the sense of living on the borderland between Nature and Supernature, between Time and Eternity, is a threshold that is irretrievably and utterly gone.

In short, the universe inhabited by this man is a world that is absolutely profane. And it is, therefore, a world that is absolutely silent. It may even be too much to speak of it as the world of "nihilism," for the *Logos* of nihilism is at least, for the nihilist, identifiable with the principle of Nothingness. But, for Meursault, the world is answerable to no principle of meaning at all: it is not even astir with nothingness. The English philosopher Ernest Gellner, in a brilliantly crotchety critique of Linguistic Analysis, says that, though this is a philosophic movement which "often considers the pursuit of world-views

11. Philip Wheelwright, *The Burning Fountain: A Study in the Language of Symbolism* (Bloomington, Indiana University Press, 1954), pp. 8, 10.

to be *the* cardinal sin of thought,"[12] it yet does have a view of the world—a view of the world which is statable in such a proposition as, "The world is what it is," or "Things are as they are," or, as it was put in the proposition by Bishop Butler—which G. E. Moore took over as a kind of motto of his own philosophy—"Everything is what it is and not another thing." And it is precisely such a banalization of reality as this that is the end-result of radical profanization: the world is experienced as silent and is conceived to be merely what it is, and not another thing.

The consequence of desacralization is, then, a general dulling, a general "platitudinizing," of everything: this is what it means to lose *all* the numinous thresholds of experience. And the further consequence that inevitably follows in the wake of banalization is a general leveling—a Cézanne apple, for instance (to what would have been the astonishment of whoever wrote the *Mustard Seed Garden Manual*), having the same monumentality as the peaks of his Mont St. Victoire; or a Beckett play having neither the beginning, middle, nor end of classical dramaturgy. The distinction between the sublime and the banal has, in other words, ceased to be a part of the furniture of the imagination: indeed, the hero of Hemingway's *A Farewell to Arms* speaks of his embarrassment by the very words sacred, glorious. And the result, if we are to give heed to the testimony of the modern artist, is a creature "full of holes and gaps, faceless, riddled with doubts and negations, starkly finite,"[13] filled with the kind of porousness that characterizes so many of the images of contemporary sculpture. The result is a creature ousted from the precincts of Grace, one something like those doomed ghosts in the pictures of the contemporary English painter Francis Bacon, who look out at the world heart-stricken and aghast. In short, the "death" of God appears to bring a kind of death to the human spirit itself: this is the

---

12. Ernest Gellner, *Words and Things: A Critical Account of Linguistic Philosophy* (London, Victor Gollancz, 1959), p. 99.

13. William Barrett, *Irrational Man: A Study in Existential Philosophy* (Garden City, Doubleday Anchor, 1958), p. 57.

very hard sort of dialectic that we are confronted by in *the profane,* as a mode of being-in-the-world.[14]

Now it is one of the interesting developments in contemporary intellectual life that the radical profanization of human existence in the modern period should begin to be deeply affirmed by Christian theology. And it must seem particularly outrageous to many secular intellectuals who are rarely prepared to accord the theologian a modicum of patronizing cordiality unless he consents to be the simple-minded literalist that it comforts them to believe he is. But, untroubled by the seeming scandalousness in secular circles of their pronouncements, many of the most significant figures in the theological community today are declaring that God is dead, that the world has at last come of age, and that now, in this late stage of things, the vocation of the Christian community must be to negate all traditional religious meaning, to affirm everything that is radically desacralized in the modern situation, and to seek for a new epiphany in precisely those corners of our world that are, in Thomas Altizer's words, most "bathed in the darkness of God's absence." In the English-speaking world, the most widely noticed piece of theological journalism since *Essays and Reviews* of 1860 is undoubtedly the book which the Bishop of Woolwich published in 1963, *Honest to God.*[15] And it would appear that the enormous amount of attention which has been given to this earnest, though unoriginal, little tract was prompted, in part, by the satisfaction which a sizable contingent within the theological community was prepared to take in the candor with which Bishop Robinson is contemplating the possibility that we may have arrived at what he calls "the end of theism."

14. Mircea Eliade has studied most profoundly the sacred and profane as "two modes of being in the world, two existential situations assumed by man in the course of his history." See *The Sacred and the Profane,* trans. Willard R. Trask (New York, Harper Torchbooks, 1961).
15. See John A. T. Robinson, *Honest to God* (Philadelphia, Westminster Press, 1963).

It is undoubtedly from Dietrich Bonhoeffer that this new evaluation of the secular in contemporary theology takes its real beginning. By the mid-forties Karl Barth, to be sure, was already envisaging the possibility that the "revelation" in which Christian faith is constituted effectively "abolishes" human religion.[16] Dr. Barth's uniqueness in theological tradition is, of course, in large part an affair of the rigor and relentlessness with which he develops the major premise of his entire thought—that the initiative in the divine-human encounter lies always with God and never with man. And thus the crux of his indictment of "religion" is that it is *man's* quest for God and is therefore a futile "grasping" rather than a "true reception." But, he insists, the authentic God-man relation entails nothing other than a "reception" on man's side of free self-disclosure on God's side, in the person of Jesus Christ. So his is a critique of religion that is undertaken for the sake of vindicating the Christian faith. Yet once the contention that religion is the enemy of true faith is divorced from what Bonhoeffer first termed the "positivism of revelation" in Karl Barth's thinking, the possibility of radical realignment in theology may then be readily perceived. And, of course, an equally radical rearrangement of theological furniture is augured by Paul Tillich's powerful critique of theistic supernaturalism, most especially when his rejection of the God of traditional theism is detached from his Augustinian kind of existentialism and from his profound commitment to ontological interpretation. Nor is it possible to give an adequate account of the dynamics of recent theology without according a large role to Rudolf Bultmann, whose insistence on the necessity of stripping the Gospel of mythological accretions from earlier periods of cultural history has introduced enormous excitement into the discussions of the past twenty years. And the revolutionary implications of Bultmann's message are most emphatically expressed by Bultmann's followers (such as Fritz Buri) who would execute the project of existential interpretation by con-

16. See Barth, *Church Dogmatics*, I/2, pp. 280–361.

tending, finally, that grace and revelation are given not in any special act of God, but are simply given with existence itself— so that, here, it would seem that the vocation of Christian theology is that of presiding over its own demise.

But, though all these various currents of radicalism in the contemporary situation have contributed to the present ferment, it is Dietrich Bonhoeffer's project of a "religionless Christianity" that has been perhaps the greatest leaven. And we begin to move towards what is decisive in a large part of the theological world today when we begin with this gifted young German theologian who was a casualty of a Nazi scaffold in the Bavarian forest in the Spring of 1945. As a good Lutheran, Bonhoeffer, especially in the late phase of his career, was determined above all else, he makes us feel, that his theology should be a *theologia crucis*, a theology consistently and deeply rooted in the Cross. For, as he said in his *Ethics*, "the central message proclaimed in the New Testament" is that "in the body of Jesus Christ God took upon himself the sin of the whole world and bore it." But, in contrast to the traditional Lutheran confessionalism of his background, Bonhoeffer did not interpret the meaning of the Cross to imply any necessity for a battle against the "world": on the contrary, said he, "Whoever sets eyes on the body of Jesus Christ in faith can never again speak of the world as though it were lost, as though it were separated from Christ; he can never again with clerical arrogance set himself apart from the world." And the world cannot be rejected by the Christian man, because, as he said, "the world belongs to Christ."[17]

So the true Church, standing as it does under the Cross, stands therefore *with* the world. This is the fundamental lesson of the two books which present the climactic expression of Bonhoeffer's thought, his *Ethics* and the *Letters and Papers from Prison*. The Church stands with the world rather than against it, because that is where Christ stood, not at the edges of life but in the very center of the human City. And so those

17. Dietrich Bonhoeffer, *Ethics*, ed. Eberhard Bethge and trans. Neville Horton Smith (New York, Macmillan, 1955), pp. 70–71.

who find the meaning of their existence in Him will not seek to create for themselves any sort of "religious space" to which the world will be expected to pay obeisance: indeed, the process of secularization is something that they shall welcome as a sign that the world has come of age, and the acknowledgment of the world's adulthood will be prompted by a Christological consideration, since it was just in the Cross of Christ that there was most fully revealed the reckless abandon with which He Himself affirmed the world.

The essential content of Christian faith for Bonhoeffer consisted not in believing difficult propositions about spooky realities but consisted rather in "conformation" with the life of Jesus of Nazareth. And if asked who Jesus was, he was prepared to offer the simplest possible answer, that Jesus was "the man for others." Indeed, it was Bonhoeffer's contention that it is precisely in the kind of radical solicitude for other life which Jesus incarnated that we meet the Transcendent. For God is not to be met in the *Deus ex machina* of traditional piety, nor in the metaphysical doctrines of classical theism: "our relation to God," he said, is "not a religious relationship to a supreme Being": this is "a spurious conception of transcendence," for God is really to be encountered not in any abstract idea, whether it be of His omnipotence or His omniscience, or even of His grace: He is rather to be met in the neighbor, in the other person, in the *Thou* who is nearest to hand—that is, He "is the 'beyond' in the midst of our life." So faith, genuinely Christian faith, is the orientation of one's being towards the other, towards the neighbor: it is "participation in the Being of God." And thus faith is in no real way imperiled in an age of total secularization: to be sure, the basic hypothesis of traditional theism—what Bonhoeffer called the "religious premise" or the "*a priori* premise"—is gone, and a religiousness based on "the two realms" is therefore no longer possible. But, nevertheless, as he asserted, Christ can still "become the Lord even of those with no religion."[18] For religion—that is, "the old doctrine,

18. Bonhoeffer, *Letters*, pp. 165, 93, 91.

based on a metaphysic of distinction between the place of God and the place of man"[19]—in this sense was never more than the "garment" of Christianity. And the great positive advantage that a religionless age brings to the Christian community is the chance to strip off a garment that has long since lost any vitally functional justification. The marvelously exhilarating challenge that is presented to Christian theology is that of working out a religionless interpretation of its faith, an interpretation which forswears all the old mythological and metaphysical views of the Transcendent and which gives itself wholly to an elaboration of how, in the manner of Jesus Christ, we can most deeply affirm the world and face our human future with confidence and prophetic hope. The Christian man, in short, is being called today to "live a worldly life as one emancipated from all false religions and obligations": the mandate under which he stands is one which in effect asks him to discover that "to be a Christian does not mean to be religious in a particular way . . . but to be a man."[20] And thus the knight of faith who may be expected to emerge from the New Reformation toward which we are heading is one who will live in the world like any other man, participating in all the characteristic cultural vitalities and intellectual movements of our time and being certain that, insofar as they are things produced by a world come of age, they are also the things of Christ.

In the Autumn of 1955, Gerhard Ebeling of Zurich, in an address delivered before a gathering of Bonhoeffer's friends in Berlin, declared that his "name is widely held today in such great respect *in spite of* the strange things that are to be found in his last Tegel letters and that were not able to destroy the credit he had earlier acquired in ecclesiastical and theological circles." Dr. Ebeling even went so far as to suggest that that credit might "now have been long overdrawn if his voice had remained longer among us and had not been silenced in a mar-

19. Ronald Gregor Smith, *The New Man: Christianity and Man's Coming of Age* (New York, Harper, 1956), p. 108.
20. Bonhoeffer, *Letters*, p. 123.

tyrdom whose gravity . . . silences any criticism that might come from those who have survived."[21] Gerhard Ebeling was, of course, speaking out of the warmest partisanship and was not at all wanting to associate himself with that conservatism of the "Establishment" which might be expected to be ranging itself in opposition to Bonhoeffer, were he alive today. But however much the theological scene of the fifties may have justified so sombre an account, the landscape of the present time could hardly be said to do so to any considerable degree. For, precisely the very high valuation which Bonhoeffer, in his last years, placed on modern secularization and precisely his coordinate emphasis on the need for a total secularization of the Gospel itself now *establish* his credit among an increasingly larger circle of younger theologians, in England and on the Continent as well as in the United States.

Indeed, it would be not at all strange if many of those, whose theological formation occurred during that fine flush of "Neo-Orthodoxy" in the late thirties and forties, were now beginning to be given a sense of vertigo by much of the talk that goes on in the theological forum. For twenty years ago they were being taught by men like Emil Brunner and Karl Barth to regard modern secularism as the great menacing giant and to understand the theological task as one of producing a Church-Dogmatic about "the divine-human encounter." But today, it seems, secularization "is no longer the menacing giant but the necessary and positive counterpoint in God's symphony."[22] And the most audacious radicals among younger theologians want no longer even to talk of God at all: they take very seriously both Bonhoeffer and the whole modern situation which he was acknowledging, and they say that the "religious premise" has indeed been corroded utterly by the acids of modernity. Like Bonhoeffer, though, they still want to listen to Jesus

21. Gerhard Ebeling, *Word and Faith*, trans. James W. Leitch (Philadelphia, Fortress Press, 1963), pp. 101–02.
22. Eberhard Bethge, "The Challenge of Dietrich Bonhoeffer's Life and Theology," *The Chicago Theological Seminary Register*, 51 (February 1961), 32.

of Nazareth: so they are prepared to colonize the strangely
novel territory of a kind of Christological atheism. But, beyond
this, they face the received tradition with an almost complete
impatience, and, on nearly any day of the week, they are likely
to attract the attention of *Time* magazine by declaring that
God has disappeared, that formal liturgical worship is a medi-
eval anachronism, that the Church is hopelessly captive to this-
or-that department of modern Philistinism, that its "solemn as-
semblies" merely make an irrelevant noise, that the new forms
of Apostolic existence will be "cells" reading plays out of the
Theatre of the Absurd or holding new kinds of jazz hootenan-
nies, and that the only norms by which our course is to be
steered are those provided by the best secular wisdom of our
age. So it is no wonder that those traditionalists whom Dr.
Ebeling was bristling against in the fifties are today shivering
with a most desperate anxiety before the new wave of "religionless Christianity" that seems prepared to spend with a
reckless profligacy the "Catholic substance" of Christian theological tradition. For, as a result of the cooperation of Bonhoeffer's influence with those elements already cited in the
work of Barth and Tillich and Bultmann, a revolution of nearly
Copernican dimensions has been slowly developing over the
past two decades, in the evaluation of modern secularism by
Christian theology.

On the American scene, perhaps the mildest expression of
the new radicalism is to be encountered in the work of the
young Baptist theologian of Colgate-Rochester, William Hamilton. His moving little book of 1961, *The New Essence of
Christianity*, affords a fine example of what begins to be the
new theological style. For, here, it appears that the primary
theological datum has, paradoxically, become the *death* of
God: so the central task of modern theology is defined as that
of reducing "the area of what is believed," of striking "the
delicate balance between what we do and can believe, what we
do not and cannot believe, and what we may hope to believe." And thus the title of Dr. Hamilton's book is very heavily fringed with irony, for, unlike those theologians of the late

nineteenth and early twentieth centuries who were hunting—in the manner, say, of Harnack—for an "essence of Christianity," he is certain that any viable "essence" that can be come by will be only a fragment of the Christian past, this being all that we can expect to be recoverable in this late, bad time to which we belong. As he says, "the special Christian burden of our time is the situation of being without God. There is . . . no possession of God for us, but only a hope, only a waiting."

Yet, even in this time of waiting, the Christian imagination can still behold in Jesus of Nazareth what is renderable only by the term "Lord." But, in Dr. Hamilton's reading of the New Testament, Jesus' lordship is an affair of humiliation and suffering and lowliness: His divinity is "exercised" from the Cross: He "is Lord by being a servant." This means that, insofar as we believe, through a decision of faith that it is God whom we are meeting in this man, we must attempt to shape everything that we say about God into the pattern of humiliation and weakness: we are saying, in other words, that "because of Jesus the Lord, God is always emptying himself to meet us where we are."[23]

It is in terms of this radically kenotic version of the form of Jesus' lordship that Dr. Hamilton proposes we build "a theology of the secular." His contention is essentially Bonhoeffer's contention, that the God who is with us refuses to be the *Deus ex machina,* or to permit Himself to be used as "a working hypothesis": instead, as Bonhoeffer puts it, He "allows himself to be edged out of the world and on to the cross."[24] So, Dr. Hamilton concludes, if Jesus' lordship teaches us that patience and suffering are God's way of dealing with man in the world, this means that it is in this way that the Christian man also deals with the secular world. He stands *with* the world, as did Jesus the Lord: he lives, in fact, a "worldly" life, and does so to such a degree that the very distinction between religion and the *saeculum,* between Church and world, disappears. The Christian man, in short, is what he is by reason of his eager-

23. Hamilton, pp. 30–31, 63, 86, 95.
24. Bonhoeffer, *Letters,* p. 122.

ness to let the world be the world, and he is distinguished by his very radical appreciation of the secular; for, in his unqualified affirmation of the world, he does, as it were, participate in the very life of God, as it was made manifest in Jesus of Nazareth.

This is, in general, the line that William Hamilton was taking in his book of 1961, and the echoes of Bonhoeffer were unmistakable. But, more recently, he seems to have been moving toward an even more complete secularization of Christianity. For, in 1964, in an essay titled "Thursday's Child: The Theologian Today and Tomorrow," he bluntly and brusquely declares that the Christian theologian is now virtually without anything at all to say to the world and that he had better simply accept the fact and make do with it as he best can. In *The New Essence of Christianity*, he had seemed prepared to envisage the possibility, at least, of a kind of eschatological hope for the Christian. God, to be sure, had disappeared, but it was being suggested that, despite the corresponding collapse of religious faith, it could still be *hoped* that some day God would reappear. But, it seems, Dr. Hamilton begins to regard our situation as more extreme than he first supposed, for now, he suggests, we have lost even the possibility of ultimate hope. Faith, he says, is "the way the Christian affirms the past and appropriates the meaning of certain past events deemed to be significant." Hope is "the way of declaring one's future to be open and assured"—whereas Love is "the way of standing before your neighbor in the present moment." And, he adds, since the Christian man is today without faith *and* hope, having lost God and the Word and the Church and the sacraments, all he can do therefore is to take up his stand alongside his neighbor, for it is love alone that is left to guide us and to chart our course. To be a Christian is simply to try to do right by one's fellow men: this is all: everything else has become too problematic even to be spoken of any longer in the forums of our public life. Dr. Hamilton seems, of course, still to believe that the Christian man is in some sense animated by the presence of Jesus. But Jesus, as he is careful to say, is not available now either as "the object or ground of faith . . . but simply as a place to be, a standpoint."[25] And that standpoint, that place, is nothing other than the position of being "alongside the neighbor."

Now this, to be sure, is a theological program that has submitted itself to an *askésis* which is extreme indeed: yet Dr. Hamilton's atheism, insofar as it is a consistently Christological atheism, strikes us as proceeding nevertheless from a genuinely Christian sensibility, despite the very drastic truncation which he is disposed to practice upon the Christian faith. And, among the new forms of religionless Christianity that have begun to emerge, his is a radicalism that will strike us as relatively mild—especially if considered in relation to the thought of so fiercely eccentric a revisionist as the young Anglican theologian, Thomas Altizer, of Emory University, who seems to find buoyancy and verve and infinite exhilaration in the news that God is dead.

The contours of a new "negative" theology were already discernible in Altizer's book of 1961, *Oriental Mysticism and Biblical Eschatology*, but the fuller statement of his position is to be found in his more recent book, *Mircea Eliade and the Dialectic of the Sacred* (1963), which is less a systematic account of Eliade than it is a presentation of Professor Altizer's own vision of the religious life; and the most succinct (though by no means a very clear) expression of his views is given in a spirited essay on "Theology and the Death of God" which appeared in *The Centennial Review* in the Spring of 1964.

Perhaps the chief difference between William Hamilton and Thomas Altizer is one of temperament and sensibility. For both take the death of God to be the primary datum of any creative theology in the modern world: but, with Hamilton, it is all an affair of elegiac nostalgia, of muted lyricism, of tentatively searching for "a provisional order, a makeshift position, a place to stay for a moment before moving on into the dark-

25. William Hamilton, "Thursday's Child: The Theologian Today and Tomorrow," *Theology Today, 20* (1964), 488–89, 494.

ness,"[26] whereas, with Altizer, the pitch of the voice is high, and everything is hot, urgent, passionate intensity. He starts from what he takes to be the given reality of the modern situation, that "God has died in *our* time, in *our* history, in *our* existence," and that any "affirmation of the traditional forms of faith" must, therefore, be "a Gnostic escape from the brute realities of history."[27] The death of God is, in other words, for him an historical event, indeed the definitive event of modern history: "this terrible 'night' " which it has created "has made incarnate the most awesome nothingness imaginable; [and] now begins the deepest *Angst* that man has ever known."[28] For all religious meaning has collapsed: the dimension of the Sacred has been lost, and human existence, as a consequence, has been radically profanized, so that whatever the men and women of our time know is known "only through the death of God, through the death of any absolute which could condition man's knowledge or experience of reality."

Now, at this hazardous new extremity of life, declares Professor Altizer, the great challenge that is presented to the Christian man (presumably by the example of Jesus and His self-identification with the world) is that of so *living* the death of God as to find "a genuinely contemporary meaning . . . of that Reality which lies at the center of the Christian faith": the problem is that of apprehending "the Christian meaning of the Kingdom of God in a situation in which God is dead." This is, to be sure, a strange and difficult paradox—the notion that the task of "the authentically contemporary Christian" is that of finding anew the meaning of an *impotent* and a *non-existent* reality—but it is a paradox from which Professor Altizer does not shrink. For, in his view, "the price of the Christian's contemporaneity" is "the confession of the death of God," the

26. Hamilton, *The New Essence*, p. 28.
27. Thomas J. J. Altizer, "Theology and the Death of God," in *The Centennial Review, 8* (1964), 129.
28. Thomas J. J. Altizer, *Mircea Eliade and the Dialectic of the Sacred* (Philadelphia, Westminster Press, 1963), p. 199.

confession that we must now live in the world without any ultimate source of meaning or security. So, as he says, "the time has come for the Christian theologian to bring an end to the [very] *idea* of God,"[29] for it is only in this way that he can truly accept the burden of his actual condition.

The floridity of Thomas Altizer's rhetoric does at times perhaps suggest sheer inebriation with chaos, with Nothingness, with the Dark Night of modern nihilism. He insists again and again that Christian theology must not say "No" to the radical profanization of our age, that it must instead most deeply affirm the secularity of a post-Christian world, that it must say "Yes" to our modern destiny. But this is an insistence that stems not merely from infatuation with the headiness of metaphysical extremism: for here is a young scholar of genuine integrity, and the "negativism" of his theological program is guided, at bottom, by the hope that, through the Christian man's descent into the abyss of Nothingness, it may be possible at last to achieve a dialectical *coincidentia oppositorum*. In this point he has been most deeply influenced by Mircea Eliade, and especially by the account that is given in Professor Eliade's many books of the kind of "dialectical synthesis of the radical sacred and the radical profane" that figures in all the great hierophanies in the history of religion. In the major philosophical and religious systems of India and China and Greece, Altizer finds the crucial principle to be one which posits the possibility that "ultimately negation is affirmation, that the opposites coincide, that the acts of radical negation and radical affirmation are finally two poles of *one* dialectical movement."[30] And his great hope is that an unhesitating excursion into the depths of our modern dereliction may yield a new epiphany, that *living* the death of God may bring us into the presence of "the God above God,"[31] that the profane may be

29. Thomas J. J. Altizer, "Nirvana and Kingdom of God," in *New Theology No. 1*, ed. Martin E. Marty and Dean G. Peerman (New York, Macmillan, 1964), pp. 153, 155, 163.
30. Altizer, *Mircea Eliade*, pp. 83, 82.
31. See Tillich, *The Courage to Be*, pp. 182–90.

for the post-Christian imagination the path that leads most authentically back into the Sacred. So, in the name of the *coincidentia oppositorum*, Altizer asks the Christian man to *will* the death of God, to negate *all* religious meaning, and to "greet the radical profane with faith,"[32] but with a faith that has emptied itself of all the traditional Christian affimations.

But precisely how Christian theology is to seek anew the meaning of Christian faith when, for the sake of contemporaneity, it has consented to abandon that faith is something that remains unclear; and it may finally require simply to be written off as one of the many elements of the opaqueness which is so much a part of that brilliant, yet willful, perversity which distinguishes Professor Altizer's style of thought. But, at least, here is a man passionately intent upon examining a great wound which the modern consciousness has suffered—himself perhaps a "wounded surgeon," but full of yearning nevertheless for the recovery of that which man has lost, namely, a connection with the *Mysterium Tremendum*, with the Holy, with the Sacred. Whereas, when we move from Thomas Altizer to another young American Anglican, Paul Van Buren, of Temple University, we approach a very nearly total secularization of Christian theology. For here is a Christian theologian whose commitments, at the level of philosophical method, lead him to declare in effect that it is illicit even to try to talk about God, about the Sacred, about, in fact, any reality whose nature prevents the empirical verification of discourse about it: indeed, here is a theologian dancing a jig on the grave of theology and finding it so dead that, as he says, he cannot even understand, as a propositional statement, Nietzsche's proclamation of the death of God.

For all of the use that he makes of contemporary analytic philosophers like R. M. Hare and Ronald Hepburn and Anthony Flew and Ian Ramsey, Professor Van Buren himself appears essentially to be a Positivist of very nearly the vintage of the early Carnap or the Ayer of the first edition of *Lan-*

32. Altizer, *Mircea Eliade*, p. 18.

guage, Truth, and Logic. At an early point in his book, *The Secular Meaning of the Gospel,* he does, to be sure, attempt to dissociate himself from "the somewhat dogmatic spirit" of Logical Positivism, but, nevertheless, it soon becomes clear that the basic assumption guiding his thought is the Positivist's assumption that statements are meaningful only insofar as they function in a context which permits their being verified in a literally empirical way. And since the language of traditional theism, insofar as it consists of statements about God, is unsusceptible of empirical verification, Professor Van Buren also assumes that it can no longer offer the Christian theologian a viable medium of reflection and communication. He proposes, therefore, to convert, without remainder, all statements about God into statements about man. For it is only in this way, he believes, that the Christian *who is himself a secular man* stands any chance of understanding the Gospel in a truly secular fashion. A "nonreligious interpretation" of the Christian faith will, in other words, for him involve no assertions about the Transcendent, about the Eternal or the Supernatural: it will instead consist wholly of statements about man and the world—statements which are in some way empirically verifiable; and, more particularly, it will consist of statements about the Christian man and about his relation to the man Jesus of Nazareth. This is the basic ground on which Van Buren stands, and it is a ground which he wins by the unprecedented tactic of wedding the Positivistic principle of verification to a drastically edited version of something like the Christocentrism of Karl Barth.

There is one particularly concise sentence in his book which gives the essence of his whole position, since it tells us at once who the Christian man is and who Jesus of Nazareth was: he says at one point, "The Christian has seen a man of remarkable and particular freedom, and this freedom has become contagious for him, as it was for the apostles on Easter." And "freedom" is, of course, the crucial word here, for freedom is the word which, in Van Buren's understanding of the historical record, defines Jesus of Nazareth: He was "a man of remarkable and particular freedom," presumably in the sense of being so free "from anxiety and the need to establish his own identity" as to have been able in a unique way to be "for his neighbor." Then, in a certain moment, says Van Buren, this freedom became "contagious"—and that moment was the moment of Easter. During the course of Jesus' earthly life, His was a freedom that exposed "by contrast" the extent to which his contemporaries were "bound by feelings of insecurity, fear, guilt, and by the desire to justify or explain themselves": so, finding their lives to be so painfully and radically judged by His life, they nailed Him to a Cross. But in the event called Easter this freedom did at last begin to be contagious, and this was "the resurrection of Jesus": for, in this "situation of discernment," as Van Buren calls it, men found a new and vivifying perspective on the meaning of their existence—and henceforward the Christian man was to be distinguished by his conviction that all of life is to be seen "in the light of the Easter proclamation concerning Jesus." This, says Van Buren, is the secular meaning of the Gospel, and in the light of this secular meaning he proceeds to produce a consistently naturalistic reinterpretation of the whole spectrum of Christian doctrine, about Creation and Providence and Atonement and the Liturgy, and all the rest.[33]

Langdon Gilkey of the University of Chicago, in an unpublished paper on the new theology[34] (by which the emphasis of this chapter has been partly inspired), has spoken of its "hard secularity." And this phrase does indeed present a fair delineation of things, for William Hamilton and Thomas Altizer and Paul Van Buren are representative of many others on the American as well as on the British and European scene who are today bent on carrying out in various ways the mandate that Dietrich Bonhoeffer laid upon us to produce a nonre-

33. Paul Van Buren, *The Secular Meaning of the Gospel* (New York, Macmillan, 1963), pp. 103, 14–15, 155, 123, 124, 199.

34. Langdon Gilkey, "Is God-Language Necessary," delivered before the Society for Theological Discussion, May 1964.

ligious interpretation of the Christian faith. These are men who have an acute sense of our involvement in what the Bishop of Woolwich has spoken of as "a currency crisis." Dr. Robinson conceives our "doctrinal formulations, moral codes, liturgical forms, and the rest" as "the paper money with which the business of communication is regularly conducted. They are backed in the last resort by certain commitments, certain 'promises to pay,' of which they are the token and expression." And he develops the metaphor by suggesting that

> In times of economic stability we do not give thought to what lies behind our paper money: we take it at its face value and use it as a ready and acceptable means of communication and exchange. So in the field of theology: we make statements about God, we issue pronouncements about morals, we set our liturgical commissions to work, we take part in debates on Church order and the rest, on the assumption that there is an area of exchange within which these symbols are accepted and valid. And, of course, there is. But in our generation people are increasingly beginning to question whether in fact they *mean anything* or stand for anything real. They ask for their backing, for their cash value.

And this is a crisis, says Dr. Robinson, which can be responded to in either of two ways. We can try "to stress the value of the old money . . . to strengthen its purchasing power by internal reforms": we can "try to extend its area of exchange." Or, as he suggests, we can meet the situation by simply admitting that the old money "probably has a limited life" and by then attempting to replace it, "while there is time, by other currency."[35]

It seems that it is this latter course—the replacing of the old currency with something new—that is being frankly undertaken by Hamilton and Altizer and Van Buren and by the

35. John A. T. Robinson, "The Debate Continues," in *The Honest to God Debate*, ed. David L. Edwards (Philadelphia, Westminster Press, 1963), pp. 243–46.

radical movement in contemporary theology of which they furnish significant American examples. For them, as it has already been noticed, the primary theological fact of our time is the death of God: this, in their judgment, is the basic precipitant of the currency crisis. And they are eager to cooperate with and to reaffirm all those elements in the secular culture of our period which are intending to deal a death-blow to traditional theism. For they are convinced that this is a system of thought which, even in its most sophisticated versions, has tended to convert Transcendence into a scientific object by positing the absurd notion of a divine *pantokrator*, a "great emperor in the skies who rules all things."[36] And this, they declare, is an utter delusion which cannot be taken seriously any longer by a man whose standards of intelligibility derive from a world of electric lights and telephones and nuclear fission. The Deus ex machina is, in other words, nothing more than a spooky phantasm of the pre-scientific imagination. And since the world we inhabit is "a world made up only of things and people," if Christian theology is to survive in any form at all, it must be by way of so transforming itself as to make whatever it says consist in statements about how matters are with man *in the world:* for the theologian to attempt any more grandiose kind of deliverance is for his speech to be simply unverifiable in the sense that nothing can count either for or against it.

Yet, however impossible it may be for the modern sensibility to acknowledge as credible the notion descending from the *fides perennis* of a God-thing whose existence is rationally demonstrable, one cannot altogether escape the feeling that the new theology (if one may be permitted so homely an analogy) is by way of throwing out the baby along with the bath water. It wants, and rightly so, to enter a vigorous protest against any literalizing of the ultimate object of religious faith: but so violently does it protest against all objectifica-

36. John Wild, "The Rebirth of the Divine," in *Christianity and Existentialism*, ed. John Wild (Evanston, Northwestern University Press, 1963), p. 170.

tions of the Transcendent that it is itself, one feels, on the way to radically reducing the human life-world. That is to say, the charge that the new theology prefers against the tradition is, in a way, the charge that classical theism consistently tended to convert Mystery into Problem, to convert the numinous Ground of reality into an entity which might become an object of theoretical knowledge. But, in the resistance that it offers to the religious *a priori,* the new theology does itself begin to stand once more on the verge of doing the same thing, of converting the radically mysterious into the merely problematical.

The distinction between Mystery and Problem has, of course, been made famous by Gabriel Marcel, and it is the device whereby he has sought to mark out the domain which must forever be inaccessible to any positivist procedure of inquiry. His clearest exposition of this idea is in the little book *Being and Having,* where he suggests that the essential difference between a problem and a mystery is that "a problem is something which I meet, which I find complete before me," "which I can therefore lay siege to and reduce. But a mystery is something in which I am myself involved, and it can therefore only be thought of as *a sphere where the distinction between what is in me and what is before me loses its meaning and its initial validity.*" And the Mysterious and the Ontological, says M. Marcel, are identical.[37] For the great primal Mystery is simply the plenitude of Being itself in which man's life is so wondrously and providentially anchored. So the domain of the ontological is not at all merely the domain of the problematical in which I undertake to dispel intellectual puzzles of one kind or another by a more strenuous exertion of my cognitive faculties: no, the province of Mystery is not one in which I fidget over what is *objectively* the case but is rather the realm in which I come to know the essential hiddenness of reality before any finite exploration, and yet it is also a realm which is suffused with a sense of encountering the

37. Gabriel Marcel, *Being and Having,* trans. Katharine Farrer (Westminster, Dacre Press, 1949), pp. 117, 101.

things and persons in my environment in the dimension of *presence*—and, here, the decisive experience is a presentiment at once of the rich inexhaustibility and of the vital responsiveness of the world that presses in upon me: here it is that a man becomes fully alive to the incalculable possibilities of creativity and innovation that are borne by the concrete occasions of our human history but which yet surpass all codes and conceptualities, and all the conventional systems of reason and explanation.

Now the new theology is eager to purify the Christian faith of what John Wild calls "those anthropomorphic dilutions" of Transcendence that are so much a part of the received tradition and that have so largely contributed in the past to the reduction of radical Mystery to the level of the merely problematical (the level on which one debates the question as to whether or not "God" can be said to "exist"). But, in the process of relegating to the discard the old anthropomorphic dilutions of Transcendence, the new theology—in its servile attitude before the norms and standards of a positivistic culture—is close to expelling the Transcendent itself from our life-horizon. And it is just at this point that we can see something of the enormous price that a religionless Christianity is about to pay for the prize of "relevance" in what is called a post-Christian world. For to say, as a theologian like Paul Van Buren is in effect prepared to do, that our world is furnished only with those realities that can be embraced by the scientific reason or by some form of quasi-scientific reason, to say that the range of our experience is limited to the public operables of empirical science and that we cannot even talk intelligibly about reality in any dimension of ultimacy, is surely to confine the human spirit within an absolutely finite province of meaning: it is to settle for a world-view quite as impoverished as that which Ernest Gellner renders by the proposition, "The world is what it is." And, in taking such a line as this, the new theology is not only in the process of committing suicide, but, in choosing thus to cooperate with what is so profoundly dehumanizing in a radically profanized world, it is in effect helping to deepen the emptiness and the consequent despair which constitute the particular affliction of the men and women of our time—an affliction such as that suffered by the poor derelict whom we meet in the protagonist of Camus' *The Stranger*, the whole root of whose malaise lies precisely in his alienation from any kind of sacral or transcendent reality, from any sort of Radical Significance.

So we are in truth today facing in, of all places, the theological world itself a secularity that is hard indeed. What is surprising and distressing is not that certain of our younger theologians should be having their difficulties with the doctrine of God and should be in something of a muddle as to how persuasively to recast the case for a theistic position. The really astonishing fact is that they should be so overborne by these difficulties as to want to redefine our human life-world in such a way that the question of ultimate reality may be adjudged an unreal and illicit question. For this is surely a most treasonous foreclosure of the real horizon that men face —which is intersected again and again by radical Mystery, by disclosures in and through the realities of our finite world of "a transfinite dimension," "a tap root which seems to connect," them "vertically as it were, with what Paul Tillich has called the ultimate Source, Ground, and Abyss of all finite reality."[38] As Dr. Tillich himself said in one of his finest sermons, "You cannot think or say: Life has no depth! Life is shallow. Being itself is surface only."[39] And the human reality cannot legitimately be either thought or said to be merely an affair of surface and without depth, because it is never anything, if profoundly experienced, that can, as it were, be seen through: the deep things of self-knowledge and love, of suffering and joy and holiness do always *withstand* exhaustive analysis, and thus they offer a kind of attestation to the environing Mystery within which our lives are set. The popular preacher

38. Theodore M. Greene, "The Ontological Dimension of Experience," in *Thought*, 29 (1954), 374.

39. Paul Tillich, *The Shaking of the Foundations* (New York, Charles Scribner's, 1948), p. 57.

has, of course, a noisy and extravagant way of talking in his pulpit about mystery, and our distaste for his kind of bumptiousness may even inculcate in us an agnostic attitude toward the dark things of life. But, when the mind has not been poisoned by a scepticism prompted by this kind of revulsion, it cannot fail occasionally to be aware that its most basic act of apprehension *is* of Mystery. For, again and again, it has the experience of beholding the ordinary realities of everyday and of finding that, all at once, they become, as it were, transparent, so that they can no longer be taken for granted—and then they take on a strange kind of novelty that elicits in us an act of marveling and a sense of astonishment. It is not, in other words, a matter of the magnificent or the sensational. For, as that remarkable Christian philosopher of Germany, Josef Pieper, has said, "the itch for sensation . . . is a sure indication of a bourgeois mind," and the man whose sense of wonder is awakened only by the exceptional is a man in whom the capacity for wonder is in a state of atrophy and decay. No, the context in which Mystery is encountered is that of the everyday and the ordinary. A man goes about talking about "my" friend or "my" wife—and then, all of a sudden, as Dr. Pieper reminds us, he is brought to a halt: his friend and his wife all at once cease to be defined by his personal needs, and he has to ask himself if one can really "have" a friend or "own" a wife, and what "having" and "owning" mean anyway: his friend and his wife finally manage to make him perform an act of true attention before them, so that they can no longer simply be taken for granted: they make their *presence* felt, and before presence a man has to stop—and to marvel.

It is in these most primitive experiences of dislocation from routinized habits of thought and feeling, it is in these most elemental experiences of wonder, that we first begin to feel the lure of Transcendence. The common, ordinary realities of our everyday existence suddenly open up and become transparent—and we are "shaken": we are "moved": and the world is disclosed as "profounder, more all-embracing and mysterious than the logic of everyday reason had taught us to believe." In such moments a man is deprived of "those penultimate certainties" that he has all along been taking for granted, and he begins to be entrained on a voyage, en route towards Transcendence: he begins to be, in Marcel's phrase, *homo viator*. So, in the kind of marveling astonishment with which, in a given finite reality, we behold the fullness of Being, there is already implicit a certain sort of hope, and perhaps even faith also. For, in the sense of wonder that our world elicits, there is already present a deep desire, a deep hope, that in the fullness of time we *shall* know fully, even if we do not now know fully: in other words, the essential structure of wonder, as Dr. Pieper teaches us, is the structure of hope and of faith.[40] And thus, when a young American theologian who has been overly impressed by the news that God is dead tells us that modern man has somehow been suddenly deprived of faith *and* hope and is now left only with love, it must simply be concluded that he has not undertaken any careful analysis, along phenomenological lines, of our actual life-world—from which Transcendence, insofar as we remain human, can never be extruded. In the great invocation with which *The Confessions* begins, Augustine says, "Great art Thou, O Lord, and greatly to be praised . . . for Thou hast formed us for Thyself, and our hearts are restless till they find rest in Thee"—and this has not suddenly become the nonsense that Messrs. Hamilton and Van Buren imagine.

But, in a time when the theological community itself has been overtaken by a great crisis of faith, how *can* it be given access to the kind of deepened ontological awareness out of which alone it can re-straighten its course? In a period when the theological imagination has entered so deeply into the climate of modern secularity as to have become convinced that man dwells in a world which, dimensionally, is as limited as

40. Josef Pieper, *Leisure the Basis of Culture*, trans. Alexander Dru (New York, New Am. Library, Mentor-Omega, 1963), pp. 100, 98, 102, 103–05.

it is represented to be in "the demi-religion of positivism,"[41] and when theology itself has begun to participate deeply in the general desacralization of life, and when it grows drunk with the news of the death of God, how can it be put once again in possession of a lively awareness and certitude of Transcendence? This is perhaps one of the deepest questions that can be pondered today by those who covet a restoration of health and sanity in that department of theological life which has fallen under the sway of a kind of ecstatic nihilism.

It is just at this juncture that I believe we ought to consider the possibility that the theological imagination of our period may find in poetic experience an important means of grace. During this present time of realignment and reconstruction, the critical disciplines which are central to the theological enterprise itself will, of course, have the greatest importance. But, now that God is in eclipse and absent and the theological imagination has even to recover, it seems, the "feel" of Transcendence and of Mystery, it may well be that its proper strength and suppleness can in part be found again by the way of *poiesis*. Vergil was able, it is true, to bring the pilgrim Dante only into the precincts of Grace, and from thereon "a spirit worthier" than he had to befriend the pilgrim's steps: but that is perhaps just where modern theology needs once more to be, within the precincts of the numinous, the Transcendent, on the threshold of the *Mysterium Tremendum*. And thus one of the most hopeful signs on the horizon today is presented by the enormous interest that the theological community is taking in the important literature of our age. This is an interest that it is customary to interpret as having been prompted by the theologian's concern to win the kind of fresh insight that is furnished by the poet and dramatist and novelist into what is called "the human condition." And, undoubtedly, much of our theology has been very greatly en-

41. The phrase is Allen Tate's: See *On the Limits of Poetry* (New York, Swallow Press and Wm. Morrow, 1948), p. 43.

riched by absorbing those dire reports on life in the modern age that the literature of this century has insisted on giving us. In much of his writing, Amos Wilder has wanted to remind the theologian that the real inwardness of our culture is most sensitively expressed by literary artists, that theology needs to learn "to diagnose the age through their insights," and he has often warned that, if the Church does not pay sufficient heed to the wrestlings and explorations of the creative writer, it may well find after a time that "the deeper movements of the age have outrun [Christian thought] . . . and left much of its . . . formulation . . . behind."[42] But, profitable as it may be for the theologian to be given the kind of alertness to the existential reality of contemporary human life that is mediated through literary art, it should be kept in mind that this is not the sole way, or perhaps even the deepest way, in which the literary imagination can fecundate theological thought. For, against all techno-empirical views of reality which would flatten it out into a single dimension, the literary imagination makes a standing testimony to the fact that ours, as Hart Crane said, is a world of "many dimensions": and thus it offers a certain support and encouragement to theology, in the kind of high drama which characterizes the story that theology wants to tell about the altitudes and depths of human existence.

Jacques Maritain, in one of the famous lessons of *Art and Scholasticism*, tells us that "poetry is ontology."[43] And yet, initially, the poetic imagination has as its most immediate end nothing more ambitious than a vivid realization of what Gerard Manley Hopkins called the "inscape" of things. By this term which he coined, Hopkins meant, it would seem, to indicate not merely an outer reality, not something auto-

42. Amos N. Wilder, *Theology and Modern Literature* (Cambridge, Harvard University Press, 1958), p. 60; and *Modern Poetry and the Christian Tradition* (New York, Charles Scribner's, 1952), p. xii.
43. See Jacques Maritain, *Art and Scholasticism*, trans. J. F. Scanlan (New York, Scribner's, 1943), pp. 87–122.

matically and inescapably present, but something to be discovered only by a seeing-*into*, by a strict and loving attention to the radical actuality of the things of earth. And this is indeed the end toward which all the rhetoric and dramatic gesture of literary art are devoted: the whole object of the poetic enterprise is to apprehend and to disclose "the character of particular things in the starkness and strangeness of their being what they are."[44] The poetic world—I mean not merely the world of verse but that of literary art in general—is rooted in the concrete particularity of lived experience; and poetic art, in its deepest aspect, is a way of loving the concrete, the particular, the individual. But, of course, to love is to enter the dimension of what Marcel calls *presence*: it is to approach a given reality out of a sense of its having the character of a *Thou*, whether that reality be "Fountains, Meadows, Hills, and Groves" or some "Attic shape . . . with brede/Of marble men and maidens overwrought" or a father who "moved through dooms of love." The intensity of its love for the quiddities and haecceities of experience conditions the poetic imagination, in other words, to view whatever it contemplates as ignited by the capacity for exchange, for reciprocity: it has the dimension of presence.

And, having the dimension of presence, things exist always for the poetic imagination in relationship: the world is a body wherein all things are "members one of another." As Coleridge reminded us in the *Biographia Literaria*, the poet does not characteristically view the things of earth as "essentially fixed and dead" but as "essentially vital": and it would appear that, in his stress on the vital quality of poetic experience, he was intending to speak of the poet's habit of confronting concrete particulars with such intensity that their significances are beheld as flowing from relations in which they stand to still other things consubstantial with themselves. As he says in the fourteenth chapter of the *Biographia*, the poet "diffuses a

44. H. D. Lewis, *Morals and Revelation* (London, Allen and Unwin, 1951), p. 212.

tone and spirit of unity, that blends, and (as it were) *fuses,* each into each, by that synthetic and magical power, to which we have exclusively appropriated the name of imagination."

Here, for example, is the illustrative instance that Wordsworth offers in the Preface to the 1815 edition of his verse. He first quotes from his poem, "Resolution and Independence," the passage which reads:

> As a huge stone sometimes is seen to lie
> Couched on the bald top of an eminence,
> Wonder to all who do the same espy
> By what means it could thither come, and whence,
> So that it seems a thing endued with sense,
> Like a sea-beast crawled forth, which on a shelf
> Of rock or sand reposeth, there to sun himself.
> Such seemed this Man; not all alive or dead,
> Nor all asleep, in his extreme old age.

Then he goes on to say, "In these images, the conferring, the abstracting and the modifying powers of the imagination immediately and mediately acting are all brought into conjunction. The stone is endowed with something of the power of life to approximate it to the sea-beast; and the sea-beast stripped of some of its vital qualities to assimilate it to the stone; which intermediate image is thus treated for the purpose of bringing the original image, that of the stone, to a nearer resemblance to the figure and condition of the aged man; who is divested of so much of the indications of life and motion as to bring him to the point where the two objects unite and coalesce in just comparison."[45]

And it is precisely such a coalescence as this within reality which, as Philip Wheelwright has also observed, is indeed a chief feature of the world when it is beheld in the terms of poetic vision. It is, to be sure, nothing larger than a concrete particular which commands upon itself an act of the poet's attention: but so intensely, then, is it contemplated that it

45. E. de Selincourt, ed., *The Poetical Works of William Wordsworth,* 2 (2nd ed. London, Oxford University Press, 1952), p. 438.

takes on the lustre of a "something more." Wordsworth confronts a decrepit old man with such intensity that he finds himself confronting, as it were, in the same moment a huge stone "couched on the bald top of an eminence" and a sea-beast "crawled forth to sun himself"—and the stone and the sea-beast and the old man are all one: they unite and coalesce in just comparison. And this is a part of the mystery of *poiesis*, that, when the concrete individual is faced with great intensity, "without losing any of its bright actuality, [it] tends also to be, or at least to suggest overtones of, something more"[46]— and thus its finite particularity affords a glass of vision into a kind of infinite depth and extension. This habit of the imagination's functioning which Coleridge called vital is, of course, very largely dependent on metaphoric modes of apprehension —and the test of a good metaphor is precisely its capacity to produce coalescence of the heterogeneities of experience and thus to evoke in us awareness of "the flowing wholeness of things"[47] and of what Wordsworth called "unknown modes of being."

It is in fact a part of the enduring greatness of Wordsworth that through the arguments of so much of his prose and poetry he should have taught the Romantic movement—and through it all the modern generations—to see the kind of attestation which poetic experience makes to an infinitude beyond "the light of sense." For what he noticed, with a singular sensitivity and perceptiveness, is that, in finding all the concrete realities of experience to point beyond themselves, the poetic imagination is restlessly driven, from "the visionary dreariness" of earth, towards "unknown modes of being." The silent way in which every particular thing, when deeply contemplated, attests to a something more, to the fragmentariness of all finite reality, the fact that everything appears to stand on the threshold of something else—this, as Wordsworth perceived, awakens in us at once a profound feeling of the essential indigence of the world that is at our disposal and

46. See Wheelwright, *Metaphor and Reality*, pp. 164–69.
47. Wheelwright, *The Burning Fountain*, p. 122.

awakens, as he calls it in the second book of *The Prelude,* an equally profound

> sentiment of Being spread
> O'er all that moves and all that seemeth still;
> O'er all that, lost beyond the reach of thought
> And human knowledge, to the human eye
> Invisible, yet liveth to the heart.

And it was in this sentiment of Being that the poet found "a never-failing principle of joy."

Now, if it is truly a sentiment of Being which is the special grace that poetic experience has it in its power to bestow upon us, it may well be that there is nothing else by which the theological imagination of our period stands to be so greatly refreshed. For what theology is now by way of losing in its latest excursion into "modernism" is that lively sense of the ontological weight and depth of the human reality, apart from which theology altogether ceases to exist as a distinctive way of understanding the human story. And facing, therefore, the threat of so deep a loss as this, it would seem that before undertaking any further act of construction or reconstruction of a distinctively theological order the strategists of systematic thought in the Christian community would be wise to consider how the most basic renewal of ontological vision may be prepared for and wherein it is, in a radically profanized world, that the appetite may be revived for a *sentiment* of Being. And, considering this, it might be expected that theology would then find promises of grace in poetry.

It is not, of course, to be supposed that the particular exemplars of the poetic imagination whom I have cited from the period of English Romanticism (namely, Wordsworth and Coleridge) represent idioms that are likely to have a persuasive influence on contemporary sensibility, even in its theological forms. Lionel Trilling, for example, has noticed how unappealing the Wordsworthian images tend to be in our time. In the brilliant essay, "Wordsworth and the Rabbis," which first appeared in *The Kenyon Review* in the Summer of

1950, Trilling suggests that it is not Wordsworth's ontological preoccupations which are foreign to the experience of our time, for twentieth-century literature, as he reminds us, bristles and explodes with a sense of ontological crisis. But, for us, the sentiment of Being has taken on the modality of hyperaesthesia and apocalypse, and this, Trilling feels, makes Wordsworth's Stoic *apatheia* and quietude seem alien and irrelevant to our modern unrest. For we have come to have, he says, a great penchant for the more violent forms of spirituality, for "the apocalyptic subject and the charismatic style," for "the powerful, the fierce, the assertive, the personally militant": and, liking "the fiercer animals," we believe that "the tigers of wrath are to be preferred to the horses of instruction."[48] So the Wordsworth who speaks in "Tintern Abbey" of "that serene and blessed mood,/In which . . ./We see into the life of things" strikes us as failing to have a certain necessary valor, and his "mildness" is only irritating. And, increasingly during the past decade, this bias of contemporary taste has caused Trilling greater and greater irritation. In these years no one has commented so steadily as he on our taste for the rare and the strange, on our preference for the great situations of extremity, on our fascination with the ambiguous and the "tragic," with evil and the demonic. With the advent of the sixties, he even began to complain of how exhausting it is for a university teacher to try to treat in his classroom the literature of the modern period, "a canon which includes Yeats, Eliot, Lawrence, Joyce, Proust, Kafka, Mann, and Gide, and which, if it is conceived in the full catholicity of its tradition, also includes Flaubert, Baudelaire, Rimbaud, as well as the later Tolstoy and Dostoievski." For this is a literature that is darkly rooted in the primitive and the chthonic: it confronts us with questions about ourselves "of a shocking intimacy,"[49] and its moral and spiritual radicalism can be so extreme as to come to the point of thrusting us outside time and history al-

48. Trilling, *The Opposing Self*, pp. 133, 132.
49. Lionel Trilling, "Commitment to the Modern," *Teachers College Record, 64* (1963), 405, 406.

together, so that we are disengaged from all the concrete, conditioned realities of ordinary experience by means of which and through which we might regain some sentiment of Being. Indeed, Professor Trilling, in many of his recent essays, does appear, for all of his customary brilliance, to be very nearly approaching such a biliousness and such an impatience toward modern literature as too frequently controlled the responses of his acknowledged master, Matthew Arnold.[50]

But maybe it would be better for us simply to decide to do the best we can with the literature that we have; and, instead of heckling it with close bargaining and captiousness, and instead of asking it to give us that sentiment of Being which the English Romantics could offer but which a Kafka or a Beckett cannot, perhaps we ought, rather, to inquire into the possibility that the poetic imagination of our day is mediating Transcendence in different modes and in different idioms. Manifestly, of course, the characteristic literature of the modern period—the literature that we claim to be *ours*—does not have the kind of positively theological tinge that surrounded the literature of Wordsworth's period. This is not to say that the age of Wordsworth presents a literature of unambiguously Christian inspiration, for Hoxie Neale Fairchild, in his massive study, *Religious Trends in English Poetry*, has been at pains to remind us that this is most assuredly not the case. But, for all its heterodoxy—by no means so thoroughgoing as Fairchild insists—the literature of Wordsworth's age does at least inhabit a sort of borderland between a Platonist humanism and an authentically biblical Christianity, and it knows that man is a creature "trailing clouds of glory." In contrast, the literature of our period is one passionately committed to its secularity: its subject, as Jean Cocteau says, is *le mystère laic*, the "lay mystery" or the secular mystery, and the representative artist of today understands himself as "neither priest nor proctor." It is, says Wallace Stevens, "a fresh spiritual that he

50. See, for example, Lionel Trilling, "On the Modern Element in Modern Literature," *Partisan Review*, 28 (1961), 9–35; also "The Fate of Pleasure," *Partisan Review*, 30 (1963), 167–91.

defines."[51] But in this fresh spiritual there is little of beauty, of loveliness, of sublimity: indeed, the song is almost aggressively devoted often to ugliness, to disfigurement, to brokenness. Far from being a creature trailing clouds of glory, man, it seems, is to be adjudged, in the phrase of Jean-Paul Sartre, as something like "a useless passion."

The predominant stress of the literature belonging to what Nathalie Sarraute calls "the age of suspicion" is a stress made up of malediction and blasphemy, of anguish and negation, of forlornness and despair of any grace beyond the reach of art. Yet, in this very abysmal sense of abandonment and dereliction that pervades our poetry and fiction and drama, there is also an infinite longing; and, in the very radicalism with which the disorders of modern life are faced by a Brecht or a Camus or a Beckett, there is implicit perhaps an invocation "to the lost harmony, like a prayer . . . corresponding to the second petition of the Lord's prayer—'Thy Kingdom come'."[52] And this is the kind of intuition of the Sacred, the kind of sentiment of Being, that the literature of our period offers us: it is, to be sure, a *negative* transcendence, but this is perhaps all that Lionel Trilling has any right to expect in a time when God is in eclipse and is felt to be absent (though to speak in this way is to speak only of a tendency of our culture and is not at all to subscribe to the myth of God's "death").

But, however much the sentiment of Being may be mediated to us by the poetic imagination of our time in a negative and dialectical way, we are, nevertheless, still not without evidence of that ontological deepening which it is of the nature of poetic experience to afford. And this is, of course, precisely what the theological imagination of our time seems now to be so desperately in need of—an ontological deepening, a recovery of the sentiment of Being, a fresh intuition of Transcendence—

51. Wallace Stevens, "An Ordinary Evening in New Haven." I am indebted to Amos Wilder for calling these lines to my attention: See his "Art and Theological Meaning," in *The New Orpheus*, p. 409.

52. Denis de Rougemont, "Religion and the Mission of the Artist," in *The New Orpheus*, p. 73.

for, apart from this, there can be no hope for it at all, given its frequently extreme present befuddlement. So, if one considers the immediate scene of our cultural life from the standpoint of how theology may once again be restored to health and sanity, it would seem that one of the most crucial transactions that can be carried on in the years just ahead is one that will involve the Christian theologian's patient tutelage unto the things of Christ by the band of Apollo: for it may well be that the first step to be taken toward resolving the crisis of faith in contemporary theology is one that will involve a prompt seizure of the promise of grace in poetic art, even in an art that is sometimes itself as heavily dominated as is the new theology by the myth of the death of God.

Chapter Six FAITH
AND ART
IN A WORLD AWRY

The recollection of the hysterias and the mass inquisitions and the ugly patriotisms of the nineteen-fifties will doubtless suggest to the student of recent American history that the style of our external life during this period involved something radically different from that of the thirties, and so indeed it did. The intervening decade was the decade of World War II and its aftermath, and the difficulties of that time made for a kind of deflection of the national spirit from the tasks of self-definition: so, as we reflect upon the quality of American life in the fifties, our first impulse is to think of it not in relation to the immediately preceding decade but in relation to the period of the Great Depression and its aftermath. And to recall the sobriety and the heroism and the good faith which generally marked our behavior as a people during that time is surely to be put in mind of the great differences in style that characterized our national life in the eras of Roosevelt and Eisenhower.

But, beneath the external differences that emphatically distinguish the two period-styles from each other, there is at least one fundamental respect in which the American experience persists along a single course. For, in both the nineteen-thirties and the nineteen-fifties, perhaps ultimately the most significant development was the journey through its own interior that the stresses of these years led the American character to undertake. There were, for example, from the years of the New

Deal the WPA guidebooks on our states and rivers and highways; the *March of Time* films; the national histories and biographies of Allan Nevins and Carl Sandburg and Douglas Freeman and Carl Van Doren; the books of social "reportage" by James Agee and Louis Adamic and George Leighton and the Lynds; and the recovery by the folklorists of the legendary heroism of the Davy Crocketts and Paul Bunyans and Daniel Boones. This vast accumulation of the historical detail and social statistics of our civilization seems now to have involved a kind of search for a national mythology and for the permanent *Geist* of our country's culture. It seems today that amid the dismay and dilapidation of those years we were in search of the living reality of the American landscape and of some element of stoutness in it that would enable it to survive the dislocations of economic disaster and social upheaval.

And this same passion for self-scrutiny distinguishes, perhaps to an even greater degree, the decade that was brought to a close by John Kennedy's accession to the American presidency. But in these more recent years one feels that our search as a people was not so much for the *land*scape as for the *soul*scape that forms our spiritual horizons. As we moved more deeply into the global insecurities of the period inaugurated by the close of the War, our great uncertainty came to be whether or not, amid the epochal disorder, man really had any good chance, as William Faulkner asserted in his Nobel Prize acceptance speech, of "prevailing." We began to discover the reality of what the Europeans call "the boundary situation," and we began to be in search of man and of some reassurance of his capacity to last. But, increasingly, what many of the more trenchant observers descried was not the grand human thing itself but, as William Whyte phrased it in *The Organization Man*, "the dehumanized collective that so haunts our thoughts." As early as the twenties this had already become a major theme in the writings of such European critics of modern culture as Jaspers and Marcel and Berdyaev and Ortega. In the relatively carefree time that we were then enjoying, however, theirs was a testimony that could be discarded as expressing merely the exhaustions of the Old World. But in these late years, as we have faced more deeply into the American scene itself, we have found that here, too, the modern populace is being reduced to the status of what Kierkegaard called "a public."

"A public," said Kierkegaard in his little book *The Present Age*, "is neither a nation nor a generation, nor a community, nor a society, nor these particular men, for all these are only what they are through the concrete; no single person who belongs to the public makes a real commitment; for some hours of the day, perhaps, he belongs to the public—at moments when he is nothing else, since when he really is what he is he does not form part of the public. Made up of such individuals, of individuals at the moments when they are nothing, a public is a kind of gigantic something, an abstract and deserted void which is everything and nothing."[1] And when the human community is overtaken by the extreme functionalization of life that is entailed in the logic of an evolving technocratic society, then men wear only the masks that are given them by the social and economic functions which they serve: they feel themselves to be anonymous and have, indeed, become anonymous, for they form a "public," and theirs is a "mass-situation," the situation of men who, in their life together, are but "a kind of gigantic something, an abstract and deserted void which is everything and nothing."

Many of the most acute observers of our culture began to tell us in the fifties, and with increasing urgency, that this is the direction that American life is taking. This was, in one way or another, the message of David Riesman's *The Lonely Crowd*, of William Whyte's *The Organization Man*, of C. Wright Mills' *White Collar*, and numerous other studies in the moral climate of contemporary American life—to say nothing of the reports that came from such gossipmongers as A. C. Spectorsky (*The Exurbanites*) and John Keats (*The Crack in the Picture Window*) and Vance Packard (*The Status*

1. Søren Kierkegaard, *The Present Age*, trans. Alexander Dru and Walter Lowrie (New York, Oxford University Press, 1940), p. 41.

Seekers). Indeed, a whole new literature began to appear whose purpose it was to insist on the inauthenticity and facelessness of the life that awaits us in an increasingly standardized mass society where the individual is caught up "into the rank and file of some operational combine," or "into some category of occupational concern with all its paraphernalia: code of behavior, standards of opinion, lingo, and so forth." "Identification of one's function," says Erich Kahler, "is the admittance ticket granting the right to exist. And so people tend more and more to touch each other with that externally established functional part of the self, that part of the self that has the right to exist, while their individually human parts, for which no legitimate place is provided in our social structure, become increasingly isolated, unrelated and alienated from each other."[2] Amid this gray, dreary anonymity of other-directedness men's goals are given them not by tradition or by their own consciences but by the social groups in which they have their assigned functions; and amid this depersonalized life of the modern public, men live by what Karl Jaspers, at the end of the twenties, was calling "a conventional ethic of association"—that is, "courteous smiles, a tranquil manner, the avoidance of haste and jostle, the adoption of a humorous attitude in strained situations, helpfulness unless the cost be unreasonable, the feeling that 'personal remarks' are in bad taste, self-discipline to promote order and easy relationships whenever people are assembled in large numbers."[3] All this constitutes, in Dr. Jaspers' phrase, the "universal language" by which the faceless, anonymous inhabitants of our contemporary wasteland shuffle through the dreary rituals of their intermingling.

Despite the somberly prophetic character of the critique that emerges from the new sociology, it does yet sometimes convey suggestions of a fatalism that very sharply differentiates it from the social criticism that was produced by the avant-garde in the thirties. For, in that earlier and simpler

2. Kahler, *The Tower and the Abyss*, pp. 23, 42.
3. Karl Jaspers, *Man in the Modern Age*, p. 49.

time, the focus of aggrievance for radical thought tended to be rather highly particularized. One knew precisely what it was that John Steinbeck was protesting against in *The Grapes of Wrath;* one knew just whom it was that Norman Thomas and the Socialist Party wanted to call into question; and there could be no uncertainty at all about the identity of those who were opposing Walter White and the N.A.A.C.P. Indeed, it may have been precisely because of the definiteness with which the source of the disorder was particularized that the critical traditions of the thirties often managed to be so genuinely radical. But the new social criticism, with its mystique of the *Masse-Mensch,* assumes that we are all involved in the malaise of an enveloping totalitarianism from which no escape is possible: it does not focus upon a particular flaw in our social structure, but, rather, it calls into question the whole fabric and design of contemporary society. The charges that are made in books like *The Lonely Crowd* and *The Organization Man* are charges that implicate us all in the depersonalizing processes of mass society, and it is the very inclusiveness of this testimony that sometimes blunts its urgency: we are all, it seems, touched by the facelessness and anonymity of an other-directed society, and the reign of the Organization is envisaged as a consequence of processes immanent within, and made necessary by, the exigencies of this present moment in modern history. The tragedy of self-loss is universal, and the new sociology sometimes seems to be saying that to suppose that any really effective resistance is possible is simply to surrender to the last illusion: no, it is sometimes implied, we are all doomed to be the helpless victims of a quietly omnipotent and unopposable totalitarianism.

It is true, of course, that, when an enterprise of cultural criticism has as its object the specification of some particular disorder or flaw in the fabric of our common life, it is relatively easy to avoid the tone and the accent of fatalistic resignation, for the very particularity of the disorder implies the existence of melioristic possibilities. But when we are dealing with a general disorder, when in some sense the tragedy is universal, when there are no longer any privileged persons and when everyone is equally distant from any sense of security—when this is the extremity of the situation that man faces, as may well to some extent now be so, then it is very difficult to do justice to the generality of the malaise without, in the process, seeming to rob the human reality of its radical imperatives and to promote a kind of euphoric fatalism. When the crowd is no longer merely an occasional phenomenon but one of the characteristic forms of human life, when men no longer feel themselves to be immediately subject to moral norms but only to the impersonal necessities of collective existence, and when the things that they do are done not because they are natural or satisfying but simply because their "radar-mechanisms" tell them that to act differently would be to violate the impersonally established laws of the social collective, then the human situation is indeed on the way to becoming an extreme situation: this is to say that, in some sense, men have begun to know the meaning of Hell. In such a time, perhaps the great danger is that men may come to be deeply enervated by a fatalistic sense of futility and defeat. And this is, I believe, an impasse that can be avoided only by our persistence in raising very bluntly some essential questions: What can be done? What concrete steps can be taken to halt the drift of life in our period towards increasing depersonalization? And if the ubiquity of the Organization is a permanent feature of life in a technocratic culture, what can be done at least to make the Organization something less demonic and more humane? What can be done, what concrete steps can be taken? These surely are the basic questions to be tackled today by any truly humanistic sociology of culture.

But, important as it undoubtedly is to resist the euphoria of fatalism, I am not at all certain that the *first* questions it will be most fruitful for the religious community to contemplate are questions of an immediately practical order. It must, of course, candidly face the issue concerning precisely how the pressures of creative intelligence can be brought to bear upon the depersonalizing structures of life in a mass society; and it must not attempt, surely, any evasion of the concrete tactical issues of reconstruction. The Christian enterprise is, in short, required to seek a deeper understanding of the stratagems whereby it may participate in the defense and reconstruction of the human community. But surely the first question to which it ought to address itself is not an immediately practical question. It is, rather, a question involving what I should call a theology of the imagination, the issue concerning how the imaginative style of a people may be renewed and reinvigorated at the concrete level of sensibility and life-orientation. Indeed, the problem of life-style, of imaginative style, may well be one of the central issues facing the theologian of culture in the years ahead, and I am convinced this is an issue to the settlement of which he will not make any very helpful contribution unless he clearly perceives how closely he must cooperate with the most vigorous movements in the art of our time.

I have mentioned the testimony being made by much of the most trenchant social criticism of our period that a new type of man has been emerging in the past generation or two on the American scene, a man the operative law of whose life is conformity and adjustment. He is a man who increasingly finds it difficult to make any real sense of such a motto as Dante's, "Go your own way and let the people talk." Nor can he make any sense of the life-perspective of Biblical faith, with its notion of the "dedicated spirit" being "singled out" and standing "over against" the world in unwavering witness to what it has beheld to be the truth: the very notion of being singled out, of standing over against the world, is resisted by him for whom adjustment and conformity define the ideal human position. Indeed, the other-directed man of our time seems to be without any real capacity for understanding the prophetic religion of Biblical faith: he simply has not the imaginative resources for understanding what the Bible is talking about. He may be an ardent supporter of church or synagogue; and yet, paradoxically, the Hebraic-Christian faith, in its moral profundity and radicalism, is something that simply surpasses his imagination. This is to say that the root-problem of our present religious situation may be one of renewing and reinvigorating that deep and interior order of human sensibility and human feeling.

But, now, what must be recognized in the religious community is that it is not within the province of the theologian, as theologian, to deal directly with the order of sensibility. This is, rather, the order in which the artist takes the steadiest, the most permanent, and the deepest interest. For, as the Roman Catholic critic Fr. William Lynch has so finely said:

> what the artist is essentially interested in is the expression, involving judgments but in the most visible and concrete terms, of the total life and movement of the soul as it engages with the reality outside of itself, especially with the reality of each current moment of history. I do not think it too much to say that . . . the artist wishes to "save" that soul in the sense that he wishes to keep its various acts of sensibility straight and real and ever moving with a freedom that really belongs to the children of God.
>
> He searches for the rhythmic and spontaneous movements that will accomplish the freedom of the soul, for it is not a set of false or cheap eternities or seductions that will win to this great objective. He so arranges his sounds and images that they judge each other, though not according to the formal judgments of the immediate moralist. He discovers the human in a thousand corners and is the revealer of the non-human for what it is. It is by the inner light of his organisms that he lights up fantasy as fantasy and reality as reality, and reaches all his power by finding and following the lines of the latter. Therefore his work is a human act in the highest and the fullest sense of the term.[4]

What the authentic artist is concerned above all else to do is to make us see the fundamental order of the world, and the account that he renders of it is given not in terms of proposi-

4. William F. Lynch, S.J., *The Image Industries* (New York, Sheed and Ward, 1959), pp. 140–41.

tions and measurements but in terms of the rich and strangely irreducible particulars of existence. We speak of synecdoche as a device which the poet occasionally uses when he wants to make a part of something stand for the whole. But, surely, synecdochism is not merely an occasional stratagem of the artist but, to some degree, is always and essentially involved in his method of handling reality. Joyce's Leopold Bloom and the ghostly finale of the string pizzicati in Stravinsky's *Petrouchka* and the cruelly impervious electric light that glares down upon the wreckage of man in Picasso's *Guernica* mural are all particulars that compel an act of attention upon themselves; but, at the same time, they tell us something about everything else in the world. And this is the perennial mystery of art, that it seeks to master the radically singular, concrete, individual aspects of reality and yet ends by somehow presenting them in such a way that they, in their concrete singularity, become resonant of the whole of reality.

St. Teresa tells us, "I require of you only to look." And this is, in a way, the single requirement of the artist also. He asks us to look, indeed to stare, at *this* boy in love, at *this* plane soaring through the sky, at *this* soldier's fright before the advance to the front—and he asks us to contemplate these images so steadily and with such intentness till we begin to perceive the story or the fragment of a story in which they are interacting. He compels us to perform an act of judgment, and this not at the top of our minds but at the deep level of feeling, of passion, of sensibility, where the men and women of our generation are perhaps most in need of reeducation. In this respect, Mark Van Doren may be right in thinking that, "The simplest evidence is the behavior of audiences at movies which are trying to be tragedies. In proportion as the attempt is successful the audiences are embarrassed, for nothing has trained them in the emotions of pity and terror; they are afraid to be afraid, and they do not know whom to pity, or when. . . . The embarrassment expresses itself in titters or in audible signs of disgust; they came to be moved a little, but not this much. They brought quantities of sentiment which they cannot use, for the work of art before them is aiming at precision, and understanding is required."[5] And not to know how to feel is to be at the mercy of dreams and fantasies and fears by which we may well be undone.

So we must say, then, that the creativity of the artist is calculated very greatly to enhance the creativity of religion, for, in the creative forces of authentic art the religious community will find an indispensable ally in promoting that health of the imagination apart from which the integrity of man can in no wise be guaranteed. And, since the order of sensibility does not lie immediately within the special purview of the theologian, he cannot but regard the artist as one of his most natural partners, for the whole office of the artist is to liberate the imagination and to train and educate us in the ways of feeling and sensibility. Indeed, perhaps one of the most constructive undertakings in the theological community in relation to the whole range of questions having to do with the collectivist drift of modern society would be to work through the first principles of what I am calling a theology of the imagination. And this will, I should hope, be an effort that will result in the development of a generation of theological critics so skilled in negotiating the transaction between art and faith that they would be capable of convincing both the artist and the theologian that nothing could be more wrongheaded than the suspiciousness with which they habitually view each other. It is wrongheaded because, in quickening the imagination, the artist trains the human intelligence to make precise discriminations about the dimensions of experience that transcend the gross materialities of life, and thus he may become one of the theologian's best allies in the liberation of man from the predominant platitudes and banalities of a positivistic culture. It is also wrongheaded for the artist and the theologian to persist in their mutual suspicion of each other because, in the artist's struggle against the blunting of our sensibilities that the popular arts of a mass culture are so skillful in bringing

5. Mark Van Doren, *Liberal Education* (New York, Henry Holt, 1943), p. 162.

about, he might find in the high drama of the Christian story
about reality a kind of support and encouragement. And, fur-
thermore, in turning their salvos upon each other, the theologian and the artist may simply all the more weaken their already none too secure status in the culture, when actually
they should be jointly engaged in warfare against the increasingly insidious control of the American imagination by the
Kitsch that is circulated in a mass society through the powerful
media of the popular arts, or of what Gilbert Seldes calls "the
public arts."

And this brings me to what ought to be the major focus in
our time of any genuinely relevant theology of the imagination. For not only ought it to entail an effort to understand what
will be involved in the collaboration between theology and the
high forms of art, but it ought also to involve an effort to submit
to the closest critical scrutiny all the archetypes and symbols
and rhythms that animate our popular literature and movies
and music. Here it is that we discover the dreams the people
feed upon and what the prophet Ezekiel called "the chambers
of imagery" in which men's souls are sometimes so insidiously
enervated that the astonished observer, on contemplating the
mere "gigantic something" they have become, must cry out
with the narrator in Eliot's *The Waste Land*, "I had not
thought death had undone so many."

I am proposing, then, that the theological community may
well conclude that something very fundamental awaits doing
before it begins to put its shoulders to any wheel of radical
and active reconstruction of the other-directed culture of our
period. And I suspect that, increasingly, the best theological
intelligence will be coming to regard the deepest cultural problem of our period as the problem of reshaping a life-style. But
a life-style is something which has its deepest sources in the
order of sensibility, in a style of imagination. And so, therefore, though the religious community must attempt to act in
many other areas by way of rehumanizing the mass-situation
of our period, I suspect that the chances of its doing something
really constructive and redemptive will be greatly increased

if it consents to begin by facing the question as to how the human imagination in a mass society may be renewed and reinvigorated. The exciting and difficult challenge that is presented to us by the human scene in our time is that of searching the cultural experience of the modern period and the rich resources of the Christian faith for the first principles of a theology of the imagination that will be prophetically relevant to a world awry. And this, I am suggesting, is a theological effort that will require a new and hitherto largely untried collaboration with the whole community of the modern arts.

What is in view here, however, when I speak of a theology of the imagination, is not anything so grandiose as might require to be spoken of as a "Christian philosophy of art." It is true, of course, that in the theological forum today one sometimes overhears expressions of confidence in the possibility and imperativeness of developing what is called by some a Christian philosophy of art. And though I shall not here attempt fully to explicate the theological grounds from which my own reservations about this kind of project stem, I do want, at least, to say flatly that I do not conceive it to be the business of the Christian, of the man whom Kierkegaard called "the knight of faith," to bully the world into granting its suffrage to some special system of propositions of his own invention. For he does not come into this world from another world like a *deus ex machina*, with a marvelous formula that can unlock all the entanglements of human culture. No, he lives in the historical order like all his fellows: the resource on which he relies is simply that particular hope and confidence to which he is given access in this world by reason of what he knows God to have done for this world. And, having this resource, his single vocation is to live, as did Jesus the Lord, in solicitude for, and in openness to, the men to whom he is related by the particular moment in history in which he happens to stand.

The Christian scholar faces the same world that is faced by

all other men; and I believe it is outrageous arrogance for him to assume that his faith provides him with some sort of privileged perspective by means of which he can integrate internally the various fields of culture and then assign to each its proper place in some tidily comprehensive arrangement that will be a Christian map of the modern mind. Indeed, for him even to attempt to produce some special *speculum mentis* for his brethren in the faith is for him profoundly to misunderstand the nature of the intellectual situation in which he must today do his work. And, here, surely the endless multiplication of metaphors based on the I-Thou philosophy of Martin Buber is something which witnesses to a deep and pervasive intuition among the most sensitive men of our age that the fragmentation of modern intellectual life commits us irrevocably to an ethos of encounter and to the stance of attentiveness and listening. It is, I take it, the recognition of precisely this that lies behind Roger Hazelton's recent definition of what the theological enterprise must entail in our time. He turns to the physiological image of the systole and diastole of the human heart and suggests that the work of the Christian theologian is, in a way, analogous to the alternate expansions and contractions of the heart. "There are times," he says, "when Christian faith has to turn inward upon itself, asking what is authentically and ultimately its own kind of truth. Then theology becomes an essay in self-discovery and self-definition." But then there are other times when "it becomes imperative for theologians to move out into the world again, on the basis of this self-understanding, seeking out and coming to grips with those modes of truth from which earlier they had strategically withdrawn." And Dr. Hazelton is alert to the fact that it is into this second phase that the theological community is moving. Nor does he see the reasons for this as being wholly cultural in character, for he takes careful cognizance of what it is in the nature of Christian faith itself that requires the attitude of attentiveness and listening to the world of culture. "Living within the circle of faith," he says, "involves the most drastic sort of exposure to unwelcome experience and unfamiliar truth. It finds charity and hope to be not simply moral but also intellectual virtues."[6]

So it would seem to behoove the Christian in his intellectual existence not to segregate himself from anyone and not to suppose that he has been given exclusive charge of the truth about any segment of human reality. In other words, he had better not come prancing into the forums of our cultural life with a Christian system of aesthetics or with a Christian system of psychology or with a Christian system of anything else. For the world is one, the same for the Christian as for all other men of whatever persuasion: if Christ is truly the *Logos*, then He is witnessed to in all apprehensions of truth, whether they occur within a framework of Christian concern or not. And, this being the case, the Christian theologian will not be in a hurry to sponsor any particular system as necessarily *the* Christian way of ordering the data in a given field of inquiry. For he will understand that the fundamental issue for Christian thought pertains not to any conceptual structure but rather, as Ronald Gregor Smith of Glasgow has said, to the question "Whence do we receive?"[7] So, then, instead of attempting to put forward anything that might be called a Christian philosophy of art, it may well be that at present the more fruitful task for the Christian humanist is the more modest task of clearly discerning what in fact the function of art truly is and how it touches the kind of imagination of reality that is distinctively Christian.

Now, in attempting to define what it is the ultimate office of art to do, it is important to avoid at least one of the answers which has continually recurred in the history of aesthetics; and this is the doctrine which, in one way or another, asserts that a work of art is an expression of the artist's subjectivity, or, as it has often been put, of his emotion. The perennial

6. Roger Hazelton, *New Accents in Contemporary Theology* (New York, Harper, 1960), pp. 11–12.
7. Ronald Gregor Smith, "A Theological Perspective of the Secular," *The Christian Scholar*, 43 (1960), 14.

attractiveness of this doctrine is, doubtless, in large part a result of the fact that we know both the creative process and the aesthetic experience to be suffused with emotion; and when a work of art is of unquestioned greatness, it does indeed very often stem from and elicit emotion of the intensest sort. But, however much emotion may be a factor both in the act of artistic creation and in the act of aesthetic appreciation, the fact remains that, finally, all emotionalist theories of art are both internally illogical and essentially untrue to the experience that we actually have when we are in the presence of a work of art that is capable of deeply engaging the imagination. The emotionalist theory is internally illogical, because it succeeds in doing precisely what it is unreasonable to expect an aesthetic theory to do—namely, to dissolve itself into some field of discourse that is not aesthetical but something else. That is to say, in viewing the work of art as significant because of what it tells us about the emotional condition of the artist, an expressionist aesthetic is always tending to convert aesthetics into a branch of psychology and thus to destroy the vital nerve of its own integrity as an independent field of humanistic inquiry. I speak of the emotionalist theory of art as untrue to our profoundest aesthetic experience because I am convinced that this is an experience which we deem to be of such high importance not at all by reason of any information it conveys about the artist, for what is exhilarating in our encounter with an authentic work of art is always the clarification and deepening we feel in our perception of the realities that constitute our world-environment. The aesthetic experience might be said always to involve an experience of what Paul Tillich calls "the shock of being,"[8] and this may be why Jacques Maritain tells us that, "Poetry is ontology."

Of course, when Maritain speaks of poetry as ontology, he does not intend to imply that the operation which the poet performs is identical, in its kind or agency, with the operation

8. See Paul Tillich, *The Protestant Era* (1948), p. 85; also *Systematic Theology,* 1 (1951), pp. 110–15, 163; both published by the University of Chicago Press.

that is performed by a philosopher. For, unlike the philosopher, the poet does not deal with *generalizations* about anything at all: his mode of statement, as Susanne Langer says in
Feeling and Form, is a "nondiscursive" mode. He does not discourse, for example, about the mortality of the human creature
with the funereal air of a young parson: no, Shakespeare
simply says:

> Golden lads and girls all must,
> As chimney-sweepers, come to dust.

Nor does he talk about the internal complications of the mind
in the labored, discursive manner of the academic psycholo-
gist: no, Hopkins tells us:

> O the mind, mind has mountains; cliffs of fall
> Frightful, sheer, no-man-fathomed. Hold them cheap
> May who ne'er hung there. Nor does long our small
> Durance deal with that steep or deep.

In short, the poet's purpose is to reveal to us the stark irrevocability of things as they are. And "things" is the word we
must use, for it is with things that the poetic transaction is carried on, since, as I suspect, it is in things that Being has its location. It is the poet's habit to be fascinated with *the singular*
—with the particular event, the unrepeatable experience, the
unique reality. "The texture of poetry is of actual things,"
says Hugh McCarron in his fine little book *Realization*. And
we should not forget that Homer dealt with the ocean and
Wordsworth with the farmland and Gerard Manley Hopkins
with "the dearest freshness deep down things." So, too, has
the imagination of all true poets been captured by things, by
that which is *other than* the human mind. Indeed, it is "the
wonder and mystery of art," as it is also of religion in the last
analysis, that it "is the revelation of something 'wholly other'
by which the inexpressible loneliness of thinking is broken
and enriched."

Poetry does not, characteristically, handle universals: instead, as H. D. Lewis has remarked, it "uncovers for us the

character of particular things in the starkness and strangeness of their being what they are."[9] And this is why the scientist, and the philosopher who conceives of philosophy as a handmaiden of science, tend to view the poet with misgivings, for the poet remains incorrigibly devoted to celebrating that rich complexity of the singular which always resists domestication within the abstract systems of scientific and philosophic ideas. We have long said that poetry's great gift to man is an affair of *katharsis,* and it may well be that that experience involves, fundamentally, the profound relief that is to be had when we succeed in gaining such release from the prison of the mind as enables us simply to contemplate the intractable givenness of reality, as this objectiveness transcends all our scientific and philosophic propositions about it, and our efforts at poetic evocation of it, making its majesty known through what Hegel called the "concrete universal."

Now, of course, modern aestheticians since Kant have often said something quite different about art—namely (as A. C. Bradley put it), that "its nature is to be not a part, nor yet a copy, of the real world . . . but to be a world by itself, independent, complete, autonomous." And this too is true. Indeed, here we come upon what is perhaps the central paradox that art presents. For, on the one hand, we must never forget that it does establish a world of its own, and, as Bradley said, "to possess it fully, you must enter that world, conform to its laws, and ignore for the time the beliefs, aims, and particular conditions which belong to you in the other world of reality."[10] On the other hand, it is equally true (and true perhaps in a very much larger order of magnitude) that the greatest and most vital art always drives us beyond itself and makes us contemplate anew, with a shock of discovery, the permanence and glory and strangeness of the circumambient world. Its purpose is to stir and quicken within us an awareness of realities that impinge upon us from beyond ourselves. It wants,

9. Lewis, *Morals and Revelation,* pp. 241, 212.
10. A. C. Bradley, *Oxford Lectures on Poetry* (London, Macmillan, 1909), p. 5.

as it were, to make all things new, in order that we might marvel at the sheer thereness of them, at the fact that they exist in one way rather than in a thousand other possible ways. "To know facts as facts in the ordinary way has, indeed, no particular power or worth. But," H. D. Lewis says, "a quickening of our awareness of the irrevocability by which a thing is what it is has such power, and it is . . . the very soul of art."[11] For the poet, as Marianne Moore puts it, is a "literalist of the imagination" who presents "for inspection 'imaginary gardens with real toads in them.' " That is, although he creates a kind of fiction, it is a fiction intended to be a vehicle by means of which there may be conveyed to us a haunting sense of some otherness in reality which impinges upon us and with which we must risk a confrontation.

Now I wonder if it is not precisely this sense of otherness in reality to which religious faith itself conduces. Gregor Smith tells us that our ultimate theological concern has to do with what is not ourselves, with what we "do not and never can possess at all," with what comes to us "all the time from beyond."[12] And this is indeed the import of vital religion. Becket, in Eliot's *Murder in the Cathedral*, says at one point:

> Only
> The fool, fixed in his folly, may think
> He can turn the wheel on which he turns.

And it is some such realization as this that all great religion promotes: it brings us news of a reality beyond all the extremities of human thought and calculation, and it speaks of a world which moves to "a rhythm which is neither the strophe nor the antistrophe of our mortal music."[13] So, though a certain kind of Philistine hostility to the arts may sometimes be expressed under the guise of having religion's sanction, the truth of the matter is that both art and religious faith share a

11. Lewis, pp. 241, 242.
12. Smith, p. 15.
13. M. Chaning-Pearce, *The Terrible Crystal* (New York, Oxford University Press, 1941), p. 143.

common intention to summon us into the presence of what is other than, and transcendent to, the human mind; and, in this, they provide each other with a kind of mutual confirmation.

But, in the particular kind of faith that Christianity entails, it is not simply sheer otherness that is confronted, however much the early teachings of Karl Barth may have seemed to represent this as being the Christian's situation. For, in the world of Christian experience, the otherness which confronts and which challenges man becomes luminously transparent in the incarnate Word of God which was Jesus Christ Himself. Which is to say that, for the Christian imagination, the ultimate reality—which is the reality of God—is disclosed in the person and in the life of Jesus Christ. And this means that, when human life is understood within the terms of the Christian faith, the primary axiom of all thought henceforward becomes the premise that what it is important for man to know about the meaning of his existence is made manifest in Jesus the Lord. In Him all Christian reflection finds its basic fulcrum, for He is the transparent center and focus of that disturbing otherness which surrounds us and pursues us and requires of us an appropriate acknowledgment.

There is no one to whom I have been more indebted for deepening my understanding of this central reality of Christian faith than to Dietrich Bonhoeffer. Above all else, what I owe to Bonhoeffer is the realization that what we meet in Jesus Christ is not the old metaphysical riddle of how the two natures, the divine and the human, could co-inhere in one person. Nor should it be supposed that Bonhoeffer's refusal to fidget over this ancient puzzle was the result of any intellectual indolence which made him want to find excuses for evading the hard, exacting labor of reading the history of Christian theology. Indeed, it was just as a result of the most careful study of the theological tradition that he reached a conclusion the revolutionary consequences of which for Christian thought in our time are only beginning to be felt. His conclusion was that on this one point the tradition has often been woefully misguided: for, said he, what we meet in Jesus Christ is not a metaphysical enigma but the simple fact of a human life that was totally pledged in responsibility for others, a life indeed so concentrated in the selflessness of its concern for all other life that it had the consequence of disclosing to the community of faith the tremendous fact that in His life the essential structure of all life had been revealed. And to this essential structure of responsible life as bound to man and to God Bonhoeffer applied the term "deputyship." For this, he declared, is the form that life takes when it is lived responsibly: one person or one group of persons acts *for* another: when a "father acts for the children, working for them, caring for them, interceding, fighting and suffering for them . . . in a real sense he is their deputy." Indeed, whenever and wherever life surrenders itself in obedience to the needs and claims of other life, there you have deputyship. And here, said Bonhoeffer, is the essential truth about Jesus Christ, that He "lived in deputyship for us as the incarnate Son of God," and, since "His living, His action and His dying was deputyship," in Him we have "the responsible person *par excellence*": "in Him there is fulfilled what the living, the action and the suffering of men ought to be."[14]

When Paul in his *Epistle to the Philippians* (1:21) tells us that "to me to live is Christ," he is simply saying, both for himself and for other men, that, insofar as we do truly live, we live in and through Christ, for He *is* life. That is, life is deputyship, or—as it was put by the Jewish thinker Martin Buber, who had a remarkable gift for expressing a sense of reality deeply akin to the Christian—real life is "meeting."[15] This is what Christ reveals the fundamental form of reality to be. And faith, as Bonhoeffer taught us to understand, is not so much believing difficult propositions about ghostly things as it is life lived in "correspondence" with the form that Christ

14. Bonhoeffer, *Ethics*, pp. 194–95.
15. See Martin Buber, *I and Thou*, trans. Ronald Gregor Smith (Edinburgh, Clark, 1937).

disclosed reality to have: the real man, as he liked to say, is "the man for others."

Now I have spoken of the dimension of otherness into which we are brought by both art and religious faith. But, as I have said, in the Christian apprehension of reality, this is an otherness whose essential character is disclosed in the person and in the life of Jesus Christ. For in Him the Christian imagination beholds the fundamental form of reality—which, adopting a central term of the late Charles Williams, we may call "exchange,"[16] or, following Martin Buber, meeting; or which we may call deputyship or, as Dietrich Bonhoeffer sometimes spoke of it, "life together."

When, however, we move from any authentically Christian account of life to that which is recorded in the representative art and literature of our period, it becomes immediately apparent that here a quite different form of reality is presented as normative in human experience. Not life together, but life fractured and broken into isolateness and solitude and loneliness: this is the reality which makes up the special kind of pathos that we meet in the most characteristic art of our time.

From the painting of this century one recalls, for example— and inevitably—those great Cubist canvases of the early Picasso in which the human image is either shattered utterly or is forsaken altogether for the pastiche of newspaper clippings and odd bits of junk extracted from some scrap heap. Or, there are those dreadful and wonderfully fascinating double-faced images which he was painting in the nineteen-thirties and which figure forth the awful dragons of the inner life that must be captured in us all. And, then, there is that beautiful and horrible immensity in black and white and gray, the *Guernica* mural, which brings to a kind of climax the scenes of disorder which the artists of our time have painted; it is a canvas which is ostensibly about a particular moment in the modern agony but which, once we have really confronted it,

16. See Charles Williams, *The Image of the City—And Other Essays* (London, Oxford University Press, 1958), Sec. V.

makes us know that it is about the whole eschatological furnace of our age. It has sometimes been said that what is most essential in Picasso is a "taste for paroxysm," but, in a way, this seems also to be what is most essential in such men as Kokoschka and Beckmann and Rouault, who were his contemporaries, and in the later generation of Pollock and de Kooning, whose vision is felt with especial immediacy at the present time. Indeed, these and many others have often been navigators negotiating a voyage that has skirted most narrowly the brink of the chaos which has threatened to overwhelm us all.

And not only have our painters fought battles with the dragons of the inner life, but so too have our poets and our novelists and dramatists. The age has been rife with nervous disorder and panic, with exile and excruciating anxieties. And it should therefore be no occasion of surprise when these are the themes that we encounter in our literature. Here is a sentence, for example, from a novel, *On This Side Nothing*, by the English writer, Alex Comfort, and it takes us immediately into the ethos which the representative writers of our age have been exploring: "I saw the same fear in her face that I should have felt if a stranger called at night, the world-wide twentieth-century fear which one sees wherever one knocks unexpectedly at any door." This is the face of the contemporary hero, whether one encounters him in the plays of Beckett and Ionesco, or in the novels of Faulkner and Camus, or in the poetry of Penn Warren and Gottfried Benn. Here and there, to be sure, there have been a few writers—like Eliot and Edith Sitwell of the older generation, or Auden and Christopher Fry of the middle generation, or Robert Lowell of a still younger group—who found sustenance in a traditional faith. But by far the great majority of those on the contemporary scene who exemplify our period-style are writers who live in much the same ambiance as that with which we associate the great classic moderns, Kafka and Pound and Joyce and Hemingway. For the fundamental form of the human reality, as they report upon it, is that of disruption and anxiety and nostalgia and loneliness.

When, therefore, the Christian community faces the whole body of testimony issuing from much of the great art of the modern period, it is confronted by a diametrical opposition between the form of reality that it knows to be the true norm of human existence and that which tends generally to be cited by the artists of our time. Yet surely it would be a great mistake for churchmen simply to reject this testimony and to withdraw into the stiff, imperious certitudes of those theologians who write systems of Church dogmatics and who expatiate on the divine-human encounter. Indeed, were this to be the prevailing Christian response to the modern movement in art, nothing would more tellingly indicate that ours is today a Church which has forgotten the Cross and all that it implies for Christian participation in the life of culture. For if, in the words of Charles Gore, the Church is an "extension and perpetuation of the Incarnation in the world"[17] (and the formula has, I suppose, at best a limited usefulness), then its relation to the world must be wholly governed by God's relation to the world, as this was disclosed in Christ Himself, and most especially in His Crucifixion. In other words, the Church is the community that lives under the Cross—it is the community which knows the fundamental form of reality to be that of deputyship, of living and acting for others. It is also, of course, the community in which there is knowledge of the "last things,"—of the fact that the final and ultimate word to be pronounced on the human situation is that man shall be justified by grace and faith alone. But, when it seeks the kind of profound identification with the world that the message of the Crucifixion demands, it may then, for the very

17. Charles Gore, *The Incarnation of the Son of God* (London, John Murray, 1891), p. 219. The formula is of limited usefulness because, though it does a rough kind of justice to the doctrine of the Mystical Body, it very seriously fails to make adequate provision for the possibility of the Church itself falling under judgment.

sake of the ultimate truth about human existence, choose not to speak about last things but rather to open itself up to what Dietrich Bonhoeffer called "the things which go before the last things"—those difficult "penultimate" experiences of humanity which are the real *preparatio* for the Gospel of Jesus Christ.[18] Indeed, the Christian community should never fail to heed Bonhoeffer's wise warning against speaking of the last things too soon. "I don't think it is Christian," he said, "to want to get to the New Testament too soon and too directly."[19] And what he meant is simply that if the Christian community closets itself in safety away from what is broken and problematic in human life then the ultimate message of the Gospel will never be grasped in its *relevance* to man's deepest predicaments. Christ's coming in grace is, to be sure, the very last thing, but we shall perceive the power and the appositeness of this ultimacy only insofar as we remain attentive to everything that is penultimate in the human story.

Therefore, on the particular frontier of culture which is here in view, the task of those who are custodians of the Christian faith in our time is not, I think, to invent something called a Christian *philosophy* of art, and thus to add to the Babel of conflicting philosophies which so much oppresses us today. We shall want, I should think, a vigorous Christian criticism in the various fields of art, and there are signs, particularly in the field of literature, that this is an effort which is beginning to be undertaken with intelligence and discrimination—and we shall want to search after something like a theology of the imagination. But a Christian philosophy of art, in the sense of a systematic phenomenology of aesthetic facts which consistently proceeds from Christian presuppositions, is not to be expected from anyone on the theological scene today of whom I have any knowledge; and I suspect that there are difficult jurisdictional questions of a theoretical order that may, in principle, rule out even the possibility of such a project. But, were it theoretically possible and were it something which we

18. See Bonhoeffer, *Ethics*, pp. 84–91.
19. Bonhoeffer, *Letters*, p. 50.

might reasonably expect the best theological intelligence of our day in time to deliver, I should still, from a strategic standpoint, question its real value at this particular juncture in our cultural life. For that which is most needed, I believe, is for theological interpreters to keep the Church alive to what in the nature of its own faith requires it to be attentive to all the somber reports and prophecies and maledictions that the arts in our time are uttering. And, if this effort is attended with success, so that the Christian community does really appear once again to be a community of deputyship, of those who are for others, then it may well be that the artist may be persuaded to move beyond what is penultimate to the things that are really the last things.

Chapter Seven SOCIETY
AND THE SELF
IN RECENT AMERICAN LITERATURE
—*for Ralph Ellison*

In Romano Guardini's famous little book, *The Spirit of the Liturgy*, there is a chapter in which we are asked to think of the Church's liturgy as a kind of play, as a kind of sacred game. Mngr. Guardini is, of course, aware that this is a perspective that will be offensive to those grave and earnest rationalists in the Church for whom every aspect of its life must have a moral purpose: they will be quick to suppose that to view the liturgy in this way is to reduce it to a mere theatrical trifle, and they will therefore want to insist that the Church's liturgical actions are channels of grace and serve the indispensable purpose of the soul's renewal and edification. But, in his sprightly wisdom, Mngr. Guardini denies that the liturgy is informed by "the austere guidance of the sense of purpose." The prayers, the gestures, the garments, the colors, the holy vessels, the complicated arrangements of the calendar are all, he asserts, simply "incomprehensible when . . . measured by the objective standard of strict suitability for a purpose." For the liturgy, in quite the same way as a child's play, has no purpose. "The child, when it plays, does not aim at anything. It has no purpose. It does not want to do anything but to exercise its youthful powers, [to] pour forth its life in an aimless series of movements, words and actions," "all of which is purposeless, but full of meaning nevertheless. . . . That is what play means; it is life, pouring itself forth without an aim." And, similarly, the liturgy "speaks measuredly and melodiously," "employs formal, rhythmic gestures," "is clothed in colours and garments foreign to everyday life," "is carried out in places and at hours which have been co-ordinated and systematised. . . . It is in the highest sense the life of a child, in which everything is picture, melody and song." It is a pouring forth of "the sacred, God-given life of the soul": it is a kind of holy play in which the soul, with utter abandon, learns how "to waste time for the sake of God."[1]

The liturgy, in short,—and Mngr. Guardini is aware of the implication here—is a form of art. For whenever the human spirit, in a deep and radical way, apprehends through the configuration of things and events a threshold beyond which is a Something More, the taproot and fecund abyss of every-thing that has reality—whenever the human spirit is granted such a moment of contact with the unplumbed Mystery from which everything is sprung—its most primitive impulse, in Jonathan Edwards' phrase, is simply to "consent to Being." This consent expresses itself at once in terms of reverence and homage and in terms of the kind of play that we call art: indeed, in their most primitive—that is, in their purest and most essential—forms, the religious and the artistic as modes of response to the fullness of reality, though distinguishable from each other, are virtually inseparable. For it is what Paul Tillich calls the shock of being that forms the matrix out of which both are born—in, as it were, the same moment, each participating immanently in the dynamism of the other.

Rudolf Otto is, of course, the great phenomenologist in modern tradition of this primitive experience of "shock" or "stupor" before the plenteous Mystery of Being, and, though he was primarily interested in its distinctively religious con-sequences, he was by no means unalive to the fact that it is also this same shock that calls forth and energizes the artistic impulse. He was also aware that primitive art was motivated by fear of the unknown forces of nature, the desire to placate hostile powers, and the desire to arrest the flux of existence by

1. Romano Guardini, *The Spirit of the Liturgy*, trans. Ada Lane (New York, Sheed and Ward, 1937), pp. 92, 95–96, 98–99, 101–102, 104, 106.

creating images of stability and rest. But he believed, as I also am persuaded, that "the change to the motive of *expression* must have been from the outset far too vividly stimulated not to [have occurred] . . . at a very early date."[2] And when one looks, say, at Paleolithic rock engravings of the Aurignacian period or at the rock-paintings of the Bushmen, one cannot help but feel that what these works express fundamentally is a kind of dance performed by the imagination, not for any purpose at all but only as a spirited utterance of consent to Being-itself.

Now it is this most primitive aspect of art—which has never been completely lost—that has doubtless led many theorists to interpret art as being essentially a form of play: this notion has cropped up in the thought of such otherwise divergent figures as Plato and Aristotle, Schiller and Hegel, Freud and Santayana, and it seems to have commended itself again and again as a fundamental hypothesis about the nature of art. The latest echoing of it that I can recall occurs, not very surprisingly, in an essay by Karl Barth on Mozart, in the course of which this distinguished Swiss theologian wants in various ways to say that the most remarkable gift that Mozart has to offer us is the strangely exciting and wonderful kind of "childlike play" that is in his music.[3] And I speak of not being surprised that Dr. Barth should take this view of Mozart, for his is a way of relating Christianity to culture which, on the side of faith, is not prepared to brook any competition at all from culture so far as the definition of man's nature and destiny is concerned; and thus, on the basis of his very radical kind of Protestantism, it only becomes possible to enfranchise art under the firmament of Christian value when it is accepted merely as a form of play.

This is a conception of art to which art itself conforms in some fashion—for as long as Being is in view. For, when it is

2. Rudolf Otto, *The Idea of the Holy*, trans. John W. Harvey (New York, Oxford University Press, 1943), p. 68.

3. Karl Barth, "Wolfgang Amadeus Mozart," in *Religion and Culture: Essays in Honor of Paul Tillich*, ed. Walter Leibrecht (New York, Harper, 1959), p. 66.

born out of an easy commerce between the artist's imagination and the mysterious depths of reality, and when it lives under "the sunlit regime of the Logos,"[4] then it is easy and unstrained: then it is all melody and song—and play—even when the song speaks of what is most profoundly tragic in life. And this may be at least a part of what Baudelaire had in mind when he said, "Great poetry is essentially *stupid, it believes,* and that is what makes its glory and its force."[5] For when art enjoys the kind of security that proceeds from a basic sense of the ontological simplicity of the world, it is relieved of any necessity to develop metaphysical aspirations. But when it loses any certitude of an irrefragable connection between man and the inner life of the world, when the deep Mystery of Being can no longer be known through affective union and connaturality, then art undergoes a *crise de conscience:* it suffers the wound that is inflicted by a time of dearth, when the light of heaven has gone into eclipse and the sun is lost. And, in the muddle that ensues, art loses its primitive innocence; it can then no longer afford to be "stupid," for, in order to survive at all, it must now take the great hazardous step into that chilly, inclement region of its period's deepest perplexity—there, as Hölderlin says, to "name" the gods all over again. In this region, where "the absence of God moves about . . . with the intimacy of a presence,"[6] art ceases, in any central and decisive sense, to be an affair of play, for here, as Eliot says in "East Coker" and "Burnt Norton," the poet is desperately

> Trying to learn to use words, and every attempt
> Is a wholly new start, and a different kind of failure. . . .
> And so each venture
> Is a new beginning, a raid on the inarticulate

and always:

4. Maritain, *Creative Intuition,* p. 231.
5. Charles Baudelaire, *Œuvres posthumes* (Paris, Mercure de France, 1908), p. 167.
6. Hopper, "Naming of the Gods," p. 158.

Words strain,
Crack and sometimes break, under the burden,
Under the tension.

This is, of course, the precarious region that the artist in our time inhabits—the region, that is, where, being wounded by our transgressions and bruised by our chastisement, he seeks to make his work a glass of vision through which new orders of meaning and hope may be discerned. It was perhaps inevitable that the artists of the word should play the leading part in this; and, among their various forms, it is undoubtedly the novel that has been the most effective agent of the modern imagination. Indeed, the regularity with which the prognosticators of the literary life annually debate whether or not the novel may be dying or already dead is perhaps itself a testimony to our anxiousness about the health of that form of art which seems more fully to comprehend the variousness and complexity of human experience than any other. "Being a novelist," said D. H. Lawrence, "I consider myself superior to the saint, the scientist, the philosopher and the poet. The novel is the one bright book of life." And insofar as Lawrence speaks for the modern novelist generally, as indeed he very considerably does, it must be said that his is a claim that we have been prepared, particularly on the American scene, more readily to grant than similar claims coming from artists working in the other great established forms of art.

American drama, it is generally agreed, continues, as it has over a long period, to be in a seriously bad way. If Tennessee Williams ever succeeds in outgrowing the frivolousness and vulgarity that have disfigured so much of his work, there is reason to suppose that the creator of *The Glass Menagerie* and *Streetcar* might well become a major presence in the modern theatre; and Thornton Wilder, in going his own quite special way, has achieved an honorable, if minor, dignity among the best playwrights of our time. But, among our living contemporaries, there is no one else whom one would dare to propose as belonging to the company of Pirandello and Brecht and

Sartre and Beckett;[7] and, among non-living contemporaries, there is only the uncertain case of O'Neill. Our poetry is, of course, another matter, and one about which a national pride is permissible. For, among the great magisterial figures of our period, we can lay claim to Eliot and Pound; nor can we forget in this galaxy Robert Frost and Hart Crane, E. E. Cummings and Marianne Moore and William Carlos Williams, and many others; and, in the current generation of Robert Lowell, there is a vigor nowhere surpassed on the contemporary scene. Frost is, of course, the only poet who has played any large role in the life of our culture, for the broad commonalty of the American people—but he has generally been admired for reasons bearing only a very slight relation to his actual achievement. So, when one thinks of the kind of quasi-scriptural eminence that belongs to such works as *The Great Gatsby* and *The Sun Also Rises* and *The Sound and the Fury*, it is difficult to resist the conclusion that in America the novel has exerted a kind of pressure on thought and sensibility more decisive than that which could be claimed by any other department of our literature.

The high prestige of the novel in American cultural life is, in part, a consequence of the impoverishment of our theatre and, in part, of the speciality of idiom and reference that has made our poetry something whose vigor was not readily perceptible in the national forum. But, more positively considered, it is doubtless in far larger part a consequence of our having supposed that the very spaciousness of the form permitted it to render a unique justice to the breadth and diversity of the land and its multi-faceted life. For a people by whom "experience" has been held in such high regard as it has amongst ourselves, the tendency of the novel in all its classic expressions to obliterate the distinction between art and experience has surely been a great point in its favor in the American climate. It has appeared to be a form of art that has a special

7. The one highly gifted newcomer is Edward Albee, but, despite the rich promise of his initial work, his career is perhaps only just beginning.

tolerance of the rough, ragged contingency and the viscous untidiness of historical existence. And where the deepest national feeling is, as Heidegger would say, that of having been "thrown" into history, it was perhaps inevitable that those artists using what Lawrence called the book of life should win something like a bardic status. So to press forward an inquiry into the testimony that is being made by American fiction at the present time is to negotiate a transaction which ought to yield evidence of a very crucial sort.

The terrain of recent American fiction is, however, one on which it is difficult to descry signs and landmarks that give an easy sense of orientation. But in the response that was made to one fairly recent event we may find at least a suggestion of what is distinctive about our literary dispensation of the last ten or fifteen years. I have in mind the gasp of resentful astonishment that was heard in 1962 when the news was released over our radio and television networks that John Steinbeck had been awarded the Nobel Prize. I have no doubt but that Arthur Mizener's guess comes close to the truth, that "the time had [simply] come around for some American to receive the award, and among Europeans Steinbeck turned out to be, for one or another reason, the most widely read American author, just as Sinclair Lewis was when he received the . . . Prize in 1930."[8] I do not, however, have any desire to offer an affront to Mr. Steinbeck, and the appropriateness of the award is not the issue with which I am presently concerned. Although if Mr. Mizener is right in thinking that 1962 was the American year, it does seem more than a little strange (if the award is intended to have any real cultural meaning) that, at a time when both Robert Frost and William Carlos Williams were still alive and neither had been offered this garland, it should have gone to Mr. Steinbeck. What I want chiefly to remark, however, is my having been persuaded at the time that the amazement that was so gen-

8. Arthur Mizener, "Does a Moral Vision of the Thirties Deserve a Nobel Prize?" *The New York Times Book Review* (December 9, 1962), p. 45.

erally expressed sprang not out of a sense of incommensurateness between the *éclat* of the Prize and the real importance of Mr. Steinbeck's achievement as an artist, but sprang rather out of a simple disbelief that the embattled social humanism that animated *The Grapes of Wrath* and *In Dubious Battle* could, as an attitude toward the world, be adjudged by anyone today as worthy of a large and handsome honor.

Now it is just such a disbelief that comprises a sort of phenomenon, a sort of tendency, in American cultural life today, most especially in our literature where it begins to be apparent that the ruling principle is a profound lack of faith in the possibility of the great, gross reality of society ever becoming anything with which the self might do any kind of significant business. Indeed, Norman Mailer—whose work presents a central example of our recent fiction—tells us that, since we are fated to live in an age which surrounds us on every side with death and destruction, "the only life-giving answer is to accept the terms of death, to live with death as immediate danger, to divorce oneself from society, to exist without roots, to set out on that uncharted journey into the rebellious imperatives of the self."[9] And it is the resolute intention to enfranchise precisely these imperatives that appears now to have been the governing motive behind our most characteristic literature of the last fifteen years. For, when we all feel the sense of impotence that we often do today before the events of our collective life, and when, therefore, the social and political order—particularly in its international aspect—is felt only as a source of gratuitous oppression and unmanageable danger, then those whose nerves are most exposed will perform a motion of recoil; and, given the disorder in the State and the unavailability of the Church except to a minority, their retreat will be into the self. Their literary spokesman will discover his task to be largely one of defining the self in relation to "the massive brute social fact . . . that surrounds and threatens to

9. Mailer, *Advertisements for Myself* (New York, New American Library, 1960), p. 304.

overwhelm it," and surely in some such way as this it has come to be the case that, "for the advanced writer of our time, the self is his supreme, even sole, referent."[10] To him the action that promises to have the most deeply renovating effect on human life is an action of entrenchment behind a barricade whose purpose is to afford protection against whatever may threaten to undo the self. "Keep your hands off my soul," says a character in James Purdy's *Malcolm* (1959). And a similar demand, as R. W. B. Lewis has also noticed,[11] is expressed in many American books of the last few years: it is the whole burden of the embittered deliverance that is hurled at the world by the nameless protagonist of Ralph Ellison's *Invisible Man*: it is the essential core of what Salinger's Holden Caulfield has to say to us in *The Catcher in the Rye*: it is the requirement of the hero of John Knowles' *A Separate Peace*, and also, in a way, of Cass Kinsolving in William Styron's *Set This House on Fire*, and of that engaging gentleman whose adventures Saul Bellow chronicles in *Herzog*. "Keep your hands off my soul": it is with this simple and radical demand that the world is faced by the most representative figures in American literature of the present time.

The whole style of mind and art of which I take James Purdy's *Malcolm* as a convenient example has of course had to suffer the exactions necessitated by its special bias. And ever since critics such as John Aldridge and Malcolm Cowley initiated discussion at the end of the forties, of our postwar fiction, they, and others, have increasingly noticed how large an area of experience our novelists are prompted to neglect by this preoccupation with the sovereign reality of the self. Already in 1954, Mr. Cowley, for example, was observing that the scene of the new fiction

> is seldom one of the centers where policy decisions are made; it is never Capitol Hill or the Pentagon or the board-room of

10. Diana Trilling, "Norman Mailer," *Encounter*, 19 (November 1962), 46.
11. R. W. B. Lewis, "American Letters: A Projection," *The Yale Review*, 51 (1962), 222.

any corporation or political London or Paris. . . . Preferring to deal with private lives, the new fiction is likely to have a remote and peripheral scene, for example . . . a lonely ranch in Colorado, a village in East Texas, a small town in Georgia, various plantation houses in Louisiana and Mississippi (all rotting into the dark loam), a country house in Maine . . . an abandoned summer hotel, two beach resorts full of homosexuals, several freshwater colleges.

And, in a similar way, Mr. Cowley also commented on the defining quality of the characters in this literature—which he specified as one of disaffiliation. The characters are, he said,

distinguished by their lack of a functional relationship with American life. They don't sow or reap, build, mine, process, promote or sell, repair, heal, plead, administer, or legislate. . . . One widely observed feature of present-day America is that the lives of most individuals are defined by their relations with an interlocking series of institutions—for example, government bureaus, churches, schools and universities, the armed services, labor unions, chambers of commerce, farm bureaus . . . and, for most of us, that center of our daily activities, the office. But characters in the new fiction are exceptional persons who keep away from offices . . . and are generally as unattached as Daniel Boone. . . . The characters likely to be treated at length are students of both sexes, young artists and writers, gentlemen on their travels, divorced or widowed mothers, gay boys, neurotic bitches . . . old women on their deathbeds, and preternaturally wise little girls.[12]

At the time Mr. Cowley wrote these lines, as at the present time, exceptions here and there could be cited as examples that refuse to fit his generalizations. These are not, however, exceptions that are to be drawn from the sleek entertainments-for-the-millions that are produced by the Cameron Hawleys

12. Malcolm Cowley, *The Literary Situation* (New York, Viking Press, 1954), pp. 45–47.

and Herman Wouks and Sloan Wilsons and Allen Drurys; for these journeymen, to be sure, use a "public" scene and handle characters affiliated with the centers of power and decision in our society, but they are writers whose unconcern with anything beyond the old stockpot of hackneyed experience and comment disqualifies them from consideration as serious artists. The exceptions—those writers who do not create "a tidy room in Bedlam"—are rather to be found in such artists as the Ralph Ellison of *Invisible Man*, the Bernard Malamud of *The Assistant*, the Frederick Buechner of *The Return of Ansel Gibbs*, the James Baldwin of *Another Country*, the Bellow of *Augie March*—for these are all writers whose focus is on the self, but on the self at that point of juncture where it encounters a significant social reality.

And in one other particular it may also be necessary to complicate somewhat Mr. Cowley's perspective. For many of those writers whose work exhibits the extreme speciality of material that he complains of do yet manage, however obliquely, to handle that material in such a way as to situate the problem of selfhood within a larger compass. One thinks, for example, of Saul Bellow's *Henderson the Rain King*, whose American millionaire protagonist is so dedicated to the inner necessities of his personal being that a voice within him is constantly crying, "I want, I want, I want." And this solitary proficient in self-realization, fleeing all attachments and loyalties, goes off to Africa, a place more remote even than any of those which Mr. Cowley enumerates in his list: yet in the African wilderness he discovers the need that we have for some great encounter with reality to "wake the spirit's sleep," and it is apparent that this is a redemptive principle in the light of which he is prepared to make a very radical kind of judgment on the somnolence that pervades his native land. Or one thinks, say, of that holy fool, Haze Motes, the young preacher of the Church Without Christ in Flannery O'Connor's *Wise Blood*, who proclaims the gospel of "no truth behind all truths." This self-ordained backwoods evangelist of an hysterical nihilism lives in darkness: yet, amidst this darkness, he is a "pinpoint of light," whose grotesque extremism of speech and behavior provides a deeply ironical measure of what is really heretical in the smug Philistinism represented by both the conventional heretics and the conventional believers. One also feels a similarly tough and serious realism in quite a different kind of book, in William Styron's brilliant novel of 1960, *Set This House on Fire*, which, through its torrid story of lust and violence and despair in an Italian village on the Mediterranean coast, seems to move toward some large metaphor on the nature of man's dispeace and how his house, afire "with agues and palsies . . . with fevers . . . and heavy apprehensions," may be put in order.

But though such observations as these may be made by way of partially extenuating Mr. Cowley's case, the main thrust of his charge remains essentially sound. For when one thinks of such representative works of the last few years as Truman Capote's *Other Voices, Other Rooms* (1948), Carson McCullers' *The Ballad of the Sad Cafe* (1951), Jean Stafford's *The Catherine Wheel* (1952), Howard Nemerov's *Federigo, Or, The Power of Love* (1954), James Purdy's *Malcolm* (1959), John Updike's *Rabbit, Run* (1960), and J. D. Salinger's *Franny and Zooey* (1961), then it does become apparent that, despite their technical brilliance and moral seriousness, they are all, in one way or another, committed to the registration of the tremors of the self's experience of its own inwardness in an adverse world. And this is a bias, as Mr. Cowley has contended, that deeply inhibits the penetration of the great Bedlam of history that literature risks when it is in full possession of its proper health and courage.

Now it may well be just this confinement to the narrow enclave of the self that makes for the peculiar irony represented by recent American fiction—namely, the irony that a literature committed above all else to the self has yet only very rarely produced any memorable characters. Salinger's Holden Caulfield and Bellow's Augie March, to be sure, have become a part of the furniture of our imaginations—but of how many other characters in American fiction of the postwar period could this be said? Hardly, I suspect, could we make such a claim with respect to any others, with possibly one or two exceptions.

Of course, even for me to remark this fact as a fact of impoverishment is to risk having my bit of testimony utterly discounted as representing an impossibly old-fashioned kind of literary primitivism. For, as I will be told by numerous bright young men teaching literature in the universities, what matters in a novel, what really matters, is "organic development of a thematic structure of images," and the complex subtlety with which "ironies" and "tensions" are held in a poised and delicate balance. This is the dreary patois in which fiction has come to be talked about in our time, and the dominant perspective is one that encourages the supposition that so primitive a quantity as character is of no consequence. For many years, for example, it has been fashionable to patronize the late A. C. Bradley as an example of such a preoccupation with character, in his case the characters of Shakespearean tragedy,[13] as inordinately moves quite beyond the limits of all decorum. And in the very title that he gave to an essay in the early nineteen-thirties— "How Many Children Had Lady Macbeth?"[14]—the English critic L. C. Knights has helped a whole generation to make Bradley and his style of criticism (despite its genuine greatness) the object of a deadly joking.

But, in this regard, we have long been engaged in a very great self-deception—as when, for example, we insist upon talking about *Bleak House* or *Germinal* or *The Portrait of a Lady* or *The Sound and the Fury* exclusively in the terms of "controlling metaphor" and "thematic structure" and "symbolic action." For surely (merely to remark so elementary a fact is embarrassing) one of the great reasons for any adult mind's consenting to devote a large measure of time to reading novels (or any other form of mimetic literature) is our insatiable craving for large images of human engagement in the life of

13. See A. C. Bradley, *Shakespearean Tragedy* (New York, Macmillan, 1904).

14. See L. C. Knights, *Explorations* (New York, George W. Stewart, 1947).

the world, and for images that have the power of increasing our own capacity for life. Nor does the Flaubert who said, *"Madame Bovary, c'est moi,"* stand as the norm of the kind of novelist into whose hands we want to put ourselves. For, when we are simple and honest, we will admit that we are most deeply drawn not to the artist whose personages are merely elements of his own personality but, rather, to him whose characters are a part of Nature and who therefore "make us feel that 'there is a world elsewhere' "[15]—that is, the world of which we are living members—and who show us something of how the human spirit goes about surviving in that world. It is a misfortune that the criticism of our own period takes so slight an interest in character, for, though Aristotle was right to remind us in the *Poetics* that character is only a means to an end, it is surely an indispensable means for effecting in us that liberating exhilaration which it is the peculiar glory of literature to accomplish when it consents to take a serious and steady interest in a Hester Prynne, an Ahab, a Huck Finn, a Jay Gatsby.

There is, I repeat, a notable irony in the fact that a literature so devoted to the self as the novel has been in America over the last two decades should be populated by so many pale and bloodless ghosts and should so generally have failed to produce any sizeable group of memorable characters—rich and full-bodied in their conduct and aspiration and eccentricity. Yet it may be that this failure is the consequence that should have been expected of the kind of retreat from the public sector that has also been a notable feature of this literature. For the self achieves definition only as it pits itself against the hard, recalcitrant stuff of social and political reality: it wins its real identity only through this kind of testing: and a fiction that is not deeply informed by knowledge of this truth is not likely to realize any profound and comprehensive images of human life.

However, the advantage that is gained when fiction finds its

15. John Bayley, *The Characters of Love: A Study in the Literature of Personality* (New York, Basic Books, 1960), p. 280.

ballast in a solid substratum of social reality is nicely illustrated by the literature that is being produced by those young Englishmen who are exactly contemporaneous with the generation of Salinger and Buechner and Purdy and Updike. What is perhaps most immediately noticeable in the novels of this younger generation across the Atlantic is, as Irving Howe remarks, their "quick apprehension and notation of contemporary life."[16] English life since World II has, of course, in many ways been sharply abraded by the entrance into the national polity of a new corps bent on finding "room at the top," the tribe of working-class and lower middle-class boys who were smart and who managed to win scholarships at red-brick universities and who now, having been divorced from their plebeian backgrounds, are pressing their noses against the glass and peeking in at the Establishment—and not merely peeking in but curtly demanding admittance. But these "dissentients," as Kenneth Allsop calls them, though they sullenly, and angrily, clamor for a larger slice of the pie, are also to be distinguished by the kind of dual vision that their alienated position affords. And theirs is of course often a most painful alienation: "they feel a mixture of guilt about renegading from their hereditary background and contempt for the oafish orthodoxy of their families," which means that "they are strangers to their own sort": yet, at the same time, "they are acutely conscious of lacking the arrogant composure of the ruling-class line."[17] And thus, in bringing the promise of "the top" near enough to "the new men" to arouse "great expectations" while yet holding it far enough away to frustrate ambition and desire, the Welfare State has created a knotty social scene, and one which gives the unassimilated a privileged perspective on the whole gamut of contemporary English life. This is the ruling perspective in much of the literature produced by the ablest younger novelists in England since the early fifties, and one's

16. Irving Howe, "Mass Society and Post-Modern Fiction," *Partisan Review*, 26 (1959), 434.
17. Kenneth Allsop, *The Angry Decade* (London, Peter Owen, 1958), Ch. 1; p. 19.

general impression is that the force and cogency of this literature are in large part the consequence of a responsiveness to
social and political actuality that is notably lacking in recent
American literature.

Nor is it at all unlikely that just here we have the chief explanation of how it has come about that there is such energy
and liveliness in many of the chief personages of recent English
fiction: the three young men at the center of William Cooper's
Scenes from Provincial Life,[18] the Jim Dixon of Kingsley
Amis' *Lucky Jim,* the Jake Donaghue of Iris Murdoch's *Under
the Net,* the Joe Lampton of John Braine's *Room at the Top,*
and the Arthur Seaton of Alan Sillitoe's *Saturday Night and
Sunday Morning,* to mention only a few, are the tough,
assertive, tangy figures they are because they know how things
look and feel, how they are organized and what they cost, and
the insolent nerve it takes to get one's proper share. In short,
they live *in* the human polity, they are creatures of history,
and, in them, the mettle of the self has been tried and proven
in the matrix of a dynamic culture: so, as images of what is
stout and vital in man, even under the pressure of partly adverse conditions, they bear the stamp of authenticity, of truth
to contemporary actuality.

It may also be this same openness to the larger scene of contemporary life that gives this literature its vital roughness of
grain and keeps it from achieving the kind of taut fragility of
poetic form that such American books as William Goyen's *The
House of Breath* and Frederick Buechner's *A Long Day's Dying* and Saul Bellow's *Seize the Day* have helped to establish as
a dominant mode of our fiction. And when I speak of our fiction taking on the form of poetry, I do not mean that its
movement has been in the direction of the kind of oddity that
T. S. Eliot chose to praise back in the thirties when he prepared
an Introduction to Djuna Barnes' *Nightwood.* On the contrary,
there is very little indication of any considerable interest

18. Mr. Cooper is somewhat older than "the angry young men," but
his work belongs to their whole ethos. *Scenes from Provincial Life*
(1950) was indeed the immediate forerunner of *Lucky Jim* (1954).

among the most serious American novelists today in what used to be called poetic prose. Though the rhetorical extravagances of James and Faulkner and Penn Warren seem occasionally to have had their influence, the language of this fiction is generally an unpretentious and soberly efficient instrument of exposition and narration. Its poetic character is rather an affair not so much of verbal inventiveness and audacity as of cunningly shaped analogical conceits in dramatic form, of highly selfconscious adaptations of traditional myth and ritual, of crankily nihilistic forms of joking and horseplay, of rigorous concision and stylization in the development of plot and action and character, and of a stringent exclusion of all those great masses of extraneous matter that give to the fiction of a Stendhal or a George Eliot or a Faulkner its special weight and density. One hesitates bluntly to denominate all this as simply a stratagem of evasion, as a kind of dandyism whose uncalculated purpose is to retreat from the inclement weather of our time. Indeed, as Albert Guerard suggested in one of the first attempts to characterize the postwar period in American fiction, it is possible for style to be "an answer to surrounding ambiguity." For, in a period when the course of history seems unalterable by the individual voice, when men are by way of being overwhelmed by the sheer gratuitousness of events, and when human life everywhere has taken on an eschatological cast, it may be "an act of resistance" for the novelist to submit "some small chosen area" to a great deal of control, since in this way at least he can "express his small human identity, the free play of his mind,"[19] and thus in effect express a kind of denial that History or Events or Civilization is all. But what needs also to be said is that, even so, this is a testimony whose muteness of style forfeits much of the masculine force and assertiveness and rhetorical power that the novel, in its most vigorous moments, has taught us to regard as a part of its peculiar genius.

19. Albert J. Guerard, "The Ivory Tower and the Dust Bowl," in *New World Writing*, 3 (New York, New American Library, 1953), 348.

In his brilliant and justly famous essay of 1948, "Art and Fortune," Lionel Trilling ventured the prediction that the novelist of the coming years would tend to forego "consciously literary," "elaborately styled" types of artistic form, and would do so in order to reclaim something of "the headlong, profuse, often careless quality of the novel" with "its bold and immediate grasp on life." "For the modern highly trained literary sensibility, form suggests completeness and the ends tucked in; resolution is seen only as all contradictions equated, and although form thus understood has its manifest charm," Mr. Trilling foresaw the novelist coming to recognize that such a notion of form "will not adequately serve the modern experience."[20] But things have, of course, not gone as Mr. Trilling predicted, and a critic of his sophistication has in all likelihood not been surprised by this fact, since his original statement was doubtless less a prediction than a recommendation of the course by which the novelist might best guarantee the future health of his form.

Yet, at our present remove of a little more than fifteen years from Mr. Trilling's prophecy, though it has not been generally fulfilled in the intervening period, it remains a good course to pin one's faith on, for the renewal of American fiction. And I am not at all convinced that the realization of this course will be furthered—indeed, I rather suspect that it will be hindered —by our granting R. W. B. Lewis the point he has made, that the ambiance of the new American novelists is an irredeemably *post*-Christian dispensation.[21] Among those who like to bandy about the *recherché* catchwords of the moment, there is surely far too much loose talk these days about ours having become a post-Christian world: it is a piece of verbiage that, in a curious way, has suddenly become very modish and pleasurable, but its relevance to religious and cultural actuality is something extremely difficult to specify with precision. And though a thinker of Mr. Lewis's brilliance is not given to loose talk, it is

20. Trilling, *The Liberal Imagination*, pp. 278, 272–73.
21. Lewis, "American Letters," p. 224.

just his customary acuteness that makes us expect him to exert a more critical pressure on the literary imagination in America at the present time.

When one recalls the disintegrated world of Norman Mailer's *Barbary Shore,* John Clellon Holmes' *Go,* Edward Loomis' *The Charcoal Horse,* William Styron's *Set This House on Fire,* and John Updike's *Rabbit, Run*—when one recalls such books as these, in which "the rebellious imperative of the self" is the single and sovereign principle, there can, of course, be no question but that our younger novelists are prepared, many of them, to settle for allegiances which, if not post-Christian, are at least far removed from the full Christian sense of reality in any of its classic versions. But what needs to be noticed is that this alienation from anything resembling the traditional Christian soulscape has carried a very great cost. St. Teresa says, "I require of you only to look." Only to *look.* And this has traditionally been the genius of Incarnational faith when it has been in full possession of its sacramental vision—to empower men to *face,* without flinching, the arduous welter of nature and historical existence, since, frail though the flesh may be, it was proven by the Incarnation to be stout enough for the tabernacling of that than which nothing is more ultimate—namely, God Himself. But when such a faith is in abeyance, when nature and history, and the flesh and the world have lost the profound import that such a faith gives them, then, should the weathers of the historical climate seem inclement or menacing, it will be difficult to avoid such a conclusion as that which is reached by Philip Roth, the gifted young author of *Goodby, Columbus* and *Letting Go,* who has said in *Commentary* that the novelist cannot "make credible much of American reality" today since "it stupefies, it sickens, it infuriates, and finally it is even a kind of embarrassment to one's own meager imagination." In other words, without something at least analogous to the sacramental vision of reality that is created for Christianity by its doctrine of Creation and of the Incarnation—without something at least analogous to this—the likelihood is that, when faced by entangled and unpromis-

ing circumstances of life, the writer may be able to manage
nothing better than a querulous retreat into the privacies of
the isolate self: the kind of querulousness that is expressed by
James Baldwin when he says that "there is no structure in
American life today and there are no human beings," or that
John Cheever, the author of *The Wapshot Chronicle*, expresses
when he complains that "life in the United States . . . is hell."

But querulousness is a most unfruitful basis for literature,
and most especially for the novel: so I suggest that we had better not be in too much of a hurry to agree with the new generation in American letters when it is inclined to assign itself to
some not-so-brave new world that is believed to be "post-
Christian." Nothing, of course, could be more futile than the
kind of debate that sometimes goes on amongst churchmen as
to how, in programmatic terms, the literary imagination in our
time may be "rebaptized": for such a work is a work for the
Holy Spirit, and the Spirit bloweth where it listeth. But,
strange and unmanageable as its workings may sometimes be,
at least we can pray for rain.

Index

Index

Index